HARVARD MED

Also by John Langone

Goodbye to Bedlam:
Understanding Mental Illness & Retardation

Bombed, Buzzed, Smashed or . . . Sober:
A Book About Alcohol

Human Engineering:
Marvel or Menace?

Like, Love, Lust:
A View of Sex & Sexuality

Violence:
Our Fastest Growing Public Health Problem

Dead End:
A Book About Suicide

AIDS:
The Facts

Vital Signs:
The Way We Die in America

Long Life:
What We Know and Are Learning About the Aging Process

Superconductivity:
The New Alchemy

Thorny Issues:
How Ethics and Morality Affect the Way We Live

Spreading Poison:
A Book About Racism and Prejudice

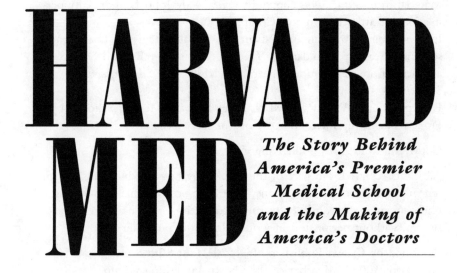

HARVARD MED

*The Story Behind
America's Premier
Medical School
and the Making of
America's Doctors*

JOHN LANGONE

Crown Publishers, Inc.
New York

Grateful acknowledgment is made to the following for permission to reprint previously published material:

The author wishes to thank the Estate of Robert Frost for permission to quote from Mr. Frost's note to Janet Forbes, January 9, 1963.
Material from *Vital Signs* copyright © 1974 by John Langone. By permission of Little, Brown and Company.
Excerpts from "Physician and Patient as a Social System" by L. J. Henderson and "Academic Standards in Medical Schools" by Bernard Davis, abstracted from information appearing in *The New England Journal of Medicine*.
Excerpts from "Why It's Hard to Enter Harvard Medical School" by Francis Burns, reprinted courtesy of *The Boston Globe*.

Published by Crown Publishers, Inc., 201 East 50th Street, New York, New York 10022. Member of the Crown Publishing Group.

Random House, Inc. New York, Toronto, London, Sydney, Auckland

CROWN is a trademark of Crown Publishers, Inc.

Manufactured in the United States of America

Design by Nancy Kenmore

Library of Congress Cataloging-in-Publication Data

Langone, John
   Harvard Med : the story behind America's premier medical school and the making of America's doctors / John Langone.
      1. Harvard Medical School.   2. Medical education—United States.   I. Title.
R747.H28L36   1995
610'.71'174461—dc20   94-44230

ISBN 0-517-59306-8

10 9 8 7 6 5 4 3 2 1

First Edition

To the Patient, and the GP,
the Good Physician, this book
is affectionately dedicated

Contents

Acknowledgments

Many sources, original and secondary, were consulted for this book, and all have been cited whenever possible. With regard to the history of Harvard Medical School, which plays a part here, the specific literature—that is, lengthy book treatments—is surprisingly scanty. The few works that have appeared are comprehensive, although maddeningly genealogical in style, and written either by alumni or committees composed of the heads of various departments. Indexes are sometimes incomplete or absent, and the writers have made little attempt to liven the works with anecdotal appoggiaturas, grace notes, of which the Harvard Medical School has many. Indeed, as someone once observed, medical schools are usually depicted in published accounts as "self-perpetuating entities guided by superhuman beings in a social vacuum."

Nonetheless, most valuable for my background purposes were the three-volume *Harvard Medical School: A Historical Narrative*, by Thomas Francis Harrington, published in 1905, and *Medicine at Harvard: The First Three Hundred Years*, by Drs. Henry K. Beecher and Mark D. Altschule, published in 1977. Equally helpful were issues of the *Harvard Medical Alumni Bulletin* and the *Harvard Medical School Focus*; bicentennial and trustees reports; old copies of the *Boston Medical and Surgical Journal*; the *Medical Essays* of Oliver Wendell Holmes; the *Addresses and Papers* of Henry Jacob Bigelow; Garrison's *History of Medicine*; Samuel Eliot Morison's *The Founding of Harvard College*; *In Celebration of Life: A Centennial Account of the Harvard Medical Alumni Association*

1891–1991, by Nora N. Nercessian; and Dr. Maurice Strauss's *Familiar Medical Quotations.*

My deepest thanks go to the busy individuals—clinicians, medical students, faculty, and hospital administrators—who agreed to be interviewed or followed about on hospital rounds, and whose comments and actions shaped this book. They were chosen not because they are superhuman, which they are not, but simply because they are human. They also do not operate in a social vacuum—as many deans and faculty at the school still choose to do—immersed as they are in the special, turbulent world of the sick.

I am also grateful to those who gave me access to individuals or the printed word: Richard J. Wolfe, curator of rare books in Harvard's Countway Library of Medicine; John Cronin, librarian of the *Boston Herald;* Adrienne Fischier, librarian of the Harvard Library in New York; Ruth Schubert, librarian at the Hingham (Massachusetts) Public Library; Martin Bander, deputy to the general director of Massachusetts General Hospital; Antony Lloyd, vice president of corporate communication of the Beth Israel Hospital, Boston; Ellen Barlow, managing editor of the *Harvard Medical Alumni Bulletin;* and Raymond Desautels, who, apart from filling his role as son-in-law, kept me from missing timely material.

While I am grateful to all who did help, I alone am responsible for the book's point of view and any errors it may contain.

JOHN LANGONE
Rowayton, Connecticut

Author's Note

As a journalist who has followed doctors and their craft, and the Harvard Medical School, for three decades, I have long been interested in their education—why they choose the profession, how they are selected, what they are taught and by whom, what the experience has done to and for them, the reasons for their choices of specialty, and what makes them compassionate or distant. Harvard Med, the nation's third-oldest medical school, serves as the backdrop here for what is an attempt to answer those questions, questions which should be of vital importance to each one of us, since doctors are the first ones most of us seek out when we are in pain. Even as students, they will see us, as one physician has observed, stark naked—physically, mentally, and morally.

I have not intended this book to be a detailed history of the school and its inner workings—that is, it is not "about" Harvard Med—nor of American medicine, which Harvard's history parallels and often outruns. Even less was I interested in depicting a routine, journal-like day in the life of a typical medical student, or the drama of an emergency room; that hackneyed genre has had far more than its deserved share of print and large- and small-screen exposure. Neither will the reader find any in-depth analysis of the role of medical education in current attempts to restructure the health-care system. These things are touched upon, but only as frames in what is meant to be a documentary that attempts to say something about how one premier school has selected and educated physicians, from its inception as a surprisingly shabby diploma factory in the grim, medically inept days at the close of the American Revolution to the science and technology–literate present; but more importantly, about how some of its students and faculty in twenty affiliated hospitals and clinical institutions are trying (and not trying) to close the gap between caregivers and patients, a gap that is ever-widening because of the intrusion of technology and market forces into medicine, and one that has created enormous conflict among students and faculty. In that regard, Harvard, which arguably outshines every other American medical school, is representative of the struggle faced by all medical schools, and its students, allegedly the best of the crop, are as concerned about their and medicine's future as medical students elsewhere in lesser-known institutions.

Through conversations, interviews, participation in rounds and classrooms, eavesdropping, and many hours in the Countway Library of Medicine, I have attempted to capture, at various stages in the education process, a bit of what it is like to be a student at Harvard Med, along with their bright hopes, deep concerns, and conflicts. I have tried, too, to show how a few exemplary faculty go about the business of impressing upon these doctors-to-be that patienthood is a social state as well as a biological one and that humanistic values are as essential as science in the making of a "good" doctor; and, conversely, how other mentors, who view a "good" doctor differently, can stand in the way of such a goal.

A word, here, about how this book took shape. The events recorded did not transpire in a neatly defined time frame; that is, the book does not follow a given class from Orientation Day to commencement. I have reordered some events, collected over several years, to form a loose narrative and a structure they did not always have in real life. The events are real, however, either witnessed by me or recounted to me and reconstructed, and the names, titles, and positions of all faculty interviewed or described are genuine; only a few of the student names, along with various markers in their lives, have been altered, at my own decision, or at their request, in order that I might enhance the narrative quality; they are, however, no less real to me, and I hope to the reader.

J.L.

HARVARD MED

1 | *"Thank You for Coming Here"*

ORIENTATION DAY FOR YET ANOTHER FRESHMAN CLASS AT HARvard Medical School and the warm, soft breeze that plays over the Boston campus of the nation's third-oldest medical school promises autumn soon, the season that eases the transition from summer laziness to hard winter work.

On the green grass of the vast lawn that sprawls toward the Avenue Louis Pasteur from the six-columned white marble palace that is the focal point of the Great White Quadrangle and the school's headquarters, a throng of students, secretaries, faculty, maintenance men, and security guards eat their lunches in quiet clusters. Nearby, a smaller group lounges in the shade of a seven-foot Oriental plane tree grown from a select cutting of the very tree on the Greek island of Kos under which Hippocrates, the father of medicine, lectured his young followers of Asclepias, the god of healing, and displayed patients undergoing treatment. True to Harvard Med's devotion to specialty care, the rare old tree once had its own private tree surgeon— a plant propagator at the Arnold Arboretum—who moved it indoors in late fall to keep it from freezing and to induce its buds to form in time for a new crop of graduates who would gather here for Class Day exercises.

Inside one of the marble halls adjacent to the lawn, in soft-lighted Amphitheater E of the Medical Education Center, the mood is also mellow. It is adjustment and transition time here, too, as an eager crop of students, fresh from a summer of anticipation and dreams and no longer precollege and premed, but ready for a season of fulfillment, file in. The seats are cushy. Compassion, camaraderie, and communication are in the air. There is a great deal of laughter, hand shaking, hugging, cheek kissing, and clapping of backs. Down front, Registrar Carol Duffey and a small army of beaming assistants are opening cartons of forms, handouts, the 119-page course catalog, the 16-page fine-print supplement, and the little red student handbook, which contains, among other necessities for navigating the school and its neighborhood, the perceptions of a few members of the second-year class. Secretaries, upperclassmen, and advisers, making nice, plunge up and down the stairs, excitedly taking questions before they're asked from the cheery students looking for seats. Handing them sheaves of papers and booklets, they assure them they can call anytime— no problem, no problem whatsoever—or just knock at the door. Computer room hours? Yup, twenty-four hours a day, just like all HMS facilities, so not to worry when you have to finish off a paper at 2:00 A.M. The audience picks up the cue and groans loudly. No, you don't have to pay to get across the Charles River. Take the shuttle bus; it's free with your ID badge. The T, the subway line, is down around midnight, which is just as well, because that's just about when you'll be memorizing all those little carpal bones. Boo. Hiss. Crime? There are more controlled substances out there than in Massachusetts General Hospital (MGH), and the "druggists" selling them don't take American Express. If you're worried after dark, call the walking escort service; they'll take you to your car, to buildings, and to the T. You'll also get a semimonthly crime report from the Harvard Police. Makes for some diversionary light reading when you're in the middle of trying to acquire your required competency in biostatistics. Yes, the Countway Library was indeed founded by the same gentleman who started Lever Brothers, Francis Countway, America's leading soap salesman and adman, who eventually made BO and Lifebuoy household words. Yes, get that immunization report in fast, and get started on the hepatitis B vaccine. You're going to be exposed to God knows what while you're here, and we don't want to lose any of you big stars.

Deans abound and mill about, each waiting his or her turn to take the microphone and greet, compliment, assure, advise, inspire, inform, caution, and entertain the new recruits. There are Dean Daniel Tosteson, and next to him another power dean, Dean of Education Daniel D. Federman, both smiling broadly and appearing as enthusiastic as though this gathering is their first. There are associate deans of student affairs, financial aid, specialty-choice counseling, public affairs, and educational services; and the ombudsperson, who provides a confidential telephone number and "an impartial, safe place of support and assistance" for victims of discrimination, harassment, or unfair treatment.

In the auditorium, too, sitting and chatting in the last and highest row, are the lords of Harvard Med's version of the privy council, the masters, associate masters, educators, senior fellows, tutors, preceptors, and advisers of the five academic societies that students will be assigned to and who will become their academic and administrative guardians. If the society members can be characterized as senior and distinguished— Harvardisms that separate Doctors from doctors—the physicians whose names adorn four of the societies' halls are enough to make even the distinguished and senior quiver, for they have scaled the rhetorical heights to *eminent:* Walter Bradford Cannon, he of "fight or flight" and homeostasis; William Bosworth Castle, almost a Nobelist for finding that a stomach factor essential for vitamin B_{12} absorption was missing in patients with anemia (fortunately or unfortunately, depending on your allegiance, two other Harvard men, George Minot and William Murphy, got the award in 1934 for prescribing large amounts of liver, which is loaded with B_{12}, to cure anemia); Francis Weld Peabody, physician, teacher, and humanitarian, "who personifies the Harvard Medical School's tradition of blending the medical scientist and the humane clinician"; and, since no society or room at Harvard Med could be complete without some mention of the man or decorated with one of his worn-leather rocking chairs, Oliver Wendell Holmes, Boston's Autocrat of the Breakfast Table, poet, wit, novelist, lecturer, and an early contributor to the *Atlantic Monthly*, a professor of anatomy at Harvard who had Daniel Tosteson's job from 1847 to 1853, and who also determined the cause and nature of childbed fever, first applied the word *Brahmin* to Boston's aristocracy, and coined the word *anesthesia*. He also found time to father the member of the U.S. Supreme Court who had the same name.

The fifth society has no distinguished name. It is simply referred to as Health Sciences–Technology, or HST, which is really more to the point than Holmes or Cannon and the other two, given that all but HST function in pretty much the same way and students are randomly assigned to them. The HST Society is more focused. It was created to "open the enormous educational resources of both MIT and Harvard to highly qualified students who seek careers at the interface of science and engineering with medicine"—another way of saying that the track is definitely Nobel-bound, that the M.D. degree the thirty-one students from this class who are enrolled in the HST program will get is for research careers in academic medicine. They will get needled a lot. If there are any nerds at Harvard Med, some of their classmates maintain, they are in HST. If anybody needs sensitivity training at this school, they're the HSTs. Everyone knows, they say, that the HST mind-set is that of an auto mechanic: Everything that pulsates in the human body—the heart, kidneys, lungs, and bladders, to name but a few of the more familiar throbbing bio-objects—is just a pump. This is perhaps why students in the other societies refer to the HST Society as the "Pump Room."

It is with members of their societies that students will have tutorials, do lab work, and—in a broad jump from Orientation Day Evenings O' Fun with desserts, videos, and music, and the dean's reception at his suburban home, to a mind-jarring landing in reality—suddenly come of age by dissecting a stiffened cadaver in the gross anatomy rooms only a couple of days from now. The shock will be like being instantly transported from a serene meadow to a slaughterhouse. For most, the experience will not only inure them to death but will also fill them with a heightened respect for, and awe of, one of God's most remarkable creations. But there will be a downside. For some, accepting the inevitability of death will bring them to the unpleasant realization that they are not, contrary to the mythology of modern medicine, god-healers, that despite the skills they will hone and no matter how much sophisticated technology they master here and can summon up, there will come a time in their dealings with the sick and the terminally ill when there will be nothing more they can do but merely prolong life for a time, and, ultimately, only counsel and support. The cadaver these youngsters will soon slice up will become a symbol of their limitations. For a few others, the detached and cavalier way they will deal with that lifeless human body—a defense mechanism that hides uneasiness—will remain with them and will translate later on into an insensitivity toward their patients.

But for today, they can enjoy the program. On the floor of the amphitheater, things are slowing. Registrar Duffey is now surrounded by nearly empty cartons. Her energetic assistants are taking a breather. "This will be painless," she promises, smiling up from the floor at the 165 young men and women who have finally settled into seats and are noisily swiveling down lap desks, their ballpoint pens and yellow markers poised to attack the myriad forms. "We're here for you."

This is a very different lot of students compared with those enrolling some twenty years ago when I was a medical reporter covering the school for a Boston newspaper and, a bit later, studying gross anatomy and medical ethics here on a fellowship. Back then, Harvard Med students were still, as they have been for generations, among the brightest, but their priorities and their fierce social consciousness had been shaped by the turbulence of the Vietnam War, by researchers who were beginning to be concerned about the ominous potential of the scary science they were doing, and by the growing emphasis on "ghetto medicine," sanitized in the classrooms of the day to "community health care."

In 1968, Students for a Democratic Society flayed the medical school for trying to buy up the neighborhood without regard for the many low-income people who lived there, and who still do; antiestablishment docs-to-be from the medical school railed against the American Medical Association, vowed never, ever to join, so help them, occupied the dean's office for a time, and refused to accept doctors' black bags and medical instruments that had traditionally been donated by pharmaceutical companies. One time, a student named Emilio Carrillo, a self-described "angry young man" of the time, who years later would become president of the New York City Health and Hospitals Corporation, scheduled a meeting with the then dean, Robert H. Ebert, to make some demands. He and his fellow students got to the meeting before Ebert, and Carrillo took the boss's chair. Ebert came in and said, "Excuse me, that's mine." Carrillo replied, "I got here first." Students even coerced the dean into letting them write their own curriculum. "I said go ahead," Ebert recalls wearily when reminded of those tumultuous days. "All you have to do is pass the exams. They did."

Novelist and film director Michael Crichton, class of 1969, author of *Jurassic Park, The Andromeda Strain, Rising Sun,* and *Disclosure,* among other works, fretted over something else—the caliber of the instructors. Later he recalled, "The lecturers were mostly winging it. One man after another would stand up with a fistful of last year's lecture notes, indicate a few scribbled changes in the margins, and start to talk. The fact that a few instructors were superb only threw the inept majority into sharper relief." Back then, too, Jonathan Beckwith, a young Harvard microbiologist, had just separated, for the first time, pure, clearly defined genes from a living organism, an achievement that set the stage for today's commonplace genetic manipulation. At a press conference, I asked Beckwith to characterize what he had done. His reply: "The more we thought about it, the more we thought about the possibility that this particular set of steps might be used the wrong way. I think it is rather obvious that the work could lead to genetic engineering. The more we think about that, the more frightening it becomes. In fact, it is more frightening than hopeful. The way things have been going up to now, however, I am afraid the bad is going to far outweigh the good." It was a day the Harvard public relations office, used to being fawned over by the media every time a new lab breakthrough was announced, nearly died of shame. Here was the school's star researcher on a guilt trip when he should have been helping the downtown copy editors write yet another page-one banner for Old Veritas.

Looking around now at this current class, feverishly and dutifully filling out the cards and sheets that will grant them entrance to a club as exclusive as the U.S. Senate, it is hard to imagine any of them giving the dean or faculty any grief. This time it is they, not their mentors, who will develop stress ulcers and irritable bowels, because no matter what they say here about the benefits of self-directed, self-motivated learning that has become Harvard Med's hallmark, the amount and complexity of scientific information each student must absorb today is overwhelming. The students are idealistic, to be sure, for that is the way it is with most medical students. But it is not the fiery idealism of the sixties, which for some who were here then was often a reflection of the strident cries of a larger, deprived society. The idealism that is here now is probably more like the sort that saves whales and speaks out against crime, environmental polluters, power lawn mowers, and preservatives. It lacks a hard edge, and so does the way the students look. Their hair is too short, they are too well scrubbed, and their new clean jeans and T-shirts, their mocs from L.L. Bean, their gorgeous print skirts, their baseball caps with *X*'s and team letters, and their Ivory-white running shoes are too trendy. There are no raised fists and middle fingers, no angry faces, no dark glasses, no backpacks, no beards, no bare feet in dirty sneakers, no obscene words; one can safely bet that there are no cigarettes in their pockets and purses, and that in their briefcases they have granola bars, car keys, credit cards, and bubble gum. And perhaps, as did the entering class a couple of years ago, they will dine in a style on campus that would have flabbergasted their earthier predecessors, even without the elaborate ice sculpture that has served as a centerpiece for the annual Christmas party. (For a tuition of $20,250 a year per head, it is all, however, the least Harvard Med can do in the way of frills.) In the last analysis, these students bear an uncanny resemblance to those retouched and airbrushed photos of today's major-league kids in *Sports Illustrated* and on baseball cards. "Well, I know my name and address, anyway," says one radiant youth, scratching his head over a perplexing question on a form. "That's something, isn't it, for a guy who did a master's in sociology at NYU?" His companion, smartly dressed in a miniskirt and heels, as though for tea and finger sandwiches at the Copley Plaza down the avenue, smirks and asks, "What's the matter, Doctor, having trouble writing a prescription?"

There is hope, however, that there may be something inside these people who seem too much like children to become doctors, in the selection process that has put them here, and in the curriculum that will guide them over the next four years that will make them better healers, perhaps, than their noisier predecessors. For this new class has been almost microscopically screened to achieve the optimum mix of scientific expertise, ethnic and racial background, and willingness to serve humanity. Indeed, nearly every student has humbly told the interviewers during the admission ritual that he or she really does want to pursue caring for people in the humanitarian sense, as well as with technical and scientific competence.

Seventy percent are, as expected, science majors, but an impressive (for Harvard Med) 11 percent are double majors—anthropology, sociology, and the humanities among them—and a few students are seriously interested in disciplines that range from choreography to English literature to music. They have been selected from 2,942 applicants and represent a contemporary mix calculated to better serve the interdependent discipline and the cloak of many colors that modern medicine has become. Twenty years ago, a typical class here had two or three women and but a handful of blacks and other minorities. The people who selected this new crowd did the right thing. The class is composed of seventy women and ninety-five men from thirty-three states, sixteen foreign countries, and sixty-three colleges; twenty-two are African-American, ten Mexican-American, thirty-eight Asian-Pacific, and two Native Americans. Thirteen of them are beginning medical school after taking time off to pursue interests in athletics, international volunteer work, research, and education. They range in age from eighteen to thirty-six. Dr. Regenia Carpenter-Edmond, an African-American instructor in medicine and an attending physician at MGH, has already helped to set the stage for the new mix as a member of the Minority Subcommittee that participates in the admission-interview process: "We are better served," she says brightly, "if we have a diverse group trained to face the challenges ahead—for example, in molecular biology, preventive medicine, and the issues of providing access to medical care for all people. We need a lot of heads in the think tank."[1]

It is a commendable goal. But at Harvard Med, the heads that think science will tip the balance, and for some students that will present great conflict. Many of those who shared the motivations of past generations of students—the selfless professionalism and the moral ideal of service—will find them nudged aside by the urgency to keep up with the explosion in scientific information, the constraints of time, and the stark reality of enormous tuition debts that will not be easily paid off by entering the general practice of medicine, what is now known as "primary care."

Although there are some promising signs of change, Harvard Med still is not the place one goes to learn primary, geriatric, and rural medicine; that distinction goes to the state-run schools in places like Michigan, Vermont, Iowa, Kentucky, and New Mexico. For years, the school and its affiliated hospitals have been driven by a fierce desire to keep the flag flying as a premier research complex, and Harvard Med is usually number one when the measure is the millions in grant money it receives from the National Institutes of Health.

Given the contributions the school has made to scientific medicine for over a century, it is difficult to fault that: to name but a few, the discovery of the mechanism of insect transmission of disease, the cause of scurvy and the concept of heat-killed vaccines; invention of the iron lung; perfection of the artificial kidney; the first successful use of chemotherapy to bring about remission in leukemia; development of the external heart pacemaker; the blood test for syphilis detection; the first use of electric current to restore the heart's rhythm; discovery of the gene that causes muscular dystrophy. Indeed, even as these new students are scribbling on their forms, a

Harvard Med upperclassman is putting in extra hours at MGH, trying to modify a key mechanism in the AIDS virus to prevent it from reproducing itself. At this moment, another Harvard researcher is leading a team that will shortly discover what the *New York Times* will front-page as the most coveted treasure in molecular biology, the gene behind Huntington's disease; right now, too, HMS scientists are successfully administering, for the first time in humans, an oral treatment for multiple sclerosis; discovering a protein that loads nerve cells for firing and may lead to better ways to manage pain and treat mental illness; and offering hope to stroke patients by identifying calcium channels unique to the brain and a natural toxin that blocks them.

And, when the day's festivities are over, many of the faculty and administrators who are here to extoll patient care will retire to their conference rooms to discuss the opening, in 1996, of the Harvard Institutes of Medicine on, appropriately, Avenue Louis Pasteur, a facility where commercial biotech laboratories and health-care companies will lease space to scientists and businessmen who will work closely with academic basic and clinical scientists, M.D.'s among them, on a range of medical mysteries from Alzheimer's disease to zoonosis. Were he alive, Oliver Wendell Holmes, unwavering in his belief that a physician's business was to doctor, would probably put a brick through a lab window. "Science," he was fond of saying, "is a first-rate piece of furniture for a man's upper chamber, if he has common sense on the ground floor."[2]

If Holmes was bothered by the intrusion of basic research science—whose goal had traditionally been the pursuit of science for its own sake—into the art of medicine, he would have been stunned to see how quickly basic science shaded into applied science, whose goal is to alleviate suffering and also to turn lab miracles into big business.

In 1975, Harvard Med took a bold step toward an aca-

demically unthinkable alliance by agreeing to collaborate with
Monsanto Company in a massive $23 million, twelve-year re-
search project aimed at supporting the work of two scientists,
M. Judah Folkman and Bert L. Vallee, both of whom had made
key discoveries in basic cancer research. At the time, the media
hailed the marriage as the forerunner of long-overdue academic-
industrial ties throughout the nation. The agreement quite
naturally stressed that the goal was the application of scientific discovery for the common good. Harvard retained the
right to pursue research clues without interference; Monsanto, the rights to commercial development of products
spun from the research. In those days, universities were not
supposed to profit from their discoveries, and any immediate
usefulness in the high pursuit of science was "but a collateral
object," as one of Holmes's colleagues, the eminent Harvard
surgeon Henry Jacob Bigelow, told graduates in a valedictory
address. (Then again, Bigelow might have foreseen the value
of new partnerships when he added, "The flood of industry
soon pours in, selects its productive spots, and tills the soil or
digs the gold.")[3]

While the historic Monsanto merger was not a profit-
making venture for Harvard, the future possibility of making
a little something from other arrangements was not ruled out.
In 1980, Harvard agonized long and hard over investing in a
new biotech company that had sprung from the research of
one of its professors of molecular biology who would be a
partner in the undertaking. After much debate, the university
eventually scrapped the plan when President Derek Bok cited
the need to preserve academic values and expressed concern
over potential conflicts of interest.

In 1988, the same year Harvard's leaders were debating
the case of Dr. Shervert Frazier—director of Harvard's McLean
Hospital and former head of the National Institute of Mental
Health, who was found guilty of plagiarizing sections of several

scientific papers and resigned—another of Harvard Med's more delicious scandals confirmed Bok's fears. This one involved a young researcher at Harvard-affiliated Massachusetts Eye and Ear Infirmary, Scheffer C. G. Tseng. Tseng had been using an experimental eye drug on hundreds of patients at the same time he was organizing a company to manufacture it. He found the drug to be largely ineffective, but he sold millions of dollars worth of stock in it before reporting the negative test results to the public.

Harvard need not resort to such shenanigans to capitalize on its research. One lucrative approach was opened by the federal government a few years ago when it transferred ownership of patents to the universities that conducted the experiments. Out of that came technology licensing, an arrangement that allows the institutions to license their patents to biotech companies for a fee. Harvard was quick to seize the moment: In 1993, it made $3.6 million from technology-licensing deals at the medical school, much of the money coming from sales of a cardiac-imaging agent and a DNA sequencer.

Harvard has found, though, that while the rarefied business atmosphere in which science now operates could fill its coffers, it sometimes clouded the scientists' minds when it came down to fiscal responsibility and accounting standards. In 1991, the medical school's dons, blushing and penitent, deducted a half a million dollars from some $28 million they had billed the feds for research costs, thereby voluntarily cutting the bill it had sent the government to cover the indirect costs of research that included space, utilities, and support and administrative costs. The school admitted it had erred on several expense-account items, among them eighteen hundred dollars for a party for a retiring dean. But then, Harvard had long ago learned how to milk a cash cow: In 1811, the school accepted twenty-nine shares of stock in a canal company, five of an insurance company, and two of a turnpike firm to form the Boylston Society—the oldest continuously operating student medical society in America, whose grand mandate was to "promote emulation and inquiry"—and used the dividends to buy an inkstand, quills, a trunk, cuspidors, and "malt beverages."[4]

"Well!" protested one loyal faculty member after the government blew the whistle on Harvard's "oversight." "At least we weren't as gluttonous as those people at Harvard West. The big guy over there got away with cut flowers and cedar closets in his home." The reference was to Stanford's president, Donald Kennedy, who had resigned amid a furor several months earlier over the school's "accounting errors." Stanford wasn't, however, the only other perpetrator; a couple dozen other big-time universities had spent money improperly. Henry Bigelow—who once rode twelve miles in an open sleigh on a freezing winter night to treat a child with scarlet fever, then refused to accept a fee—would not have approved.

The forms are completed now and handed down to Duffey, and the deans are onstage, preparing to deliver their welcoming addresses. The warm-up act is Daniel Federman, HMS class of 1953. He spent four years at Stanford as chairman of the department of medicine but was wooed back to Harvard in 1977. Federman's peers call him comfortably eloquent, an enthusiastic and challenging teacher with a keen interest in student concerns. Here, he is the crowd-pleaser, with all the timing and quippery of a stand-up comedian. He looks up and around for a moment, acknowledges the trainees, and strokes their egos, telling them what they knew all the time. "We didn't just pull your names out of the Yellow Pages, you know," he says.

He gives them standard-issue Harvard Med, a brief history of the school, and its optimum educational ratio, in its early days, of three professors to two students. "That kind of rich, personal connection still exists here, in new ways," he says, pointing out that the ratio is still great, three thousand full-time faculty to seven hundred students. He says it's Harvard's job to take a group of young people who couldn't get a job, at least a job they could like, and turn them into some of the most valued, respected members of society. En masse, they swell visibly. "We know that change is latent in all of you," Federman goes on. "The admissions process is dedicated to recognizing that. We watch it occur. Nobody understands it fully. Gradually, you're ready to serve, dedicated to others, juggling family and responsibility, no one knows how." He echoes what he has said in his letter to the entering class in the red student handbook that is now sitting open in every-one's lap. "Our curriculum is based on the assumption that there are certain things all doctors share. The very word *doctor* conjures up a set of expectations, and the faculty accepts the responsibility of providing an educational framework within which you can meet those hopes. Our planning is rooted in biomedical science, but aware that knowledge is steadily ad-vancing; it is focused on relationships with individual patients, and yet aware that no two of these are the same; and it is dyed to a social fabric that is being constantly rewoven. We believe that each student is the key to mastering these shifting circumstances, and that our principal role is to guide you to a lifetime of dedication and learning in medicine."

To dispel any notion that Harvard Med is a stress shop, Federman ends on a pleasant note, observing that 99 percent of the students graduate, and the ones who leave before that probably didn't want to be here in the first place. "You are in for such a delightful time. We are very glad that whatever else you have considered, you made the right choice. We are thrilled that you are joining us as students, colleagues, and teachers." Next to me, a student wearing a UC cap mutters, "That's right, it's great to be here at the Stanford of the East."

Dean Tosteson, HMS class of 1949, a former football player at the University of Wisconsin, confirms yet again the school's pleasure in accepting them. He alludes to the financial aid ("One of the more lamentable dimensions of going to Harvard") that 70 percent of the students will require from wealthy donors and the taxpayers to get through it all, and, turning up the seriousness level, he quotes Aristotle: "Medicine begins in philosophy, philosophy ends in medicine." He paraphrases the distinguished Harvard biochemist Lawrence Henderson to the effect that in a social system, what Henderson called "sentiment" is as important and as powerful as gravity in solar systems. "This physician-chemist makes the point that it is very important for a doctor to learn to use sentiment, the feeling of one person for another, for the benefit, the health of his or her patient. It's a heavy responsibility and a difficult art. Perhaps the most important skill is learning to communicate with other human beings in a valid and effective way, and through that kind of communication help both of you to learn."

Tosteson pays traditional Harvard homage to science, telling the students they are incredibly fortunate to be entering medicine at the crest of one of the great waves that have occurred in all of human history, the emergence of a truly molecular and cellular biology hand in hand with medicine. "By the time you are out there practicing whatever you're going to practice, the human genome will have been, to all intents and purposes, mapped and sequenced. The implications of that for your patients will be incalculable. You'll have a view of man as organism informed by the natural sciences and particularly this new biology."

But that, he says, will not be enough. "You must also come to grips with the reality that we live in groups, that each human being, each patient, is a member of society, that we make each other sick, stress each other out."

Then, Tosteson raises the especially thorny issue of racial and ethnic animosity. It is an appropriate topic, for Harvard Medical School, since its very founding, has had to deal with it as both an institutionalized and a spontaneous problem. "The genes responsible for disease do not segregate," he says. "While predisposition may differ between racial groups, sickle-cell anemia and cystic fibrosis, for example, the phenomenon of genetic predisposition is common to all. It is this unified view of our nature that medical science can bring to the discourse of ethnic and racial conflict."

Tosteson turns it over to Dr. Alvin Poussaint, an African-American and associate dean for student affairs. He picks up on the race issue, telling the story of a colleague who went looking for work in a Boston suburb that would fit his interest in serving a diverse group of patients. He applied for one post, with nothing in his application to indicate he was black. On the phone with the doctor in charge, he asked, "Are you serving blacks and Latinos there?" "No, relax," was the reply. "We can assure you we have none of those kinds of patients, and in fact, we have ways of controlling that situation." Poussaint says he hopes none of the people there were Harvard grads, and he explains that he raises the issue because it indicates the realities of medical practice. "Even here," he says, lowering his voice as though letting a skeleton out of Harvard's closet, "even here, there have been many, many incidents, not just ethnic, either, but things that have happened to probably every single group, and over gender differences and sexual orientation. You are apt to see them much more in the hospitals, and you have to decide how brave you're going to be in facing up to it and talking about it." Remember, Poussaint says, none of us has any purity on this issue. "Psychologists tell us that we all have the propensity to be prejudiced about something."

Will the messages sent by Tosteson and Poussaint on this

hopeful day get through? Perhaps. Will they be remembered? That will depend not on what they hear today but on who they were before they came here, and on whom they work for and with when their hospital time comes, and on whether they accept and implement what they are expected to learn in their doctor-patient classes, such as getting to know their black and Hispanic patients as individuals with problems that may be shared by everyone, and not as members of a group that may have a predisposition to certain illnesses. But stereotypes are not, unfortunately, always responsive to education, even a Harvard one. A year before this new class heard these messages, an incident inspired by the Clarence Thomas–Anita Hill confrontation—and was perhaps behind what some freshmen will later feel was an overkill of sensitivity training during this Orientation Week—surfaced here. Two second-year white medical students—a young man dressed as Thomas and a woman as Hill, and both in blackface—showed up at the annual Halloween costume party. A first-year black student took offense at the students' darkened faces, flung beer on the woman's dress, and punched the male in the face, creating a gash that required seventeen stitches. Harvard's response was swift. A review committee recommended that the black student be placed on probation for two years, spend a year in "constructive work that carries no academic credit," enter a counseling program "in order to understand and control his aggressive behavior," engage in twenty hours of community service a month for twelve months, working with victims of violence in the community, and be suspended if he demonstrated any further aggressive tendencies. The white couple, too, felt Harvard's scorn; they were informed that Harvard was "appalled by their insensitivity to the feelings of their black classmates," and they were assigned to prepare a syllabus and bibliography on medicine in a multiethnic society for their own education and that of their classmates. The dean's committee concluded: "The

Harvard Medical School finds completely unacceptable this loss of self-control; this inexcusable resort to violence is totally inappropriate for one who wishes to become a physician. The profession of medicine is an art and science based upon human compassion, and violence is therefore completely antithetical to this central foundation of medical practice. So contrary to medical behavior is an act of violence that any such act must receive the most severe expression of our community's condemnation."

Poussaint does not mention the incident in his message to the students, nor does he mention that others at the party were made up as Senator Edward Kennedy and Mary Jo Kopechne, and Long Dong Silver and a flasher. He does not defend now, as did students and some graduates after the incident, the right of the white students to choose their costumes at a Halloween party, nor does he take issue, as others did, with their punitive assignments, their punishment for expressing their views, however insensitive. Not everyone on the faculty was as zipped up over the incident. "Hey, this was a Halloween party, Jack," an irate member of the faculty observed soon after. "The dean and some faculty, mostly the Northeast Corridor types, had their thumbs in their ass and their fingers up their nose, and they just didn't want to do bad to anyone black. So what do they do? They send the black guy to counseling—did you ever hear of counseling helping anyone who pokes someone in the mouth?—and they make the white kids write a thesis, which is a wonderful way to learn a lesson, isn't it? Sort of like writing the Ten Commandments on the blackboard five hundred times. What they did on both sides wasn't treating the offenders; it was treating the dean and the faculty, making them feel better. The guy who got hit should have sued and recovered for damages, and if it was really as bad as it appeared, they should have either given the other guy five milligrams of dingaling or thrown him out."

Nor does Poussaint, as a member of the class of 1960 would do in an issue of the *Alumni Bulletin,* link the nature of the punishment meted out to the black student to its impact on the doctor-patient relationship that is the heart of what this new freshman class, for all the gee-whiz science that will engulf them, is here to learn about. In the *Alumni Bulletin* article, the writer said:

> What I find particularly egregious is the requirement for psychiatric counseling. . . . The use of psychiatry to quash unwelcome behavior smacks very strongly of the former Soviet Union. . . . Coerced psychiatric counseling contaminates the psychiatrist/client relationship and prevents the uncensored flow of information from patient to doctor since the goal of the relationship is no longer the best interest of the patient, but rather a stipulated judgment that the patient is no longer a threat to others. . . . What I am most sorry about is that some old-fashioned common sense, combined with a spirit of reconciliation and community, was displaced by an academic pageant of committees, hearings, and enforced psychiatry, the sum of which is more depressing than the incident itself. I honestly thought Harvard could do better.[5]

Before Poussaint concludes his remarks, he commits a gaffe. He is talking about ethnic strife here and abroad. "Well, it's happening all over Boston, and what's happening in Nazi Germany is—" To loud laughter and stamping of feet, he stops abruptly, startled and embarrassed by what he has just said. He recoups nicely. "No, not *Nazi* Germany . . . As I said, nobody is pure."

Poussaint steps down and the mood changes abruptly, shifting from the gloom of racism to the joys of professional and personal development. The speaker is Dr. Edward Hundert, a psychiatrist and associate dean for student affairs. He is soft-spoken, and his message is reassuring. If they are intimidated by Harvard, he says, that is normal. "You figure that the person on your right probably has two doctorates in molecular genetics, and the person on your left has probably discovered a cure for four rare tropical diseases, and you're wondering if you're really supposed to be here. So, look at the person on your left and on your right, and be warned that we anticipate that all three of you are expected to graduate." As the students laugh and applaud, Hundert says that Harvard has tried to create a curriculum and an educational environment where collaboration rather than competition guides the learning and leads to excellence. It is what they need to hear, considering that during their intensive premed exams and their competition for grades and favorable letters of recommendation for admission to this and other medical schools their stomachs knotted over the warning of successful applicants: "Don't ever drop your pencil during the premed tests, because somebody is going to kick it away from you."

Hundert lets them know that even if Harvard Med had any kind of class ranking, which it does not, they should consider a question. He puts it to them in carefully measured tones: "What do you call . . . the last person . . . who graduates . . . from . . . Harvard Medical School?" Like fired-up strikers on a picket line responding in unison to the union boss's prompt, they shout out the answer as though it had been scripted: "DOCTOR!" The cheerleader smiles approvingly, makes a hammer fist, and adds proudly, "And a very good one at that!" In the student audience, the youngest member of the class, Clark Schierle, eighteen years old now, but only sixteen when he interviewed for admission, swells with pride. He is thinking how incredibly fortunate he is to be here, not intimidated in the least by all the reputed talent surrounding him, just overwhelmingly happy. "There is just, like, a mystique about this place," he will say later. "I mean, like, when you're reading about a doctor in the papers, you never read about where he trained unless it's Harvard. You don't hear Cornell-trained. Definitely. This is, like, a mecca. This is the place to be."

Hundert winds it up. He wishes the students the best of luck and imparts his impression of medicine, which, if it could be heard by exhausted upperclassmen cramming in their dorms and the case-hardened residents and interns plugging up gunshot wounds and detoxing crack addicts at this very moment in the emergency rooms around the city, would raise a wailing Greek chorus. "What a blast it is to be a doctor!" he exults. "Most of us find that treating patients is so much fun! Every day! It is hard to believe that you really get paid for it."

Dr. Poussaint cannot let it pass. He steps up to the microphone again and brings the youngsters back to reality. "Fun? Remember that when you're a fourth-year med student at three o'clock in the morning, and you need to sleep for two days. Then tell yourself it's fun. Deep, slow breathing is what our own Herb Benson over there at the Mind/Body Medical Institute will be teaching you in a couple days so you can counteract the harmful effects of stress—we prefer to call it Valium-deficiency—that'll come when you're out there caring. Deep breathing, remember that. Only problem is that when we try it on medical students, they all start hyperventilating."

A brief presentation follows, by a cheerful woman from financial aid, who talks about student responsibility for the funds they'll be using. It's really about paying the piper. She says, "We don't only try to find the resources; we try to help you develop habits of financial responsibility that will contribute to your personal and financial well-being now and in the future. You have responsibility to be steward over those funds while you are here and later when you'll be repaying your

loans, and when you'll be a donor yourself, to help the students who come behind you."

The speeches are over for the day. It is time for lunch
with the masters and associate masters. Then, just two hours
from now, the students will have their first exposure to what
the next four years are supposed to be all about—sick people.
Though the encounter, billed as an introductory clinic, will be
carefully orchestrated, it will give these doctors-to-be a chance
to see how the pros handle both ends of the lifeline, youth
and age, to ask questions, and, perhaps, learn something
about empathy.

2 The Fatigue Lab and the Good Doctor

I WAS TWELVE YEARS OLD WHEN I FIRST ENCOUNTERED HARvard Medical School students and some of the men who were helping to turn them into arguably the best doctors in the world. It was 1942, the year I started going to a peep show that introduced me to the inside of a unique laboratory near the Harvard Stadium on the Boston side of the Charles River, as well as to other labs on the Cambridge side that lay hidden behind the nearly mile-long, nine-foot-high fence-wall of wrought iron and textured red brick and the ornate, rustencrusted gates that enclosed the Yard.

The fence and walls and gates, and the Georgian Revival buildings, protected the twenty-two-acre Yard, the heart of Harvard College, from the Square outside. Out there in those days, electric streetcars, with side panels of orange-painted wood and seats of woven straw, shuddered and screeched along on steel rails that encircled the oldest institution of higher education in the United States. Horses drew wagons full of coal, ice, fruits, vegetables—remnants of a past mode of transport still serviceable and, indeed, essential in a time of war-induced shortages. There were Harvard students in blue button-down shirts, crimson rep ties or plaid bow ties, tan slacks, and three-button tweed jackets from the haberdashers to the Ivies, J. Press and J. August, Leopold Morse and Brooks Brothers.

Within the ivy-covered walls was, and still is, an oasis of tranquillity and order, of tree-lined paths and private autumns, and a school (only a native Cantabrigian has the courage to give it so humble a name) with an absolutely avaricious roster of graduates: Increase Mather, the hellfire-and-damnation Colonial divine, and his witch-hunting son, Cotton; Ralph Waldo Emerson; Henry David Thoreau; James Russell Lowell; the brothers James, Henry and Will; the Holmeses, Oliver Wendell, dean of the medical school and man of letters, and his son, Oliver Wendell, the Supreme Court jurist; and six U.S. Presidents, John and John Quincy Adams, Teddy Roosevelt, Franklin D. Roosevelt, Rutherford B. Hayes, and John F. Kennedy.

From brick and stone castles, the dons and doyennes of old Cambridge had once presided—a mandate secured as much through money and privilege as through learning—over a nearby fiefdom of stately yellow clapboard mansions, among them the Vassall-Craigie-Longfellow House on Brattle Street, where George Washington drew up his battle plan against the British, where Henry Wadsworth Longfellow waxed poetic and wrote *Paul Revere's Ride* and "The Village Blacksmith" (the smithy's site remains), and where the rich and visible served frog soup, mutton chops, and truffles to distinguished guests. Years later, the feudal barons of academe would still reign over the Yard and the Square, and their presence, if not their influence, would be felt even farther down the trolley line in "the other part" of Cambridge, where I and my mother were born and raised—the less lavish enclaves, where geraniums grew in tomato cans on the rickety porches of the Irish, Italian, Portuguese, and Polish immigrants who worked in the smelly rubber and soap factories, the slaughterhouses and pork-packing plants, and who staffed the city and county buildings whose consolidation in East Cambridge and Cambridgeport had established another, meaner kind of power base. It was from this part of the city, alien to this day to tourists who think of Cambridge only as the home of an educational aristocracy based in Harvard Square, the old Cambridge once tried to secede, but, for all its power and position, it could not, because it simply wasn't streetwise and didn't have the votes. Political clout wielded by lesser mortals dissolved Brahmin fantasies and made Cambridge one city in 1846.

It was to the Yard and Square of my childhood that my friends and I would go—it was only a twenty-minute walk, but the cultural distance between the two disparate neighborhoods was far greater than that—to see how people literally on the other side of the tracks lived. We would marvel at the same ancient buildings in which Colonial-era scholars educated English and American youth "in knowledge and godliness," requisites for entering the Puritan ministry; among those buildings was Harvard Hall, where blue-uniformed patriot soldiers were quartered in the spring of 1775 and where the Medical Institution of Harvard University got its start in 1782 in a dank basement room with but two students and three professors.

A visit to the Yard was a pilgrimage to a shrine, a repository of superlatives matched only by its Boston branch in the Great White Quadrangle, which, we all knew, turned out the only doctors you could ever have, the best of the best.

We'd get our science education by tramping through the Museum of Comparative Zoology, founded in 1859 by the Swiss-American naturalist Jean Louis Agassiz, who was a professor of natural history at Harvard. Clanging up and down the museum's open and precipitous iron stairways was a scary expedition, and oggling the dusty, musty collections in dark, cavernous rooms smelling of formaldehyde and mildewed cloth was an education in the ancient, the remarkable, and the arcane: dinosaur bones strewn like jackstraws in a volcanic matrix; a stuffed menagerie of gorillas, rhinos, giraffes, and lions; a giant octopus suspended from the ceiling, ominously spreading its preserved and varnished tentacles over spectators cringing beneath; case upon case of fragile glass flowers, some broken, of the world-renowned Ware Collection; slices of meteors, the nickel inside smooth and polished, just like the real nickels we carried in our pockets; gold, silver, and bejeweled ornaments, artifacts of the Mayans, Aztecs, and Utes. There was also the grimy case that penned two stuffed boa constrictors wrapped around a tree limb—which, when they were alive, had traveled with my uncle up from Panama in a railroad boxcar and had to stay the weekend in the cellar of our home, slithering in and out of their crates, because the museum was closed when they arrived. The most chilling part of this story, which made me the envy of my friends, had to do with my mother's lifelong refusal ever to go into that dark cellar, because she believed that the snakes, females, were carrying eggs that had hatched there and that boas slithered about in the gloomy areas between my grandfather's wine barrels.

Clustered near the museum were the laboratories of chemistry, biology, physiology, botany, and physics, where medical and premedical students studied and worked. Although they were off-limits to my gang, I had visited a few of these, courtesy of two of my mother's brothers (one of whom brought back the snakes), who were beginning research careers at another Harvard facility across the Charles River. I visited there eagerly twice a week almost till the end of the war and it became my personal playground and after-school refuge, as well as the stimulus for a lifelong interest in medicine and science.

There, in the basement of a brick building near the Business School and the stadium, a massive oaken door bearing a stenciled sign, HARVARD FATIGUE LABORATORY, opened into a very large room that was, in my young eyes, an Alice's Wonderland of science, fantastic and illogical. Inside, clusters of students and scientists hunched over at benches, working amid the steady blue flames of Bunsen burners, the piercing stench of butyl-alcohol solvent, and the mysterious bubbling and hissing arrangements of sparkling beakers and flasks linked together with twisted lengths of glass and rubber tubing. In one corner of the room, treadmills clattered backward under the feet of yelping dogs and panting young men; in another, the heavy steel door on a bulky walk-in chamber screeched open to admit a smiling student in shorts and T-shirt and clanged shut to lock him in. In other parts of the room, naked men dozed on padded tables, intravenous lines in their arms; gagging men who had slugged down jugs of syrupy guck urinated in bottles or, marvel of marvels, actually watched as their blood was drawn, their eyes fixed intently on the needle and the puffed vein, even as they retched from the stuff they had drunk; others just vomited into buckets or shivered uncontrollably.

The Fatigue Lab had been founded in 1927, a facility the likes of which organized science will probably never see again. Hardly known even to those who lived nearby, and all but forgotten today, the laboratory, in its nearly twenty years of existence, greatly influenced the careers of a generation of physiologists, biochemists, and physicians, left a legacy that shaped the thinking of many of today's medical educators, and helped give legitimacy to organized medicine's stepchild, what we know today as social medicine.

The lab grew out of the inspiration of its first director, the biochemist and sometime social scientist, Lawrence J. Henderson, whose huge red beard and matching tie, rumpled woolens, and the way he peered sternly over the round glasses perched forward on his nose, made his presence quite awesome to a preteen. His enormous intelligence, measured manner of speaking, cold logic, and friendship with Harvard's most powerful administrators—among them even, late in his life, Charles W. Eliot, who, as president in 1869, transformed Harvard Medical School from a disgraceful diploma mill to a model of medical education—made him a demanding mentor to the small army of chemists, biologists, psychologists, anthropologists, and medical students whom he counseled and who did his bidding.

Henderson, known simply as "L.J." to the multidisciplinary team he had assembled, was born north of Boston, in Lynn, in 1878, the son of a ship chandler who worked in the port city of Salem. He graduated from Harvard College in 1898 and from the medical school in 1902 and immediately launched into a career as a basic scientist. Although he would become one of the first physicians to speak out against the tendency to dehumanize and depersonalize medicine, in the way of Harvard medical research tradition he never practiced medicine. Indeed, those who knew him well said he had never even taken a patient's pulse or blood pressure after he got his medical degree. Rather, as soon as he graduated from Harvard Medical School, he went to the University of Strasbourg, for two years of study and research in the fledgling field of biochemistry. For most of his life, Henderson's primary tools would be a blackboard, a notebook, and a slide rule. Even when doing science, he left the bench work to others.

Henderson became a full professor of physical chemistry at the medical school, which had moved to Boston in 1810, and taught at the college in Cambridge, as well. A true Renaissance scientist versed not only in chemistry, biology, and clinical medicine but in sociology, philosophy, literature, theology, and several languages, he was as comfortable teaching his popular Sociology 23 to undergraduates at the college as he was lecturing on his other area of expertise, the physical chemistry of blood. His lofty position at Harvard and his restless, penetrating, eclectic mind shaped a personality that was often arrogant, judgmental, and impatient. Unable to suffer fools, he minced no words when it came to some of his colleagues, and he seemed to delight in quick, acerbic generalizations. One German physiologist, he dismissed as a "good third-rate man."

Someone else, he described as "pathologically modest." He could call a noted mathematician "remarkable," adding, "He can construct a formula that will fit any set of data, however erroneous." George C. Homans, Harvard's distinguished professor of sociology, who was Henderson's teaching assistant in Sociology 23, once said of L.J., "His method in discussion is feebly imitated by the pile-driver. His passion was hottest when his logic was coldest."[1]

Henderson's critical nature did not spare medicine. A fervent admirer of Hippocrates because he was a constant, skillful observer who saw his patients as social beings and not "mere cases," he was an admonisher of physicians who had dismissed or forgotten the Hippocratic view and went coldly about their business, as though compassion was not an obligation; and he was a counselor to medical students who, he feared, would emulate those officious physicians and neglect a patient's social pathology as they focused on his or her physical disease. "In your relations with your patients," he once warned medical students and physicians, "you will inevitably do much harm, and this will be by no means confined to your strictly medical blunders. It will arise also from what you say and what you fail to say. But try to do as little harm as possible, not only in treatment with drugs, or with the knife, but also in treatment with words, with the expression of your sentiments and emotions. Try at all times to act upon the patient so as to modify his sentiments to his own advantage, and remember that, to this end, nothing is more effective than arousing in him the belief that you are concerned wholeheartedly and exclusively for his welfare."[2] For Henderson, the good doctor was a decisive and skilled practitioner whose judgments were a product of science, intuition, and experience, and who was reflective about his own behavior. A summation of Henderson by Steven M. Horvath of the Institute of Environmental

Stress at the University of California at Santa Barbara, who worked in the Fatigue Lab, addressed such sentiments, as well as the man's contradictory nature:

"Henderson seemed a very impressive gentleman in the old sense, certainly majestic, obviously of superior intellect, imposing physically, sometimes frightening in his manner of questioning and criticism, but [was] essentially a warm, humane person who made a conscious effort to stimulate the development of the best in everyone with whom he had contact. Possibly, he envisioned himself as a modern day Socrates; a function he did perform and perform well."[3]

Initially, Henderson did not reveal his feelings about the shortcomings of medical practice. He pursued his first love, basic science, applying his knowledge of physical chemistry and biology to general physiology and to human response to physical and mental stress. His friend and colleague at Harvard Medical School, Walter B. Cannon, had already paved the way by defining, for the first time in physiological terms, the body's remarkable ability to respond appropriately to a physical threat or emotional disturbance—what is known popularly as the "fight or flight" response. It was Cannon, too, who developed the concept that would not only further influence Henderson but also promote the growth of the whole field of physiology: that of homeostasis, the intricate process by which the body maintains itself in a state of internal equilibrium, despite fluctuations of the outside environment.

The notion of an internal physiological environment and the mechanisms of interaction and equilibrium within an organism had long interested others besides Cannon and Henderson, among them the Russian physiologist, Ivan Pavlov, and, before that, the great nineteenth-century French physiologist Claude Bernard, who originated the term *internal secretion* and pioneered in the study of the endocrine glands and their hormones. Bernard, known as the "father of experimental medicine" came up with the idea of a *milieu interieur,* based on an organism's stable and self-regulating internal system.

Armed with new research tools and techniques of chemistry and physics that Bernard lacked, Henderson and Cannon developed Bernard's concept.[4] In 1908, Henderson applied his own ideas about homeostasis and equilibrium to the chemistry of blood, notably on the interaction of oxygen and carbon dioxide. The significance of the interaction had apparently escaped the physiologists of Henderson's day, who were studying blood's respiratory function. But to Henderson, it was obvious that since carbon dioxide influences the oxygen equilibrium in blood, oxygen must also influence the carbon-dioxide equilibrium. When he studied the interaction of the two more closely, he concluded that it was vital not to regard the change in one simply as cause and change in the other simply as effect.[5]

Out of it all came the Henderson-Hasselbach Equation, a precise formula used to calculate the pH of blood, a principle that has been in the notes and minds of every medical student studying acid-base balance since early in this century. At first, Henderson confined such methodology to man's internal environment, his aim being to establish a more scientific version of clinical medicine, an approach that had begun and continued to develop during his lifetime. Soon, however, he began to apply his deep interest in equilibrium, systems, and mutual dependence to the study of social science. The system that now interested him was not only the inner physiological complex but also the social one, and the equilibrium and interaction was no longer between oxygen and carbon dioxide but between organisms and their environment, too, and the relationship between individuals. Eventually, he would define another system, one that would become crucial to the development of the good doctor—the notion of the physician and patient as a social system.

Henderson's view of the sociologists of his day was what one might have expected from a biochemist. With the exception of perhaps one man—an Italian economist-engineer-mathematician, Vilfredo Pareto, who wrote a sometimes tedious four-volume work on general sociology—social theorists, Henderson believed, relied too heavily on a pretentious and elaborate systematization of knowledge that had little solid foundation in fact, did not clearly observe real life and human behavior, lacked "intuitive familiarity with things," and did not take into account the importance of Hippocrates's emphasis on close observation. Pareto, on the other hand, applied the stern rules of mathematics to sociologic theory in an effort to explain human nature, social action, and the rise and fall of a governing elite. With his substitutability curves, his notions of equal aggregate utility and general equilibrium, Pareto laid claim to be the first to study human relations and motives as a true scientist. He postulated a structured sociological system that was similar to a physical one, with its own interdependent parts and equilibrium, and that could be methodically analyzed. For Pareto, who died in 1923 and who worked for a time for Benito Mussolini (for which his many detractors referred to him as the "Karl Marx of the bourgeoisie"), society was driven, and kept in balance, by ideals, values, emotions, and sentiments.

It was not surprising that Henderson, as devoted as he was to the importance of mutual dependence and equilibrium in his own science, easily accepted the concept as appropriate on a social level, refined it, and applied it to his own beliefs about the complex relationships of human beings. "He appears to have said," Horvath observes, "that so long as environmental changes or attacks upon a system are not catastrophic, so as to lead to death of the organism or deterioration of a society, the physiology of the organism or the structure of a society will adjust to maintain its existence. And, further, that the two presumably dissimilar systems do this by similar laws through which we should be able to diagnose and prognosticate a society's ills and prescribe the treatment, if only we would study sociology as the natural sciences are studied."[6]

The Harvard Fatigue Lab blended research in human physiology with sociology, and as it grew it became a cooperative venture involving private industry, universities, the military, and other government agencies. Its original purpose was to research physical and mental stress in workers, not only to determine one's fitness for work but also to better understand a person's limitations and the physical and emotional changes—disease among them—that not only work but also economic and sociological factors produce. Underlying all of the work was Henderson's view that the systems and organs that comprise a biological organism are interrelated and must be studied in that context if its biological and social functioning is to be fully understood.

Interestingly, the lab was established not under the more likely aegis of Harvard's schools of medicine or public health, nor the faculties of the biological sciences, but was supported by the Business School. One reason for the association was the work of Dr. Elton Mayo, a psychologist and sociologist with whom Henderson had worked and who had been doing research in industrial psychology. Horvath points out that the collaboration was well timed, because industry had just realized that it could not ignore the human factor if it was to make economic progress. There was also the shared belief of Henderson and Mayo that group psychology, social problems, and the physiology of human fatigue had to be studied, not only as individual factors in determining physical and mental health but, more especially, to determine their interrelatedness and the effect upon work.

The sources of physical and mental stresses that occupied the lab staff were an amazingly mixed bag that included athletic competition, factory labor under unusually harsh circumstances, construction work at high altitudes and in intense cold and heat, confinement in submarines, and exposure to the battlefield conditions common to much of the world at the time. On a more practical level, during wartime the scientists developed and tested protective clothing, oxygen masks, defenses against poison gas, sleeping bags, load-carrying equipment, survival rations, and synthetic foods.

Doing the work were some of Harvard's brightest researchers, medical students, foreign fellows, and visiting scientists: Arlie V. Bock, a skilled blood and exercise investigator at Harvard's flagship hospital, Massachusetts General, described by Henderson as "the best physiologist amongst the clinicians, and the best clinician amongst the physiologists"; David Bruce Dill, perhaps America's preeminent exercise physiologist, the lab's research director, and later the scientific director of the Army Chemical Corps's medical laboratories; John H. Talbott, who would become editor of the *Journal of the American Medical Association;* Jean Mayer, the late president of Tufts University and former professor of nutrition at Harvard, who was a Henderson student and protégé; Ancel Keys, who conducted a famed study of twelve thousand men in several developed countries and discovered that the Finns had the highest percentage of animal fats in their diets and the highest blood-cholesterol levels, as well as the highest death rate from coronary artery disease; A. Clifford Barger, then a Harvard undergraduate, who became professor of physiology at Harvard Medical School; and my uncles, V. William Consolazio, who worked with Bock at MGH and was a founder of the National Science Foundation in 1951, and his brother, Frank, who held the lab's record for the number of accurate blood analyses done in an hour, much of it from his own arm, and who would become chief of the bioenergetics division at the Letterman Army Institute of Research.

Drawing one's own blood, as Frank Consolazio did so often, was the least of what most of the lab staff was required to do to themselves. Indeed, one of the rules for the medical students—who were there to learn basic research techniques, serve as human guinea pigs, and to earn a little spending money—was that you did to yourself the things you would one day do to your patients. Obedient to Henderson's stern belief that medicine needed a large dose of sociology, they would put themselves in the skins of the sick and the stressed, literally as well as figuratively, so that when medical school was done with they'd have picked up a bit more about how to be more caring, concerned doctors, along with all the hard science. In those days, they got away with self-stressing in the interest of science for its own sake because there were not yet any federal guidelines or codes of ethics governing human, including self-, experimentation. Tinkering with one's own metabolism also came with the territory if one wanted to be a human physiologist. "We're subject-experimenters," Frank would tell me as I squeamishly watched him wrap a rubber tourniquet tightly around his bicep and hold one end in his teeth like a heroin junkie, preparing to jab a needle into a vein. "You don't need brains when you do it this way. All you need is two hands." In later years, he would lament federal intrusion into human experimentation, shake his head, and say mournfully, "For God's sake, you can't even give yourself food poisoning without having to fill out ninety-three forms. Where the heck does it say that it's against the law to make yourself sick? All medical students should try it. Get sick, throw up, get the trots, stay in a hospital, use a bedpan, get stuck with a cath. That's how you make a good doc."

Getting sick and stuck, it sometimes seemed, was what the lab was all about. The medical students and staff researchers, along with a horde of enlisted-men volunteers from the U.S. Army, were enrolled in a course in scientifically controlled sadomasochism. They were punctured and prodded, roasted and frozen and hyperventilated. Pushed to the edge of human endurance, they rarely drew a normal, peaceful breath. They were regularly relieved of their blood and urine so that the physical chemistry of these fluids could be charted; their lungs and leg muscles were strained to the bursting point on treadmills so the researchers could collect sweat for analysis and measure respiration and fatigue-inducing lactic-acid accumulation; their bodies were chilled and heated in the steel climate chambers to determine the effects and limits of cold and heat. Wearing oxygen masks developed at the Harvard School of Public Health, they were taken to the equivalent of thirty thousand feet in altitude chambers; the masks fit poorly on some faces, and the men lost consciousness, proof that if they had been wearing the leaky masks while in flight, they would have died. (Harvard egos being what they are, the finding made the lab staff most unpopular with the Public Health scientists responsible for the mask.) Lab volunteers were forced to stand at attention for long periods to monitor the accumulation of lymph in their legs and the speed at which their blood returned to the heart; marched, panting, around the stadium on warm days, wearing heavy wool clothing to boost heart rates and speed exhaustion; and, for the field study portion of their excruciating work, sent to deserts, the tropics, mountaintops, polar regions, and the steel mills of Youngstown, Ohio, to add to what they'd learned in the lab about the effects of heat and cold and altitude.

One time, in a cholesterol study on Cape Cod, Frank Consolazio and a couple of students gorged themselves exclusively on lobster and pints of melted butter for days, a diet that probably ruined more than the subjects' waistlines. "We didn't know then that there was a short-term hypercoagulating effect on the blood," Frank would say later. "Even if we had, we'd probably still have gone on with it. Our arteries might get clogged, but that's what they were paying us for." Another time, they existed on a dozen different kinds of shellfish—trying to find the one that would make them sick. (They did, and the reaction, according to those who were there, laid them all flat, instantaneously.) On yet another occasion, in a test of military rations designed for emergency use, Fatigue Lab scientists, who had been living for days on the then popular K rations, had to devour the newly developed D-bar. This was a one-pound bar of semisweet chocolate that had been made available to air crews in the event of a bailout, and it was being reappraised because Gen. Henry "Hap" Arnold of the Army Air Corps had sent word from the Pacific that survivors of air crashes reported it "looks like hell and tastes worse." Volunteers ate part of the bar for breakfast, part for lunch, and planned to finish it off at dinner. But before they got to the last chunk, everyone had a blazing headache, was nauseous, and was vomiting profusely. They'd been poisoned by theobromine, a bitter alkaloid related to caffeine and having stimulant and diuretic effects, effects that could have been predicted by pharmacologists, who should have been aware that if anyone eats a pound of chocolate within twelve hours, they run a risk of raising theobromine levels in the body to toxic levels. The D-bar was quickly withdrawn.[7]

But one planned experiment was too much, even for the derring-doers of the Fatigue Lab. Learning that German scientists were doing direct heart puncture to determine cardiac output—these were the days before cardiac catheterization, in which a thin catheter is routinely threaded through an artery in the groin and up into the heart—Bock decided to take a drastic step: He would puncture his own heart to draw a sample of mixed venous blood. Word of the plan reached Henderson, who was far more comfortable with a notepad and an easy chair than with a hypodermic. "Arlie," he droned. "I hear you're going to jab a needle into your heart to get some blood." "Yes," said Bock as offhandedly as though he was going after a couple of drops from a patient's fingertip. "Well, Arlie," said Henderson, before he stormed out of the room, "I am afraid I have to forbid it."[8] Bock gave it up grudgingly. Years later, when I mentioned the incident to my uncle Will, his response was, "All I know is that Arlie was pissed that the Germans developed cardiac catheterization right afterward. Took the steam right out of his experiment."

Occasionally, a researcher's zeal created problems. Once, a visitor to the lab was hurried into a room, his vital signs checked, and an arterial puncture made in an arm. When the technicians then tried to load him onto a scale, he fainted dead away, smashing costly laboratory apparatus. When he came to, he groaned that he was just a visiting philosopher from Wales and had come in to be interviewed by Henderson. In recounting the story, Henderson added, "He has never come back, which under the circumstances is quite understandable, for there is no reason why a philosopher should enjoy having his artery punctured. He might well think it an undue interference with personal liberty."[9] Hypochondria did not exist in the group—what the subjects got was real, not imagined. If there was any doubt about that, a hand-lettered sign on a wall in the lab that paraphrased Dante's inscription over the gates of hell reminded the volunteers of what they could expect: "All hope abandon of avoiding the bends, the runs, heat cramps, emboli, or the tossing of your cookies, ye who enter here."

I did not participate in any of these tortures—youth, apparently, was the one guideline the lab's stress-inducers observed as inviolate. Nor do I recall much of what the lab people said to me or to one another. My memories of the sights and smells and sounds of the place are, however, wondrous and fixed. I was there to hang out, an unofficial mascot for the lab team, to play touch football in the stadium, to ask what this or that mysterious gadget was, what caused all that smoke pouring from a mad chemist's Florence flask, why that marathon runner had collapsed, gasping, in the corner, why that guy on loan from the Pittsburgh Pirates, naked except for his shorts and locked in a chamber, was banging frantically on the frosted window, why they were getting all those hysterical calls from people who saw pictures of the dog treadmill. ("These people are like sin," my uncle Frank would say, shaking his head because he couldn't understand animal rightists. "They'll never go away.") I was allowed, and encouraged, to roam about, wash lab glassware with long bristle brushes, poke my nose into jars of vile-smelling liquids, eat lunch while sitting in a soft leather chair in an altitude chamber, and set up my own "experiment bench" complete with a Bunsen burner, in whose flame I'd bend rods of glass, melt the ends of hollow glass tubes, then blow bubbles in them. I'd play around with small bottles of solutions like that most impressive indicator of all, phenolphthalein, which, when you added an alkali, turned an eye-popping red, and, when you mixed in an acid, was instantly drained of all color. I'd take a tube of it home for my bedroom lab, and magic like that went into the tricks with which I further impressed my pals on the corner. I also got to bring home a jug or two of pure ethyl alcohol for my grandfather, who, when he wasn't pressing 150 gallons of wine a year in his cellar, would mix it with extracts of vermouth and anisette, the homemade liqueurs to be served proudly to the lab scientists when my uncles brought them around to the tenement for macaroni suppers. Because my grandmother, the cook for these mammoth feasts, didn't have enough pots and pans to hold the gallons of tomato sauce and the meatballs as big as fists she'd have to make—the meal preparation should have been included in the Syllabus of Fatigue Laboratory Methods, which my uncle Will wrote with Dill and Horvath— Harvard would supply her with appropriate labware. There'd be boxlike metal sterilizers for the sauce and meat, army kitchen pots for the water, Florence flasks for the wine, even a huge slab of lab-bench slate on which the cook could roll out her handmade pasta. My uncle Will, who also doubled as a driver for Henderson, brought him by for a couple of these banquets, and my grandfather—who didn't know (and couldn't have cared less had he known) that this imposing man with the red beard was, among other things, a counselor to the president of Harvard and a great influence on scientists, sociologists, and philosophers—would address him with his own peculiar form of casual respect as Dottore Barbarossa. Then he'd ritually pour him the first glass of lab-spiked liqueur, because his sons had told him that the guy with the beard would be the lab padrone. Henderson, who had translated Pareto, would smile approvingly at the un-Harvardian doctorate, take a taste, and, when informed by a staffer that his lab had supplied the alcohol, remark, *"Bella roba,"* meaning "good stuff." My grandfather would beam, probably reveling in the knowledge that he, too, could mix a few chemicals together and come up with something that would pass the big lab boss's test. The compliment may also have changed his impressions of doctors in general as men who, as an old Italian proverb put it, became doctors because they couldn't handle a trade. My grandfather was a simple man who came to conclusions about people on the first meeting. It was enough that a man of Henderson's position could come to Brick Bottom—our section of the city, which furnished the muscle and the material that built Old Veritas, and where the Prohibition-era distillers, in their tenement cellars, made vodka from potatoes and water—trudge up three flights of squeaky stairs to a tenement apartment heated by a coal stove, address him in his own language, and knock back some potent home brew with a lesser mortal. Dottore Barbarossa just had to be a good doctor, really *prima classe*.

Only a handful of the men who ran the Fatigue Lab, or

worked there, are alive, among them Cliff Barger, long retired, but who still has writing space at Harvard's Countway Library of Medicine. Henderson died of a pulmonary embolism shortly after I started visiting the lab. Dill was in his nineties when he died a few years ago; up until his death, he was still monitoring his own vital signs, as he had done for nearly sixty years, pedaling a stationary bike in 110-degree heat at the University of Nevada's Desert Biology Research Center, where he was working under a government grant to study the effects of aging on physical performance.

Few, if any, of the students at Harvard Medical School today talk much about Bruce Dill and the others who sweated in the Fatigue Lab. Indeed, on the rare occasions when the name of the facility is mentioned in casual conversation these days, someone invariably wonders whether it's a rhetorical comment on the drudgery of labwork at Harvard in general. As for Henderson, except for his equation, a brief salute to him in a Tosteson orientation address, and occasional references to his scientific work by someone who's stumbled over his writings in the bowels of the Countway Library while researching buffer solutions, not many students know that he was a force behind the physiology they must study, and behind the other thing they must learn, and often do not—that it is not possible to know the patient without knowing his or her environment.

Such neglect is unfortunate, because more than ever today, in an age of transplants and genetic manipulation, of laser and laparoscopic surgery, with medicine so often hostage to the awesome power and tools of technology, with many of its students and practitioners too busy to "care" for their patients, the Fatigue Lab's underlying philosophy—of health as a social product, of a medicine that deals with human beings in a personal way, and of scientific study that realizes human activities and their interrelationships are "associated with human welfare in the normal activities of life as well as in the treatment of the sick"—is as important in a medical curriculum as anatomy, biochemistry, microbiology, and pharmacology.

Henderson's words, too, are appropriate these days when the primary-care physician, the family doctor of yesterday, remains under attack by the overseers of overspecialization. "It is the business of the physician," he once said, "never to forget the social factors; to acquire skill in the diagnosis of social conditions and in the recognition of the social elements in the etiology of disease. . . . The practice, teaching, and science of medicine have never been isolated from the affairs of men, but have modified them and been modified by them."[10]

3 | *Clinic*

IT IS THE AFTERNOON OF ORIENTATION DAY, AND CLARK Schierle, the teenage embodiment of Charles William Eliot's vision of the new Harvard doctor carried to extreme, and the youngest member of this Harvard Med class, has joined his fellow students now filing into the amphitheater at Brigham and Women's Hospital. It was here in 1954, when the place was smaller and known as Peter Bent Brigham, that a team of surgeons performed the world's first successful kidney transplant, moving a healthy kidney from a twin to his brother, an achievement that paved the way for what is now a routine procedure and that helped win one of the surgeons, Joseph E. Murray, a Nobel Prize in 1990. Here, too, in 1963, the poet Robert Frost died, two days after having scribbled a gracious and appreciative note to Janet Forbes, a staff nurse in the kidney unit: "Miss Forbes I met you on a cloudy dark day and when you smiled and spoke my room was filled with sunshine. 'The way you smiled at me/has given my heart a/change of mood/and saved some part/of a day I had rued.' "

The note and bit of verse, its homage to Forbes's tender, loving care notwithstanding, eventually showed up in a Boston bookstore; it had been sold for two thousand dollars.

Schierle does not know of the scrap of poetry or its fate, nor does he yet know where he will be or what he will be doing when his education is completed. What he is certain of is that he is fortunate to be here and grateful for the options Harvard has kept open for his future. Later, when pressed after he's been at the grind for a few months, he will respond equivocally. "It flips around from day to day, depending on what day you ask me. I might go into clinical practice, become, like, you know, a cardiologist or something. That would be really fascinating, the patient contact and all that. Other times, I'm really into, like, the scientific breakthrough, and I want to be on that cutting edge. Whatever, it's another source of joy being here. All the resources . . . You've got the guy who published the world's first paper on this and that. There's a lot of information. It's overwhelming, and draining, but I keep up. I'm studying and it's good, and I'm learning really cool stuff."

For his tender years, Schierle is a veteran of the learning process. When he was about eleven, he was watching a *20/20* interview on TV with a nine-year-old who was going to the University of Arizona. It upset him, especially since he knew his own IQ at age five—the tester stopped it at 180—was testing like the nine-year-old's. "Who is this kid?" he asked. "I'm, like, mine was higher than his, and I'm jealous of this kid who's going to do organic chem and calculus, and, like I'm stuck in high school and not really liking it much, kinda bored. 'I wanta do that,' I said. So, going to college at age twelve was actually my idea."

Schierle entered UCLA's early-college-admissions program as a microbiology major. "One of the things they had me do when I first got in was to walk," he recalled. "Like, get up and walk? Back and forth across the room to make sure I wouldn't look like I'd stick out."

Microbiology was a good premed major because it meant a small and closely knit band of students. "Biology and biochem are the big premeds," Schierle reasoned, "with huge departments and lots of bureaucracy." His grades were pretty good, although the first couple of years were admittedly a bit strange. "I was essentially, like, basically, asocial? I just, totally, didn't have a clue as to what was going on outside of class. I'd just go home and watch TV, and it wasn't until my late sophomore and junior year that I had this, like, awakening? Like there was this life outside of school? So I started hanging out with friends more, and went through a sort of, basically, like, adolescent, high school, social-type integration. That's when I started working in labs, and managed to find little groups of people who were kind of off-center enough to see beyond my age, people who liked me for who I am. It wasn't like . . . some people in the program became, like, mascots, child-prodigy types. It's a problem for some people, getting rid of that label."

Schierle comes from a family of architects—mother, father, uncle, and grandfather. His mother, who met her husband when they were both students at Berkeley, was born in China; his dad, a Ph.D. and professor at USC, is from Stuttgart. Schierle describes them both as "kinda mellow, laid-back, who wanted to be sure this was what I wanted and that I was happy."

As an undergrad, Schierle got more and more interested in research, and eventually he heard about Harvard Med's combination Ph.D.–M.D. program. "It seemed ideal to me. As long as I can remember, I've always enjoyed school, education, stuff like that, and medicine seemed to exemplify some kind of pinnacle or zenith, like, you have to spend years in school, and it's a respected profession, and you're doing a good thing helping your fellow man. I always aspired to that. What makes a good doctor is having a certain level of knowledge and applying that in a really all-encompassing way to health care. We have to take into account the patient's emotional health as well as curing disease. There should be mutual respect between the doctor and the patient. For a doctor to be on a pedestal is an unequal relationship, as harmful to the physician as to the patient. Sure, you have to have the knowledge, but the patient has the problem, and they'll tell you things you can't read in textbooks."

He applied to fifteen medical schools, "sort of hoping for a smaller school to get warmed up," and was accepted at five, Harvard among them.

The age oddity trailed him to Harvard Med. "It did come up during my interviews, like, how was it for me fitting into college? And I sort of used my age as a crutch during the interviews, because a lot of them were interested in that part of my life, like how I dealt with it, how I would deal with it here. My friends at UCLA had told me that at Harvard Med I couldn't expect to be a prize prodigy child anymore. Like, I wouldn't be pampered? Because everyone here has, like, amazing stories, like you go to a party and, like, one guy's climbed Mount Everest, and another guy's written a novel, someone else has a wife and two kids, and there's a Ph.D. in biology. Here you can find little niches that you're comfortable with. It would be a mistake to say my age is a nonissue, but people do take it as another facet of who I am."

The amphitheater is filled now, and Schierle is about to have his first exposure to patients. Dean of Education Daniel Federman is onstage again. His suit jacket has been exchanged for a white coat, but the bow tie is still in place. With him is Dr. Patricia Donohoe. She is as rare around Harvard Med as a *B* student: The school's only female full professor of surgery, she is also chief of Pediatric Surgical Services at MGH and an internationally known researcher in developmental and reproductive biology. She is not wearing a white coat, but a blue print dress.

With them on the stage are Liz Soccorso, a nurse, and her three-year-old son, Steven Soccorso-McCoy. Her husband, a builder, is sitting in the front row in the auditorium, along with Harriet Cohn, age eighty-seven, and her husband, Haskell, ninety. Young Steven has been Dr. Donohoe's patient ever since she removed a fibrosarcoma—a rare type of malignant tumor—from his chest when he was three months old. The Cohns, who have beaten back a lot of medical challenges, have been under the care of Federman. They have also been through this many times before, volunteering for the annual Orientation Clinic for the last several years.

This gathering is a traditional set piece designed to introduce the beginners to how the pros deal with their patients and to allow the students to ask all of them some questions. Steven has been chosen for the session because young patients generally have the advantage of being healthy overall; the Cohns because, as Federman will tell the audience, "Every year that they join us here, they have a different story to tell."

Donohoe takes the microphone and outlines Steven's case. The McCoys were on vacation when they noticed a small lump on Steven's chest. They went to an emergency room. The doctor told them it should be checked out, and they were referred to MGH. Donohoe did a lumpectomy on what turned out to be a tumor—a low-grade malignancy, which was good news—the size of a quarter. To get it all out, she had to remove the pectoralis major muscle from Steven's chest, and except for physical therapy, he needed no other treatment— no radiation, no chemotherapy. Steven shows no signs of cancer, but he is examined regularly.

Donohoe tells the students how she and Liz Soccorso have become good friends. She spends a good deal of time with her, and examines her child regularly. She hugs Steven, tousles his hair, smiles indulgently as he continually interrupts the presentation by darting about the stage, pulling at his mom's dress, and leaping into her lap. Donohoe introduces the mother, and they embrace each other, and the child. Soccorso recalls the fear she felt when she realized Steven's problem was potentially dangerous, how she searched for the best doctor to do the job, how she checked out Donohoe, and she expresses the deep regard she has for the surgeon. Her husband comes to the stage. He is nervous; tears come to his eyes as he tries to address his feelings about his son's predicament.

"You have to . . . okay . . . I was, well . . ." He praises Donohoe, says he and his wife will never forget her. She took the time to care, he says. "The greatest thing she did was . . . she hugged us and kissed us."

Donohoe asks for questions from the students. Several hands go up.

"I have a family member with a similar cancer," says one young woman. "And we have not gotten along well with the doctor. What made you trust yours and feel secure with her?"

Soccorso says she was comfortable from the moment she met Donohoe. "There was a relationship. The fact that she was a woman, a mother, made me relate to her. But more than that, she talked to us—not just about the scientific aspects of the tumor but about the experience, like, she knew how devastating it must be."

Donohoe picks up on that. She tells the students that the mothers and fathers of the child patients are the best doctors, that they should always listen to them as well as to the patients, because they all know more than the doctor does. "Always deal with them as equals; don't set yourself up as a physician on a pedestal; don't say to a parent or a patient, 'Don't worry your pretty little head and I'll take care of it.' Understand all the nuances. Most patients are well informed about medicine. I have never met an uninformed, unintelligent one."

Another student asks Soccorso if her position as a nurse helped her get the right doctor. Soccorso admits she had access, "unusual resources," a lot of people who fortunately referred her. "I don't know what it might be like for patients who don't have the connections."

A female student questions Donohoe: "I'm surprised at how emotionally involved you were. Would you have kept a safer distance if the prognosis wasn't as good as it was?" Donohoe seems taken aback, but only briefly. "It makes me a better person," she says, responding to the first part.

Another student presses her. Her tone, too, is incredulous: "Can you afford to give the same amount of time to all your patients?" Donohoe answers quickly, as though anticipating the question. "I guess we can, because we do," she says. Her eyes narrow a bit. "You're all very smart," she says evenly, "but you have to be sensitive doctors as well as smart ones."

Federman and the Cohns wrap up the show. Federman is perfect for this segment. He plays it like a TV talk-show host, and the students appear to enjoy his chatty rapport with his aged patients. Psychiatrist Ned Cassem has referred to him as a paragon, a very skillful doctor who has a way of extracting the right information from his patients. An understandable gift, since Federman was not interested in medicine at the beginning, but in becoming a lay analyst. Without an M.D. degree, though, it would have been difficult, so he went to Harvard to become a psychoanalyst. In the second half of his first year, while studying physiology, he switched onto a path to internal medicine, got interested in pulmonary medicine, then endocrinology, his field now. He teaches students, counsels them, accompanies them to clinics and to the bedside, sees patients, coordinates educational programs, and hobnobs with the dean, the deans of specific disciplines, the chairmen of departments of medicine and surgery, and with those who manage the daily activities of the school.

His emphasis now on the multiple ills that beset the elderly and the temptation to write them off as merely symptoms of old age are timely. Twelve out of every one hundred people in the United States are over sixty-five; by the year 2020, it will be twenty out of a hundred. Five years after that, the elderly will outnumber teenagers by two to one. But traditionally, the elderly patient has been a mere crock or a turkey or a geriatric case to generations of medical students and young physicians, who, though they may have been taught otherwise when they were taught at all, rarely remind themselves that

they have been aging since birth and will most likely be looking up at a young doctor from a hospital or nursing home
bed one day themselves. Even now, as the United States is
graying rapidly, as three out of four of the elderly are afflicted
with at least one chronic disease, when one out of four is
malnourished or suffers some degree of hearing loss, and when
more than half of the blind people in the country are over
sixty-five, medical schools often give only passing attention
to caring for the elderly. The elderly continue to have more
osteoporosis and hip fractures, are twice as likely to develop
complications than younger people, are especially susceptible
to heart disease, alcoholism, depression, suicide, and the disease that ranks fourth in what kills them, Alzheimer's. But few,
if any, medical schools routinely rotate their students through
nursing homes, even though there are now more people in
those homes than in hospitals and despite the fact that more
than a fourth of all drugs taken are taken by the aged in those
homes and wherever else they live. Instead, the schools' biochemists tinker with cellular mechanisms, trying to discover an
elusive biological clock of aging, and, with the same faith and
fervor as the medieval alchemists, pursue the quest for the
drugs and antioxidants that will give them an *elixir vitae,* often
without a thought, as they probe all the biology of senes-
cence—vital as it is to understanding the process of aging—to
trying to alter some of the negative cultural attitudes toward
aging and giving the elderly a healthier, as well as a longer,
life. Harvard Med appears to be trying at least. Geriatrics is
listed in the course catalog as a selective, a course that can be
chosen out of a list of mandatory electives. There are three
under geriatrics. One exposes students to a variety of clinical
activities and settings in which the elderly receive health care.
The second covers the biology of the aging brain, neurologic
and mental illness in late life, family dynamics with an elderly
family member, the relation between medical and psychiatric

illness, and the importance of a comprehensive interdisciplinary approach in geriatric medicine. The third examines the process of aging and health problems and teaches treatment approaches. The prerequisite for taking the course is stated simply in the catalog: "An interest in working with the aged." Not too many of the students sitting here now listening to Federman will display any such interest and opt for the geriatric selective. For one thing, it doesn't pay as well as the other specialties because it comes under the rubric of primary care, which Harvard Med has generally treated as a stepchild, and conventional wisdom holds that every doctor is supposed to be able to handle that sort of thing anyway. And since so many of the elderly suffer from the same disorders that the young do, why focus on it? A dead-end practice to some, a sea of lost ships of patients and doctors, geriatrics is not an ego boost for bright young doctors who need to get on with a fast career track and get themselves out of debt faster. Erroneously, they see all the elderly as wasted and terminal, plagued by incurable diseases. One has to wonder, as did Dr. Robert N. Butler, who served as director of the National Institute on Aging, whether medical students would so quickly choose to be pediatricians if they saw only babies suffering from irreversible conditions.

"So, Mr. Cohn," says Federman. "Tell us your problems." Haskell obliges. He has had hypertension, he says, undiagnosed until a routine physical turned it up; a stroke; bowel problems; and a hematoma on the left side of his brain, probably the result of a fall. The hematoma, not the diagnosis of advanced age that most of the students and not a few physicians would be tempted to offer, was probably why Haskell was growing weaker and listless after his stroke. "At the worst," he says, "I couldn't even dress myself." With treatment, he has improved markedly.

Haskell also wears a hearing aid. His wife wears two. She

also lost the sight of one eye. There is a tumor growing in the other, but, as Federman points out, she can still see. She is a foreign language translator. There are fewer questions for the Cohns, and Federman's message to these students seventy years younger than the two patients is quite clear: "When you are treating an elderly patient, anything you can do to improve what can be improved is valuable."

Federman demonstrates how getting at the root of a problem often depends not on what the ailing individual says, but on a family member. "So, Mr. Cohn, did you realize you were being hard on your children, as your wife says?" He is responding to Mrs. Cohn's observation that her husband worked hard and was under a lot of tension when he came home at night. He'd get upset when the kids practiced piano and said things like, "Don't even ask me what I did today."

Haskell answers sharply. "They did, but I didn't."

"Well," says his wife, "I hear you were always relaxed at work."

Haskell smiles, accepting the implicit causative factor.

"So, Mr. Cohn," Federman asks, "what happened when you called the doctor about your stomach pain?"

Cohn thinks a moment, looks slyly at Federman, and gives him an answer that countless patients would appreciate. "I called on a weekend, and he was on vacation. He tells me to go to the hospital." The students roar, applauding loudly. Their sympathetic response is a small sign that they are not yet overburdened doctors, the sort whom folks allegedly prefer moldy, as Oliver Wendell Holmes put it, like their cheese.

As the students file out—next stop the welcoming reception at the dean's home, followed by meeting second-year advisers and touring Boston and Cambridge—Clark Schierle is thinking, Wow. He turns to a colleague, a medical student who already has a Ph.D., and says, "You know, it's a good thing we're doing." Later, he was to say, "Coming out of that auditorium, I had the most ridiculous sense of just, like, love for my fellow human beings. I was feeling so incredibly, like, cornball. Being able to improve the quality of someone's life, that was incredibly moving and inspiring to hear."

A year before, among the first-year students who heard this same presentation was Shawn Nasseri, twenty-one. He was especially riveted by Pat Donohoe and her comments about parents knowing more about their kids than the doctors, so much so that on the very next day he started hanging out with her in her lab and while she operated. "With her, you get a feel for how illness impacts on one's life," he would observe, "and you soon see that there are things the kids are never going to tell you, that if the kids' parents are not actively involved—kids on antibiotics and on gastric tubes, for instance, require a lot of maintenance on the part of the parents—any surgery you do is never ever going to take."

4 | *Getting In*

A YEAR BEFORE THIS FRESHMAN CLASS BEGAN GLIDING THROUGH Orientation Week, Dr. Gerald Foster, who is an associate clinical professor of medicine, a practicing gastroenterologist at MGH, and, more to the point, Harvard Med's director of admissions, was behind his desk on the second floor of Building A, the school's headquarters in the Great White Quadrangle. It was a day in August, and the applications were pouring in to meet yet another October 15 deadline. By the cutoff date, there would be 3,260 petitions for admittance to the "Medical School of America," and soon afterward the complicated, labor-intensive screening that Foster oversees would begin, ending with the relative handful of students now listening to welcoming speeches in Amphitheater E.

An unopened envelope lying on the heap of letters drew Foster's attention. Doing this job for some ten years has made him something of a handwriting expert, and he could tell by the studied penmanship that it was from someone who deserved a personal reply. Not everyone receives such a courtesy, certainly not the ones who write and promise him that if they are admitted to Harvard Med, they'll find a cure for AIDS or a blood test for intelligence and that such discoveries would make the school famous and a lot of money. This letter was, as Foster suspected, from a youngster, a fifth-grade girl, and she was asking how she should go about getting into Harvard Medical School. Risking the chance that he'd be adding another juvenile pen pal to an already good-sized list, Foster took a break from the pile of applications and dashed off this note to the child:

Dear Amy:

Thank you very much for your letter. I am glad to hear that you are interested in being a doctor, because I think there is nothing better than taking care of sick people.

You should be a good student and do the best you can in your course work. But it's also important to be a good person, helpful to your parents and to your classmates, because these are the things we look for in people who apply to medical school.

I hope that we will hear from you again some day. Good luck in your plans.

Foster did not specifically mention the science these kids will need to get into this school, nor, though it was not exactly on the mark, the observation of another fifth grader, who wrote to give him her opinion that when someone wants to become a doctor at Harvard, "they have this here test in which they put you in a room with dead bodies and see if you can take it." Foster sent that one along to the woman who was developing a new medical college admission test and told her, "Check it out. This is it."

In 1992, according to the Association of American Medical Colleges, the 123 accredited medical schools in the United States and the three in Puerto Rico received some 354,000 applications from undergraduates who wanted to become doctors. Because each young man and woman who has chosen a medical career contacts an average of ten schools, there were actually some 35,000 individuals competing for around 16,000 spots. The number is not as high as it was in the early seventies, something then on the order of 42,000, spurred, some suggest, by students seeking draft exemptions from Vietnam service. At that time, there were three applicants for every medical school spot. Nor is the new applicant pool as low as it was some five years ago; then it declined to 26,000, making the odds of getting in excellent, 1.5 applicants per place. Today the ratio is still very good from the candidate's standpoint.

Moreover, once a student is in, flunking out is almost as impossible as flunking high school lunch break. The pass-fail system is prevalent; at Harvard Med, "marginal" grades are not used . . . officially. A rare student who merits such a humiliating blow gets a letter from the course director, with copies to the master of his or her society and the registrar.

The bottom line, however, is that once a student gets into Harvard Med, he or she is expected to pay the school back for the favor and graduate. Indeed, Michael Crichton has reported that in his days there, anyone who wanted to quit had to see the school shrink. Tell the shrink you hated it, and he'd be apt to say, "So?"

To ensure that enrollees make it, Harvard Med has developed what it calls a "constructive program for the individual student," which considers special problems and needs. A Preclinical Promotion Board appointed by the dean oversees the punctilious process that includes promotion without qualification, promotion with reexamination, "or other modification of the schedule," repeat of a semester or year with specific conditions, and, horror of horrors, withdrawal from the school. Students are asked to withdraw from the school if they are repeating an academic year and fail two courses, are on probation and do not complete conditions imposed by the promotion board, or have flunked step one of the National Boards (steps one and two must be passed before graduating) on their third try.

If flunking out because of bad grades is quite unlikely, leaving medical school because of the cost is even more so. A medical education generally does not come cheap—it can range from, say, as low as $5,394 a year at the University of Kentucky ($17,324 for nonresidents) to $20,250 at Harvard—but while the primary responsibility for financing schooling rests with the student and/or the family, borrowing is the most common form of assistance. There are all sorts of guaranteed loans, health-assistance loans, state and federal loans, and minority and other fellowships. Again, once a student is in, bursars see to it that he or she manages to pay, and live, too. At Harvard Med, where the $20,250 is only the base tuition—add-ons like health insurance, living expenses, fees, books, and lab and diagnostic equipment make it around $36,000 a year—the financial needs of a candidate are never considered during the selection process, and, the school's officers assure students, the effort to assist is "vigorously pursued." As one insider's guide to medical school admissions advises candidates, "Don't worry about signing for loans, either. You'll be able to repay the loan for your tuition pretty easily—and eventually you might have enough left over to buy mom and dad a nice Mercedes-Benz." To further reassure the candidate, the guide lists some median yearly salaries: $420,000 for a cardiovascular surgeon, $338,000 for a neurosurgeon, $274,000 for an orthopedist, $246,000 for a radiologist, right down to the paltry $101,000 for the family practitioner.

Most medical school applicants know early on that they want a medical career. These are the biokids, the brainoids, the organodweebs, the ones generally afflicted with that sickness known as the "premed syndrome," an illness characterized by a fiercely competitive, noncooperative race for science facts, which, if carried over into medical school, leads to what one Harvard Med alumni survey committee called an "excessively cynical, dehumanized, over-specialized and narrow individual." A few premeds do have the breadth of interests that medical schools say they are seeking today. Indeed, Harvard's premeds, perhaps more than those in many other schools, must take a wide range of nonscience courses, as must anyone who enters.

Still, medicine remains virtually alone among the professions in requiring a specific lineup of courses, science courses, at the undergraduate level. Despite oft-heard comments from college administrators that it is the premeds themselves who have serious misconceptions about premed and medical school requirements—and the vehement denials that the premed syndrome even exists—the fact is that the undergraduate colleges and the medical schools feed the entrance frenzy by their not-so-subtle emphasis on admissions requirements. And although the stereotypic description of a premed as an exam-stealing, experiment-wrecking, grade-grabbing overachiever may be a bit too harsh, everyone who has encountered them agrees that they are indeed a highly motivated lot.

At Harvard Med, little if anything is done to dispel the image of the school as primarily a training ground for medical scientists and specialists, and one has to rummage to find anything in official print beyond an occasional cursory acknowledgment that graduates are also in general practice, in public health, and doing low-visibility surgery somewhere in the hinterland. Indeed, even as the new freshman class was listening to Dean Tosteson's orientation speech, preparations were under way for dedication ceremonies the next day for a new 200,000-square-foot, five-story research building on the Quadrangle. Honorary degrees and medals would be conferred by the dean and the new president of Harvard, Neil Rudenstine. There would be papers presented on "Parental Imprinting in the Mouse," "B-Cell Development as a Problem of Cellular Selection," and, the high point of the program, "Quantal and Molecular Components of Excitatory Synaptic Transmission in the Mammalian CNS," by a scientist from the Max Planck Institute in Germany. And yet, not a few grads sometimes feel left out. Dr. George Bascom, a Harvard Med–trained surgeon practicing in Manhattan, Kansas, and the poet laureate of his class of 1952, has summed up the feelings of the school's unsung physicians this way:

> We practicing physicians have a perspective different in degree from the research scientist or the academic physician that needs to be articulated. The practicing alumni are the faces you cannot see. We sit in darkness before the beautiful and impressive transparencies when you lecture to us. We are not stupid, though we often feel that way in the presence of academic physicians. We are the ones through whom the marvelous gifts of science are made available to our patients. We don't discover much in the way of scientific knowledge. We try to understand the individual patient and help him in his misery. Our discoveries are the small local ones of diagnosis. Our lectures are to patients and their families. They are elementary, poorly illustrated and largely forgotten. Our rewards are the gratitude of people we help, the fees we collect, and the satisfaction of competence.[1]

On Alumni Day in 1992, Bascom rubbed the boys at the top a bit harder, declaring in his poetic-essay address, "I feel like a deer caught in headlights, who will soon get back to the dark of the forest where the practicing physician usually resides."

If the biokids stick with the narrow, accepted premed program—a program imposed as much on them by the schools' perception of modern medicine as by themselves—they will get in, but a great many of them will give up the fun of learning. They will survive the grind, but through it all, and later—during the three years and more of one-hundred-hour workweeks as residents in a hospital after graduation, the additional years of fine-tuning their specialties, and as they confront an average indebtedness of fifty thousand dollars and the deferred income—they will become frustrated, disillusioned even, by what medicine has become, a morass of paperwork, Medicaid, Medicare, and malpractice liability, a far more restricted and complex calling than it was when Oliver Wendell Holmes was telling his Harvard Med students that medical schools were not science schools and that medicine, at least on the curative side, was an art.

Most applicants to medical schools are between twenty-one and twenty-three years old, a handful are as young as eighteen, and in recent years some 8 percent have been thirty-two or older. Whites still dominate, though their numbers have declined somewhat: from 79.9 percent of the applicants in 1982 to around 66 percent today. There are also more female applicants, better than 40 percent of the total, and more underrepresented minorities—Native Americans, Alaskan Indians, Chicanos, mainland and commonwealth Puerto Ricans, and Asian/Pacific islanders.

The vast majority, nearly 70 percent, are admitted to medical schools in their own states, most of them public schools. Harvard Med, one of the so-called national schools, takes up to 90 percent out-of-staters. Given that many capable students don't make it in on the first try, the ones who do will probably have a lot of luck and charm along with their excellent college grades—more than 65 percent will have undergraduate grade point averages of 3.26 or better—and even if they're average students, they'll be helped considerably if they've tested high on the other essential screening device, the nationally standardized multiple-choice preadmission exam, the MCAT, which is supposed to enable admission committees to predict which applicants will perform adequately. Some four thousand of the candidates who failed to secure a place on their first try will try again, and close to 40 percent will make it. Others, generally older students, will apply to schools overseas or to one of the ten to twenty "offshore" schools in the Caribbean, risking limitations on how, where, and what they can practice in the United States.

The MCAT, required by most U.S. and Canadian schools, is generally taken eighteen months before entering. Administered on a Saturday twice a year, in the spring and fall, the test costs $140 and is broken into four parts: Verbal Reasoning, Physical Sciences, Writing Sample, and Biological Sciences. It is a grueling five-and-three-quarter-hour exam, with such questions as, "What are the highest and lowest values of resistance (in ohms) that one can construct using three 2-ohm resistors?" and "What is the maximum tangential speed of the subject along the circular path at the maximum angular velocity of 4 radians/s?" There are questions asking whether an elastic bandage will bring on increased oncotic pressure difference, increased flow into the capillary, increased interstitial volume, or a larger hydrostatic pressure difference; the definition of a zwitterion; and whether Plato's sense of truth was revealed by God, limited to mathematical proofs, agreed to by consensus, or underlies principles in any field.

Whether all the scientific arcana that saturates the MCAT is worthwhile is a question of continual debate. Some doctors, among them, understandably, those who entered medical school when scientific knowledge was confined to what could be observed under an optical microscope or from slicing up a frog, opt for the more nonintellectual essentials they consider relevant to medicine and to producing good doctors. While a few may have failed to grasp the importance of basic research to the advancement of modern medicine—for these, training at the bedside is the magic formula for students—they are not all that wrong. Indeed, a dozen years ago, an alumni survey committee assessing the selection and education of students at Harvard Medical School recommended that the school's requirement for MCAT scores be eliminated. Criticizing Harvard College's "undesirable pre-med syndrome," the committee said this about MCATs:

> Standardized hurdles are clear deterrents to creativity, ingenuity, inventiveness, and curiosity. Quantitative testing of the applicant's aptitudes and achievements (MCATs) is given considerable weight in the decision reached by the Admissions Committee. There is no sound evidence to support the conclusion that MCAT grades have true predictive value with respect to a given student's performance (either in medical school, in the clinical years, or thereafter). The existence of cram courses specifically designed to improve a student's MCAT score is ample evidence that the MCATs are not tests of aptitude but rather of information retention. It is also sobering to learn that the content of premedical science courses at Harvard College is constrained by the composition of the MCAT tests.[2]

Lest anyone forget that Harvard College values math competence, consider that of the 13,865 students who applied for admission to the class of 1997, nearly 7,000 scored 700 or higher on the SAT mathematics test and more than 1,500 earned a perfect 800 score on the Math II Achievement Test.

Although the goal and design of the MCAT has not changed—and neither has its importance in the roster of medical school entrance requirements—the Association of American Medical Colleges and medical school administrators have become painfully aware that science literacy alone does not a good doctor make, that breadth of education and the ability to write more than prescriptions and notes on a medical chart—both sorely lacking in generations of physicians—are equally important. The current test, thus, is also designed at least to encourage students interested in medicine to pursue broad undergraduate study in the natural and social sciences and the humanities. Moreover, the updated MCAT, which added an essay section to the test in 1991, assesses facility with scientific problem solving, critical thinking, and writing skills, as well as an understanding of science concepts and principles identified as prerequisites to the study of modern medicine. The Verbal Reasoning section of the test draws on the humanities, social sciences, and the natural sciences, presents the material in lengthy passages, and encourages the student to comprehend, reason, and think critically when answering specific questions. "They are trying to give people who may not consider themselves typical medical students a chance to compete," Richard Green, a spokesman for the AAMC, has said. "And they are trying to send a message to the typical science geeks and say you will have to know more than organic chemistry, you'll have to know how to think and write."[3]

Everyone who wants to become a doctor must consult, among the avalanche of popular paperback strategy guides that cover all the requirements from grades to ranking as an Eagle Scout (seriously), the candidates' bible: the annual four-hundred-page *Medical School Admission Requirements* put out by the AAMC. Along with specific information on all the fully accredited schools, the compilation offers reams of data on the composition of admissions committees, financial aid, and the timing of applications. It also has something to say about personal qualities and attributes, highly developed communications skills, and a solid background in the social sciences and the humanities. It tells the candidates that evidence of maturity, self-discipline, concern with helping others, and leadership is sought through information obtained from the personal statement on applications, evaluations by premedical advisers and college faculty members, and interviews. It advises that in writing a personal statement, the applicant should record not only the reasons for desiring a career in medicine but also extracurricular and work accomplishments, and that activities deemed particularly significant should be described clearly and succinctly.

While educational programs and philosophy differ markedly from school to school, entrance requirements vary only slightly. Most require a minimum of three years of undergraduate work and either "recommend" or "prefer" a baccalaureate degree. But for all the comforting commentary on the humanities—and all the dire warnings from educators about medical students in peril of becoming slaves to rampant technology—science is still necessarily king, and don't believe anybody who tells you otherwise. The wry observation some years ago of medical essayist Lewis Thomas holds true today: "There is still some talk in medical deans' offices about the need for general culture, but nobody really means it, and certainly the premedical students don't believe it. They concentrate on science with a fury, and they live for grades."

If there is a sameness in medical school prerequisites, however, comparing Harvard Med's entrance requirements with those of other schools reveals that Harvard demands more in-depth science than virtually any other. Harvard Med's demands are akin to a Dead Sea scroll, while those of its competitors are but *Watchtower* broadsides. Most of the schools list the necessary course work fairly succinctly. For example, the University of Kentucky College of Medicine, which admitted its first class in 1960, does it in about three lines: "Biology with lab, 2 semesters; Chemistry with lab, 4 semesters; Physics with lab, 2; English with emphasis on communication skills, 2." The University of Massachusetts, one of the few that actually advertises training for practice in primary care, in the public sector and in underserved areas of Massachusetts, simply lists a year each of biology, inorganic chemistry, organic chemistry, physics, and English.

Harvard Med's requirements are on a grander, Harvardian scale:

> Biology: One year with laboratory experience. Courses taken should deal with the cellular and molecular aspects as well as the structure and function of living organisms.
>
> Chemistry: Two years with laboratory experience. Full-year courses in general (or inorganic) and organic chemistry meet this requirement. Other options that adequately prepare students for the study of biochemistry and molecular biology in medical school will be acceptable.
>
> Physics: One year.
>
> Mathematics: One year of calculus.
>
> Expository Writing: One year. May be met with writing, English, or nonscience courses that involve expository writing.

The HST program requires even more science: "Requirements are the same as above except that calculus through differential equations and calculus based physics is required. A course in biochemistry is encouraged."

Forty years ago, a candidate might have gotten away with less. One had to have (relatively) spectacular science and college records, the admissions test, extracurricular activities, and letters of recommendation. But there were other, more mundane considerations when someone wanted to enter Harvard Med. "It boils down here to scholars who are gentlemen," Dr. Kendall Emerson, Jr., an assistant professor of medicine once suggested. He continued:

And by gentlemen we mean men with those intangible qualities that will make them good doctors. Perhaps it is a good idea to go to Harvard College because 43 of the 114 in next year's class are graduates. That does not mean there is favoritism. More of them apply. We know their recommenders better. There are no geographical limits [but] perhaps the best places to come from are Iraq, Iran and Australia, each of which got fifty to 100 percent of its applicants in— Australia had one. There is no advantage at all in having an advanced degree. We also don't recommend that alumni throw their weight around too much. Praise from parents is always suspect. The alumnus who writes that his son is a drunkard and a rounder but he'd like to see him admitted to medical school may make the committee prick up its ears and pay more attention than if he cites his son's virtues.

Regarding the "gentlemen" aspect of admissions policy, Emerson added that the incoming class had twenty-two glee club members, thirteen varsity lettermen (including four major varsity captains), a cartoonist, an Arctic explorer, and a glockenspiel player.[4]

Harvard Med has had a long history of such diverse expertise in its student body—not that it now makes a habit of accepting professional accordion players, world-class bungee jumpers, and graffito artists who are looking for some job security in a time of high unemployment. Over the years, the school has admitted a piano soloist with the Pittsburgh Symphony, a member of the American Ballet Theater, lawyers, the head of an art gallery, a founder of a Quiz Bowl team that appeared nationally, and one foreman in the roofing business. For Harvard Med, that roster represents a trend.

From the heap of applications on his desk, Foster and two hawk-eyed members of his sixteen-member admissions committee rather quickly selected eight hundred who met Harvard's exacting requirements. How had these candidates challenged themselves academically? Had they taken more than the minimum-level courses? Had they done the things that signal a love of lifelong learning—had they written a thesis, gone for honors, pursued independent study or research? But there is much more than grades and pursuing a project in depth. "What we really look for is a balance between intellectual and personal qualities. Contrary to mythology, we really do spend a lot of time looking for personal qualities. We look at what they've done with their time when out of class, how they spend their summers, their life experiences, their values, where they come from, what people say about them. But what distinguishes them is the extras, not just doing things to put in their resumes, but the things they've really been involved with—community service, inner-city schools, soup kitchens in Chinatown, teaching English as a second language, giving something to their country, and to the college community as tutors, counselors, AIDS educators—all of the things that indicate a concern about societal issues."

Foster and his committee picked out a couple of solid *B* students and put them in the pile of eight hundred. "There are trade-offs sometimes. Some people have come a great distance from some tragic circumstances in their backgrounds, have overcome some terrible obstacles, have been real leaders in service to their communities, and have such outstanding personal goals. Their academic credentials may not be spectacular—they still have to be very good—but they have that mix. We make an effort to have a diverse class, and not everyone over here is a superstar with a straight *A* average and an astronomical score on the MCAT."

As the committee sorted and selected, they tossed aside

the things that did not carry much weight. Letters of evaluation from premedical advisers and college faculty members who know the applicant rate high. Letters of recommendation from friends, family members, clergymen, or political figures do not. Neither does having a physician parent.

The weeding out was finished, and the eight hundred will be asked to come in for personal interviews. Most will come to Boston, staying with medical students who have similar interests and who have been chosen from a student council host list. Some candidates will opt to be interviewed at regional sites throughout the United States by Harvard Med alumni and committee members. In the meantime, the names and vital statistics of these eight hundred will have been sorted out by college and then assigned for further evaluation to one of five admissions subcommittees, each associated with one of the five academic societies and each made up of faculty, nonfaculty, and students.

The interviews will be painstaking affairs, handled with all the seriousness and trepidation that accompanies any job of deciding who is better than who. "You're never really quite sure you've made the right selection," Robert Ebert says, "which is exactly what keeps exasperated members of the selection committees awake at night after they've made their picks. You do the best you can. Choosing between individuals is especially hard because the ones who have been invited in for interviews all have such impressive credentials. I used to say that to get into Harvard Medical School you have to be first in your class, a concert violinist, an Olympic skating champ, and live in a tree hut in the Amazon."

Nobody gets into Harvard Med without two face-to-face interviews. HST candidates get an extra one. "It's hard to validate an interview scientifically," says Foster, "because it is so subjective. It does give us a glimpse of how these people communicate, and it gives them an opportunity to tell us what they think is important. We can also explore their values. We like to get a sense that they know just what they're getting into, that they have some sense of what's going on in medicine. If one of them doesn't have an awareness of medical current events, we have to question their motives for wanting in. It's so involved now. When I was in medical school, all you thought was that you'd be a clinician or a scientist. Now the number of careers in the medical field has exploded, what with the interface of law, public health, public and fiscal policy, and ethics."

The interviews will be conducted between September and February by some seventy faculty, handpicked by Foster from a wide range of medical disciplines, and twenty students. If the candidates have been around Harvard as undergrads, chances are they've thumbed through the "How to Prepare for Your Interview" section in the well-worn premed guide put out by the school's Office of Career Counseling.

The meetings are free-flowing and informal and not, as they once were, the rigid Q and A that tested a student's medical knowledge or, in some instances, the pro forma sit-downs to admit a candidate who'd already been admitted because he had the right connections. Today, interviewers are more apt to get candidates to talk about relationships and describe meaningful personal experiences. They want listeners—perhaps students who have had contact with sick relatives or other ailing people—who can respond to a patient's needs and also deliver bad news.

While the admirable goal of finding the student with the best chance of becoming a good doctor has been a consistent one for most of Harvard Med's existence, the current approach to identifying the right students is more refined than it used to be. There is a wealth of stories, apocryphal and unbelievably true, about the way it was. There was the Harvard faculty member who would invite a trembling candidate to take a seat—in an office bare except for the interviewer's desk and chair. If the student just stood there looking blank and baffled, he was out. Make a lousy diagnostician, fit only for some chiropractic college out in East Jesus. If he sat on the floor or the edge of the desk, he was also out. Too presumptuous, sign of a second-guessing pharmacist. The candidate was in, however, if he displayed honesty, either by stating that there weren't any chairs for him or by dumping the interviewer out on his ass. The student was also in if he sat on the interviewer's lap. Demonstrates an ability to adapt quickly to stressful situations. If the student who did that was a woman, well, she'd make a helluva empathic psychiatrist, and she was definitely in. There was the ringing-phone ploy. Kid walks in for his interview with a prominent surgeon, and no one is there. He takes a seat and the phone rings. If he picks up right away, he's out. The kind of guy who wants to be doctor because he couldn't make king. Kid is also out if he just lets the phone ring. Stupid bastard could have killed someone if it was an emergency call requiring "the Presence." But if the student picks up on the fourth ring, he's in. Understands that this is the office of the Presence, and answering his phone to take a message that requests him to deal with an emergency will not only get the Presence to the ward but allow him, after he's dealt successfully with the problem, to transfix patient with a stern gaze and murmur, as he holds out his steady palms, "Madame, do you see these hands? They saved your life!" There was the prof who always asked scornfully, "You want in so you can hang the big red H on your wall and make a lot of money, isn't that so?" Answer no and you were on the bricks. Unrealistic, given the financial state you'd be in when you graduated. Someone else wanted to know whether a male candidate could do a vaginal exam without getting aroused, and if not, why not? A yes or a no meant he was out. Then there was the doctor who, dragging on a cigarette and inhaling deeply, offered one. When refused, he muttered, "I hate guys like you," which meant the candidate was in. (On the other hand, some say if the student accepted the cigarette, he was in. Willing to take chances, like when they're evaluating black-widow bites and jellyfish toxin on student volunteers over there in Tropical Medicine.) There was the fake-you-out gambit. Doc: "Of course, as you know, that Italian—what's his name—Dr. Lascivio Amoretto, was among those who discovered the mechanism behind the engorgement of erectile tissue with blood." Student: "Uh-huh." Doc, leaping to his feet and pointing to the door: "Out, you goddamned bluffing podiatrist!" Finally, there was the legendary grand intimidator, who would suddenly quit in the middle of an interview, start to pant, loosen his tie, clutch his chest, and moan, "God, I'm having a heart attack. Help me!" Depending on the version of the tale, the student so challenged (a) runs out of the room for help from the formidable array of medical expertise in the immediate vicinity, (b) tries CPR, the Heimlich maneuver, or a tourniquet, depending on his qualifications to be a doctor, (c) tries frantically to open a window to let in some fresh air but finds it nailed shut and passes out, and (d) hurls a chair through the glass of the sealed window; it hits a workman below; workman sues and wins not only a sizable settlement but gets the interviewer dismissed. All except the Heimlich maneuver and a tourniquet get you in.

Ebert says most of the stories are probably all "beautiful fibs." Not so, however, the experiences of some who will never forget their interviews at Harvard Med. Cliff Barger, who was admitted to the school in 1939, remembers his agonizing, insulting meeting with an assistant dean who was reportedly quite openly anti-Semitic. Such sentiment was not unusual, particularly in eastern schools, during the twenties and thirties, and Harvard College was among those that paved the way by establishing a Jewish quota system at the urging of Harvard president Abbott Lawrence Lowell. Lowell, the sixth generation of Lowells to attend Harvard, had firm ideas about exclusion—they basically revolved around what we know today as the separate-but-equal doctrine—and Jews were not the only ones who fitted that format. "We owe to the colored man the same opportunity for education that we do to the white man," he said, "but we do not owe to him to force him and the white man into social relations that are not, or may not, be mutually congenial."[5] Lowell considered the Jews at Harvard—their enrollment had increased from 6 percent in 1908 to 20 percent in 1922—"an actual problem," which, if ignored or not dealt with courageously, "would be unworthy of a university." According to one account, admission committees were instructed to admit to house residence only students from the sainted Episcopal schools: St. George's, St. Mark's, and St. Paul's, as well as Groton and Middlesex.

Saul Benison, a medical historian who collaborated with Barger on a biography of Walter Cannon, points to the "open warfare certain Harvard hospital members had mounted against Oscar Schloss as Harvard's first Jewish professor of pediatrics, which within a short period of time succeeded in driving him back to Cornell, from whence he came."[6] Of his own experience, Barger recalls: "My interview experience was traumatic as hell for me. Things were different then, an era in which ten Jews were taken per class. I had letters of recommendation from Bruce Dill at the Fatigue Lab, from another top man over there, and from the lieutenant governor of Massachusetts, who was from my hometown of Greenfield. The assistant dean, Dr. Worth Hale, pulled them out and said, quite gruffly, 'Barger, what are you trying to do, impress us?' I said, 'No, sir, these are the people I've worked with and who know me the best.' He didn't ask me anything else, if you can believe it, and I didn't think I was going to make it, because he was the whole admission committee. It worked out, and it's probably why I got so involved in minority admissions in the sixties."

On the Harvard Med admissions committee, Barger had to overcome the reservations of some provincial faculty members about admitting a young man named Roman DeSanctis, now MGH's director of Clinical Cardiology, a clinical professor of medicine, Barger's personal physician, and one of a handful of heart specialists Boston-area physicians would go to themselves. "There was some question about whether we should take a chance on anyone from Tucson, this very bright kid from a poor immigrant Italian family who was summa cum laude. 'Is the University of Arizona comparable to Yale or Princeton?' they'd say. Well, I and some others went to bat for him because we were very impressed. It became obvious that most people on the admission committees shouldn't be there. There was that psychiatrist who used to nail down the window? Terrible. I used to argue with him about that. I suppose it was to determine how a student would react to stress. Terrible. They had no feeling for what makes a good physician, even though they were physicians themselves. What saves the process is the students themselves. They're so extraordinary, they want to come here, and we've often been lucky when we made our choices."

The interviews are over. The interviewer dashes off a summary and rates a candidate on a numerical scale. It all goes back to one of the subcommittees for more scrutiny. The subcommittee will vote on whether to reject, or send the application up to the main committee, which will give the successful candidates' records another meticulous going over. Each member will then vote secretly on a student by entering a numerical value in a book. The average number is calculated, and six months from the August day on which it all began for this particular class,

228 applicants, 95 women and 133 men, a slightly higher number than will actually matriculate, will be mailed treasured letters of acceptance. They will be given three weeks to respond. Foster knows from experience how many will accept, defer, or attend elsewhere. Unless there are extenuating circumstances, not on your life will too many who are accepted by Harvard Med choose another school that has also accepted them. This year, 165 slots at the "Medical School of America" will be filled.

Foster is not yet finished. He has letters to write, and not just to the successful candidates. There are the rejections, a job he does not relish. He shakes his head. "It is difficult to predict what the people we have selected will do in the next stage of their lives, but I can say we have a lot of talent here, and a real diversity. We have gone on what our candidates have done so far, and that is the best we can do. This selection procession is not an absolute science."

Soon, Foster will have another job to do while he's waiting for the next crop of students to come in, one that might even make amends to someone who didn't make it into Harvard Med but who was accepted elsewhere. He also sits on the MGH selection committee for interns. "Look," he says with a slight smile that signals he really doesn't believe it, "we're not the only great medical school in this country."

5 | Detachment

HARVARD MED'S FIRST-YEAR CORE COURSE IN HUMAN BIOLOGY is billed in the school's catalog as an intensive introduction to the basic sciences, centering on the structure of biological systems from molecules to organisms and with a focus on the integration of structural principles across all levels of magnification; the aim is to build a fundamental knowledge of structure/function correlation and general systems rules. The course will be taught using problem solving, case-based methods in small tutorial sessions and labs. Occasional lectures will focus on general principles, but it is in the laboratories that the new students will gain experience in solving structural problems in cell biology and histology, radiology, and gross anatomy. It will be in the gross lab alone, though, that these medical catechumens will experience a bonding with their "body buddies," an unforgettable baptism, not in blood, because the cadavers that are waiting in stillness for them now while the gala Orientation Week festivities are under way will have been drained of that, but in the preservative, formalin, which will bathe their hands as they work and leave traces of its pungent fumes in their nostrils as a constant reminder of where they have been, especially on these fall days when the campus leaves are dying.

First day in class. Introductory lecture by Dr. F., who doesn't at all look like someone Burke and Hare would have done business with, a pleasant man, not without a (sexist) sense of humor, who opens with a story about medical students fleeing en masse from the anatomy laboratory when they recognized a cadaver as a popular hooker. He delivers the punch line with appropriate dramatic pause: "She had a very large . . . clientele."

All, except me, in the auditorium will be physicians one day, and this course, which will add significantly to their mechanical expertise, is to be their first professional experience with a dead human being. The laughter at Dr. F.'s little joke seems exaggerated, but it is difficult to tell whether the students are masking uneasiness, as I am, by playing the insensitive role tradition dictates or whether, because of their prior exposure to the detailed study of lab animals, they are truly desensitized in matters of death and well on their way to becoming good doctors of machinery.

My participation in the course some years back, as a medical journalist, had been permitted for background purposes, to plug an educational gap. There were, however, other and more personal motivations. There was a gnawing need to shake off the fear and revulsion the dead had planted in me. As a novice reporter, I had seen death, but always it was violent and at a distance. The charred remains of the victims of a jetliner crash strewn about an Illinois cornfield like burned and broken jackstraws. The bloated body of a child, drowned under the ice on which he had played. The severed head of a drunken driver who tried to beat a train to a New Hampshire crossing in the middle of the night. A gangland victim, the side of his head blown out, bloody and brain-scattered, by a shotgun blast fired at close range. The young woman impaled, faceup and arms outstretched, on the spikes of an iron gate beneath the window from which she had leapt. The contorted face of a lineman shocked to death on his high-wire job. Museum images of Bosch and Durer and Holbein, the horrible Dance of Death theme, cavorting demons and skeletons leading unfortunates to the infernal regions. The childhood dread of coffins and candles and draperies of black, of muffled drums and the creaking gates of a cemetery, and the chilling words of the Mass of the Dead. Bottomless pit. Sharp flames. Torments of hell. Day of wrath. Mouth of the lion.

I had seen death and smelled it, and always I had turned away, and I had never touched it. My grandfather lying in an ornate casket, his face painted, the hint of a smile he hardly ever smiled fixed in place for years to come, smiling underground when he had no reason to, and I could not touch him as my mother had done, or kiss his white forehead after my mother, and I thought now that somehow a course in anatomy might help me face and touch death without fear and help me understand, just as the babies I saw being born and the patients I watched undergo surgery were fulfilling experiences, helping me know a little more about birth and suffering and how close to the edge humans tread in the striving for the ultimate goal, and that of all living things, survival. No textbook, no lecture series, no beautifully executed anatomic drawings, I was convinced, could substitute for the specimen that had to be observed, touched, and dissected before any logical conclusions could be drawn.

The medical student, says Dr. F., has to acquaint himself with some ten thousand special terms, and gross anatomy is responsible for about eight thousand of them. He discusses the early development of the science, the difficulty making progress at first because of ancient taboos against desecration of the human body. Egyptian mummy makers, who contributed a good deal to the future knowledge of anatomy, used to pack the bodies in salt, immerse them in honey, and coat them with wax. They got better at it later on. They'd extract the brains, open the body by incising the left flank, and remove the viscera, except for the heart; then they'd double up the corpse and jam it into a jar filled with a salt solution, where it would remain for several days. Dr. F. confesses the process reminds him of an old New England recipe for corning beef, where you take a piece of brisket, weight it down in a crock full of water, salt, saltpeter, saleratus, and brown sugar, and in a month it's ready.

After the epidermis and fat were dissolved, the body would be taken from the jar, straightened out, and dried. The cavities and skull were packed with herbs and myrrh, and the whole thing was then smeared with a paste of resin and fat and wrapped in bandages. None of this, he says, will be found in Gray's or Grant's anatomy texts, but he thinks it should be thrown in in case the dropouts decide on embalming.

Then it is on to Aristotle, the father of anatomy, whose conclusions were drawn from studies of lower animals and probably not from actual dissection. Warming up, Dr. F. tells us about Herophilus of Chalcedon, who, in 300 B.C., worked his way into the brain and recognized it as the seat of intellect; of Erasistratus, who had a theory that the whole body was made of tubes; and of another Greek, Galen, who took apes and hogs apart and wrote a very inaccurate but convincing anatomy book. Da Vinci did thirty dissections, until the Pope made him stop. But it was Andreas Vesalius, a Belgian, who was responsible for modern descriptive anatomy. In 1543, he published the first comprehensive analysis of the human body based on detailed observation. Vesalius stole his cadavers when he had to, employed a naked attendant when he needed a live subject for his "pubic, ah, public demonstrations," proved that Galen "knew an ape's ass from his elbow and nothing more," managed to stay out of the clutches of the Inquisition, although someone started a nasty rumor that he got religion "after some thumb-screwing by the Church," and went on a pilgrimage to Jerusalem, all because he supposedly opened a woman's chest to determine the cause of death and found the heart still beating. Dr. F. says that even though Vesalius confused nerves and ligaments, he was, let there be no mistake about it, the first anatomist to quarrel with the existence of pores in the interventricular septum.

Dr. F. is into the resurrectionists, who snatched bodies for medical schools, Holy Harvard among them, before laws made it legal. Contrary to popular opinion, he says brightly, and what we may have seen in the movies, they didn't raise the coffin. They simply dug down by the head, broke a hole into the front end of the box, yanked the body through the hole with a hook sunk under the chin, "which raised hell with the thyroid cartilage, not to mention the depressor anguli oris," replaced the dirt, and rearranged the stone and flowers on top. Dr. F. mentions someone named Cunningham, "Old Cunny," they called him, who was a notorious body snatcher of the 1800s. He used to dress his stolen cadavers in old clothes, sit them up on the buggy seat with him, and admonish them loudly for drunken behavior. Once, he tried to ship a body long distance over the rails, but the express company opened the box and sent it back to Cunny. Medical students used to play practical jokes on him, and to get back at them, he once snatched the body of a smallpox victim and had it sent to the school. He was delighted when a number of students contracted the disease. His widow had the last laugh. She sold his body to the Medical College of Ohio for fifteen dollars. William Burke, Dr. F. informs us, got up to fourteen pounds sterling for a body. Then he quotes a Dr. Donald Forman of Northwestern University Medical School, who says that the approximate value of all chemicals in the average adult human body is three dollars and fifty cents. Dr. Forman says this represents a 257 percent increase over the same chemicals' estimated Depression-era value of ninety-eight cents in 1936.

The Medical College of Ohio crops up again, which figures, because Old Cunny was from Cincinnati. Before he was President, Dr. F. says, Benjamin Harrison went to the college to look for the stolen body of a friend. Instead, he found the body of his father, U.S. senator John Scott Harrison. The public furor that erupted helped stimulate anatomy acts that allowed universities to have unclaimed bodies from asylums and almshouses. Speaking of relatives' bodies, a rather grotesque Harvard aside: Before John Collins Warren died—he was the man who performed the historic operation in the MGH Ether Dome and was the son of Harvard Med's first professor of anatomy and surgery—he wrote up a will, in which he stated that his bones should be "carefully whitened, preserved, articulated and placed in the Medical College near my bust, affording, I hope, a lesson useful, at the same time, to morality and science." There the bones stand today, in a closet, hidden from all of our eyes unless we are Warren family descendants.

Dr. F. emphasizes that medical schools do not buy bodies, and it is now possible to donate all or parts of one's body to schools and hospitals under the Uniform Anatomical Gift Act. Fifty percent of the bodies at this school have been donated, he says proudly; the rest come from state institutions. There is, however, a shortage of anatomic material. Dr. F. blames the funeral director's lobby for stressing the therapeutic value of funerals and for invoking visions of Nazi experiments on humans, as well as the relative affluence that enables virtually everyone with a friend or insurance policy to be buried. In the Depression, enough unclaimed bodies turned up in the city morgues to supply the needs of the medical schools. Dr. F. characterizes the donation of a body as a noble gift because dissection is the only way future physicians can gain the basic information essential to the diagnosis and treatment of disease, and he sees it as a way to beat the high cost of dying. While the nearest of kin must bear all the expenses of cremation or private burial, he explains, the remains may be buried without expense to the donor or to his estate in cemeteries owned by the medical schools. What is gained, he asks, when a body is placed in a casket, buried in the ground, and allowed to disintegrate? Better that the dead should teach the living. There are no religious prohibitions, he says, save that the dissection be carried out with scientific objectivity and that the remains be respectfully interred and not disposed of as ordinary biological refuse.

An informal survey has revealed that the vast majority of physicians do not practice what they preach to their patients about the need for donating bodies and organs for research and transplantation.

Their reticence to do so, some suggest, is inappropriate at a time when both the number of bodies donated for anatomical study and organs for grafting are in critically short supply.

The survey disclosed that few doctors are members of hospital organ banks, organizations formed to promote the procurement, preservation, and distribution of tissues and organs for transplantation. Few doctors have willed their bodies to medical schools and of those who are interested in performing this unique service to mankind, most are more willing to donate organs than the whole body.

"It's the old story," commented Professor William J. Curran of Harvard's Department of Legal Medicine. "The physician is usually the last one to get a cancer checkup. My impression is that many doctors would be willing to donate their organs rather than their bodies, and I think a lot of this stems back to their days in anatomy class. There's a lot of denial in the medical community."

Dr. F. tells us that for centuries dissection was a dangerous procedure, but he says that we shouldn't worry about contracting any kind of disease or infection, because modern embalming techniques have wiped out any problems. Several gallons of formaldehyde, glycerol, borax, and dye are injected into the arteries. The common sites of injection are the armpits, the neck, and the groin. The solution spreads through the vascular system and reaches the tissues, and the blood displaced by it is drained off by opening a vein at the place of injection. The abdominal wall is incised and gases are allowed to escape and fluids aspirated. Hollow organs are perforated, as is the diaphragm, and in the case of cadavers for dissection, latex is pumped into the arteries, puffing them out for easy identification and handling.

Dr. F. has one last thing to say, and that is that we not ask the identity of the cadavers. They are owed their anonymity, he says. They are paupers and professors, and it makes not a bit of difference whether we know who they were. He urges us to approach the investigation of the dead with dignity and reverence. He says he is not telling us this out of any belief that the body is the repository of the soul, for that is a personal thing. Respect, he says, is owed, rather, on sound moral humanistic grounds. He dismisses us to the laboratory, and there is a disquieting overtone to his words as he tells us that for a generation that has been crying out for relevance, here it is, at last.

I am aware of the gross lab before I get inside. The doorknobs are greasy to the touch, and there is a penetrating, pungent odor of preservative in the hall. In the room are the bodies. There are twenty-five or thirty of them, most of them white and old, with gray tufts of pubic hair that draw gazes like a magnet because we are all crotch-fixated from Eden, and the hair is on dead people, and death and sex preoccupy most of humanity more than anything else. So here it is, combined, in this room full of dead, helpless, pulseless, defenseless, breathless, maybe victorious people, all lying naked and stiff and wet and glistening on hard black tables, their heads and hands swathed in bundles of cloth to prevent drying. That, says Dr. M., who has taken over this phase of instruction, is because we won't get into the hand until late March, and the face not until sometime in April, which is just as well, because they don't seem as dead, masked as they are. There are skeletons hanging in corners of the huge, high-ceilinged room, bright lights overhead, deep sinks, wheeled, plastic-lined baskets near each table; buckets hanging from the tables, hacksaws, wooden mallets, bone forceps, scalpels, squirt bottles filled with preservative, rolls of paper towels on wooden tables, blackboards against windows whose lower halves are painted black on the street and campus side, and this is just as well, too. Outside, it is bitter, crystal cold, and the hard sunlight that streams through the tops of the windows does not warm; it is enveloped by the controlled chill of the room and neutralized. Winter's dormancy is victorious.

Standing on a high stool among bodies that were not about to rest in peace, Dr. M. says we are to go at it region by region—abdomen, thorax, upper limb, vertebral column and vertebrae, head and neck, perineum and pelvis, lower limb—and forget the sugar, spice, and everything nice, because we'll know soon enough, if we didn't already, that Avicebron was right when he said that man was a carcass fouled and trodden. He says we will work four students to a body. Two will dissect one area, two another, and then all will swap information at the end of the day. There will be an hour lecture each lab day, followed by six hours in the lab, with review lectures once a week. He talks about the architectural plan of the body, the intricate piece of machinery, the engineering marvel, the highest product of the evolutionary process. He says it will take us about 150 hours to break it all down. A crash course in demolition. He says he shouldn't have to go into that the body is a large unit made up of lesser ones, that cells form tissues, tissues form organs, and organs and other parts make systems, and that these, it goes without saying, are the skeletal, muscular, digestive, circulatory, respiratory, integumentary, nervous, urinary, reproductive, and endocrine.

He says we shouldn't look for more, because anatomy is anatomy, although Neanderthal man is strikingly different from later *Homo sapiens,* as we all know, with an average brain size of 1,450 cubic centimeters as opposed to modern man's 1,350, but then there is—he is sure we are all familiar with this—the people of the middle Acheulean hand-ax culture, not significantly divergent from modern man in anatomical features. He dashes through, with proper apologies for taking us over such familiar ground, human topography and map reading and planes and cavities, superior, inferior, anterior, posterior, quadrants, cranial, medial, caudal, proximal, midsagittal, frontal, transverse, the dorsal and ventral, separated by the diaphragm. He advises us to approach our work as geologists seeking to establish a stratigraphic framework, and that just as Department of Interior surveyors probe large masses of sedimentary rocks beneath the Atlantic Coastal Plain and Shelf to assess the petroleum possibilities of this unexplored province, so, too, should we probe these (he sweeps his hand over them), who will teach us in silence, who reach back to the australopithecines of the early Pleistocene—not for petroleum, of course, he wants to make it clear.

Some medical students, psychiatrists say, are overly concerned about their own health and well-being, an attitude that may be linked to a fear of death.

"The average medical student in this country comes from a family in the middle or upper-middle class," Dr. Charles H. Goodrich, a community specialist at Mount Sinai Hospital, once told a euthanasia conference. "He has probably lived a sheltered life in regard to death, questions of death, certain physical representations of death, and frequently he enters the medical school with the idealistic notion that what he wants to do is help people. And the first thing he is presented with is a cadaver, a dead body. Now, that should be the beginning of his education about death. Yet I don't know of any medical school with the exception of isolated experiments which has on any concerted basis tried to deal with this first contact with death. Those of you who have seen a cadaver that has been in cold storage for months will understand that this student not only unlearns any feelings he may have had about death, but represses them rapidly. He usually assigns the cadaver a nickname to permit him to deal with it as a thing rather than as a person. His repressed feelings come out as a kind of gallows humor usual among medical students. This inadequate training for death is then reinforced: in the second year, the student has his first encounter with the autopsy, where the patient has so recently died that it's hard to deny he was a person. The only help in terms of his feelings is being taught to concentrate his attention upon the organs rather than the person. By the time he gets to his clinical training, when for the third time he sees the human body being assaulted by the knife on the surgical table, it is not surprising that he is detached from it as having anything to do with human life or death.

The best we can say is that we have tried to train him in something called detached concern."

We are assigned our cadavers, my partners and I to a short, slight female with shriveled breasts and milk white skin and crinkly gray hair caught in the folds of the head wrapping. As I look at her lying in state, without the security of a coffin or clothing or the vault of a cathedral, unstimulating in her dead, aged nudity, examined curiously now but soon to be brought to a second end, her cloth-covered head like a white beehive propped upon a wooden block, her legs together, arms stiffly down by her sides, her mind mute and blind, her body drained, I ask myself, because humans are unconsciously convinced of their own immortality, where she has gone. Does she continue to exist, not as a woman, but in some other organic or inorganic form? If her soul is standing by and knows what we are about to do, is it saddened that its old home is to be torn down, or is it uncaring, because its new dwelling place is bright and beautiful? Or is there no one standing here but students and instructors, and she as well as her body are truly dead? I ask one of my partners what he thinks she would say were she watching us, and he answers directly, "She'd probably say, Man, I've still got it. Everyone's still trying to get into me."

Dr. M. distributes scalpels, probes, forceps, small scissors, and sheets outlining the lesson plan for the next few months. Two members of each team are to begin with the surface anatomy of the thorax, the pectoral region, and the thoracic and upper abdominal walls. The other two are to start on the surface anatomy of the thigh, skin the lower extremity, and begin the femoral sheath. He picks up a small plastic squirt gun from the head of one table, points it at a cadaver, and squeezes out a stream of formalin, playing it over the body as though he is at an outdoor barbecue squirting lighter fluid over charcoal. He tells us we should reflect only that skin over the area to be studied because skin, the largest organ in the human body, he reminds us, affords the best protection against drying of the parts beneath. We are to see that our charges do not dry out, and a few squirts from the bottle every so often, he demonstrates again, will keep everything nice and moist. When we are done for the afternoon, he says, we should give the remains a good dousing, lay paper towels over the underlying parts, and if we've left skin flaps attached along one border so that they can be folded back over what is beneath, then we could close up shop, so to speak, with a clear conscience.

We open our anatomy atlases, prop them against the cadaver's head, and listen intently as Dr. M. advises us that before we do any cutting we should get the lay of the land and, with apologies to the ladies, this means that in the pectoral region we are first to palpate the chests of the cadavers as though we were palpating the chests of our girlfriends, identify the bony parts, the prominent medial ends of the clavicle, the sternum, the sternal angle marking the junction of the manubrium and the corpus sterni, the position of the nipple, which usually corresponds to the fourth intercostal space, four inches or so from the sternum, situated in the female atop a rounded mound made up of superficial fascia containing the mammary gland, and we *Playboy* readers ought to know what that is all right.

We lay our hands on the flattened chest—my partner as gingerly as I, it is pleasing to note. We begin, loudly at first, shouting questions at Dr. M. or the roving instructors, as we slice into leathery skin. Wondering who she is, what killed her, who had loved her, I do a superficial dissection of the pectoral region, making a chest flap, tracing around the nipple so it will stay perched on the fascia beneath when the flap is pulled back, cutting through the deeper fascia to expose the pectoralis major, muscle that looks like flank steak, chunks of fat layering the area like the soft salt pork in baked beans, and it is like cutting through linoleum. Stopping to turn the pages of the atlas and peer inside, matching the color plates to the body, I suddenly realize, with some dismay, that the neatly mapped textbook is as near to the real thing as a Vargas nude is to the model.

Dr. M. advises us not to be discouraged, that Mother Nature hasn't read the textbook—in fact, she hasn't taken the course—and that people don't always have everything in the right place, and even if they did, we probably wouldn't find it all, because there are just some things that cannot be seen in a fixed body, only in a fresh one. Cutting, I ask silently, Does this hurt? adding, If it does, I am sorry. How frustrating it must be if her consciousness remains intact and she knows what we are about and can do nothing—like a stroke victim who cannot move or speak but who understands and sees; like being accused falsely and no one will hear you. Death checkmates. Had she died before she could apologize? Or before someone could apologize to her? Had she been fulfilled? Had she died before her body died? Had she never won by winning and now had won by losing? When the circus performer has defied death and beat it on the high wire, the spotlight that has held him for the crowd is extinguished and quickly beamed on again to capture another act. Her act, too, is ended, and yet the light still holds her. How can she rest in peace?

It goes slowly—cutting and probing, tissue by tissue, hands chilled as when trying to work partially thawed hamburger from the freezer into a meat loaf, the medicinal stench of formaldehyde rising up and smarting the eyes; reflecting the skin, checking the underlying fascia, picking it away tediously, trying not to harm the structures embedded in it, dropping bits and pieces of tissue into the buckets. Organs and muscles go into the plastic-lined barrel as I wonder which bucket gets the lumps of red latex that pop from every severed artery, then stop for a look and a probe at a male cadaver on the next table, they looking at ours, identifying each muscle, each vein, each nerve and artery, tempted to forget what cannot be found, because, after all, we tell one another, parading knowledge of a sort, there are about 60,000 miles of blood vessels in this lady, along with 600 muscles, 2 million sweat glands, 35 million gastric glands, and 12 billion nerve cells in the brain alone to worry about when we get there, and hey, not to mention 200 bones and joints, 6 billion fibers, and 72 feet of nerves in a square inch of the skin we have knifed into. But we are brought to our senses by Dr. M., who keeps showing up at each table to tell us not to be careless, because the more thoroughly we clean an area, the easier it will be later on when we are in deeper.

It is over for the day, and we have invaded her privacy. Laid open to some depth, her chest and leg in tatters, she is a poorly dressed scarecrow, a nameless, faceless instructor stretched stiffly on this slab, shamelessly exposing herself, sharing her deepest secrets with total strangers, allowing us to see what neither she nor any of her loved ones could ever have seen. I think of a jingle about Victorians and how they would react if they could see her. "They asked no social questions, they probed no hidden shame, they never talked obstetrics when the little stranger came." She and all the others are methodically moistened with the squirt bottles, paper towels are layered on, the skin flaps carefully rearranged but not fitting anymore. We cover our cadavers with huge sheets of plastic, then wrap them in purple cloth. It is as though we have undone someone's handiwork, have second thoughts, and are now trying to restore the finish we have marred, or, knowing that we cannot, are trying to hide what we have put asunder so callously.

Later, on the subway going home, the smell of formaldehyde sticking to my nostrils, I feel strangely exhilarated and yet somewhat shaken, as if I had just cheated on my wife for the first time. Smug or guilty, I cannot tell which, I look into bored faces, trying to arrest a pair of eyes, wanting to shout out, Hey, if only you knew what I've been doing, you wouldn't look so damned dull. At home, it grows dark and I thumb through the anatomy book. Brute memory. Jargon. Fifth costal cartilage, serratus anterior, rectus sheath, tendinous intersection; origin of the obliquus internus, fleshy from the outer half of Pouppart's ligament, anterior two-thirds of the middle lip of the iliac crest and posterior lamella of the lumbar fascia; its insertion, crest, and pectineal line of os pubis with transversalis muscle—forming the conjoined tendon, part of the posterior boundary of the external abdominal ring—cartilages of the three lower ribs, and by an aponeurosis, which splits for its upper three-fourths to rectus muscle, into linea alba . . . I'm deep into it until snapped to by yellow smudges on the slick white pages, and I think of her again as *her* and not *it,* cuts and wounds swathed in bandages, never to heal. I wonder how it would be if I went back to the school at this late hour, as some do, let myself into the lab, and stood alone in that room, and I know I could never.

The course wears on. Revulsion is sublimated in the work and patois but suddenly resurfaces—like the pain that lies dully beneath the morphine until the drug wears off. A student waves a scalpel while I lean on the swathed head with my elbows, in calculated cool, listening to his commentary on the Super Bowl. "Put down that knife, son," says Dr. M., ducking. "You're among friends."

The stench is familiar now, and I am more comfortable.

It is like the apprehension that nags when a new job is begun and new friends are to be made, and in two weeks or less, it is as though you've always done it, always known them.

Lower abdominal wall and inguinal canal, introduction to the arm, forearm, and hand. Finish the femoral sheath, canal, triangle, and adductors.

"What's the matter, can't find the fascial midline?" asks Dr. M., approaching a table where four harried students are attacking an obese cadaver. "Forget it. Just dig that stuff out or you'll be here next semester, too. Get in there! Go! You're not surgeons yet; you're high-class butchers. Don't pat yourself too hard. If that guy down at the corner market could have gotten up the dough, he might have made it into a classy place like this."

We pull her arms out from her sides with effort, and I listen, jaws clenched, for the creak, but there is none. We shove boards under the shoulders and stretch the arms out on them and tie them at the wrists to the board. Dr. M. drones. Identify and clean the cephalic vein. It's in the present area of dissection, in the groove between the upper border of the pectoralis major and the deltoid. Watch it. It disappears from view behind the clavicle in the delto-pectoral triangle. "I got it. I got it!" someone shouts. Globs of fat, like chicken fat, are removed with fingers that feel for the deltoid branch of the thoraco-acrominal artery, which, Dr. M. reminds us, accompanies the cephalic laterally, supplying the anterior border of the deltoid. Veins and nerves are stringy, buried in fat and muscle and fascia, a pulpy computer with its case removed, exposing the maze of wire.

Back and dorsal shoulder, and we turn her on her face. She is rickety and slippery. Hip joint, gluteal region, and hamstrings. Hands groping inside, I realize the sartorius muscle reminds me of a chunk of dark turkey drumstick, and Dr. M. tells us of the woman who telephoned to ask for the dental plate of her sister, whose body had been donated to Harvard, and of the students who, at the close of a day's dissecting, inserted a severed penis into the vagina of a female student's cadaver, covered her up, and the next morning, when the woman uncovered the body, how she was only momentarily shaken and delivered a great put-down: "Looks like one of you guys really left here in a hurry last night."

Lateral neck, pleura, superior mediastinum, and pericardium. A student across the room frees the sternum, ties a string to an end, and raises the breastbone by pulling the string through an overhead light. "Hey, man, that's engineering," says another. Introduction to the cervical fascia. Outline triangles of the neck. Posterior triangle. Interesting area. Thyroid gland. "If you go in," says Dr. M., "it's going to be lost to you. Don't skin it too much or it'll dehydrate, and you've got to come back to it later. Look for the external jugular. It's an invaluable landmark." Someone finds it first and says so, and someone else says, "Hey, give that man a box of balls." An exasperating dissection filled with lots of fat, and fibrous nerves and connective tissue look alike. Dense, but with diligent picking, says Dr. M., we'll get through. "But don't be discouraged. We'll be in the heart after vacation." Do you help your patients, doctor, the old man, the old woman, because they cannot help themselves, or do you do it because you are trained to do it? Do you get angry at patients for being sick?

A researcher from the university was discussing his recent project. He waved a hand to the projectionist and said, "And now—slide—this funny little group with congestive heart failure."

He was interrupted by a question from the floor.

"Doctor, were the prisoners in your study co-operative?"

"Oh yes," he replied. "Very. They loved it, actually. They got paid, you know, and they could use the money to buy candy and gum."

We attend a surgical film. It is about surgical approaches to the hip joint and is produced by the Veterans Administration. There are cheers and a few hisses when a narrator tells us that a team from the University of California Medical School is involved. There is laughter when he says, "Before we go on with the operation, let's look closely at these parts in our drawing." Laughter erupts again when he tells us to notice that the patient is lying in the prone position.

In the lab, a student says, "She couldn't have done much necking" as he struggles to bend the neck to get at lateral dissection. Hard work, no give. Students lean on foreheads and faces of cadavers as they discuss the next move. Heads uncovered, and ours looks like the face had done isometrics before it died. She is old, nutcracker face, chin turned up to meet down-turned and flattened nose. I do not know her. We move her again and her ripped skin flaps heavily. A student wants to take home a piece of bone for a keepsake, and a woman admonishes him, "These people appreciate being buried with all their parts." Later, she cuts herself with a scalpel and someone tells her to watch out, she'll get cadaveritis.

Vacation, and back to an exam. "The following questions are offered to help you assess your progress and intended to help you relate your knowledge to function and to clinical application, and to give you some familiarity with the kinds of information sought in state and national board examinations for medical licensure. Give the course, branches, and function of a typical thoracic nerve. The attachments, innervation, blood supply, and actions of the pectoralis major. Describe a possible route of collateral circulation from the subclavian ar-

tery to the vessels of the leg if the aorta is congenitally con-
stricted or narrowed by disease. List the coverings and contents
of the spermatic cord. If you are seated and cross right leg
over the left leg, what muscles would be principally involved
in executing this movement?

In the lab, I look at the heart, brownish red and hard, for
the first time, nestled in the chest cavity. Sections of ribs, with
muscle adhering, are broken off, like spare ribs. Lecture by
Dr. L., a crowd-pleaser who calls students "kids" and the heart
"headquarters." He stops by our table, chides me for being
too meticulous. He removes the scalpel blade and blunts away
at the juicy fat on the heart's surface. "You haven't got the
time," he says.

The heart is out, and holding it in my hand, I feel that it
is cold, and I think of hard-hearted Hannah, the vamp of
Savannah, and heart of my heart and Valentine cards and love,
courage, and the strength of kings and lions. I look closer at
this stilled engine that has pumped tons of life in its lifetime
and I think of the Living Theatre and its obsession with nudity, its actors who rip off their clothes and scream of honesty
and proclaim that this is the way it is, and I say, No it isn't.
This is it, this heart, this cadaver torn open for all to see,
recesses that have been hidden all through life; but then, as I
hold the heart and squint at it, I have my doubts about even
this piece of truth, because it may be filled with latex.

Dr. M. is in high gear, telling us, Come off it, Denton,
the name of this game isn't surgery; it's systematic destruction.
Get your hands in; you're the worms of Job. You're not going
to be sued by that one, so don't be dainty. It's too bad you
have to learn all this stuff, isn't it? Should have all been chiro-
practors, learned it in six months. Bright kids like you would
learn it in two. You've got a textbook body there, boy, open
it up! Come on, lady, look at it! It's not pornographic on the
inside. Remember, the lab cadaver is going out of style some-

day. Be a historical oddity, so get in there before it's too late. Enjoy your necromania.

We finish the heart, which has been dissected open, washed in the sink of its fibrin and sludgy blood, simple intricacy. Gallows humor picking up, out of a necessity to offset the grim work, or something deeply hidden, inadmissible. "Here, catch," says a student, lobbing a heart across the room. "How about a transplant?" asks another. Someone else says, "Cough," inserting a finger up under an esophagus. A woman walks into the lab and approaches one of the students. Unruffled in this place of split-open and frayed cadavers, she discusses something in a low voice, and I am angry because she is oblivious in this privileged preserve, because she has come into this house of carnal knowledge with that same air of detachment that teenage girls assume so well at a dance. Screw her.

"Let's juice her up," says someone loudly, squirting preservative. It sloshes on his partner's feet and he yells, "Hey, man, what are you trying to do, preserve my balls?" The slosher says, "No, just want to keep 'em cool." How melancholy at a funeral, how lighthearted here, and I wonder which is real, or are both displays a fraud?

Lungs and posterior medisastinum. Slice through the ligamentum arteriosum, through the cartilaginous trachea a few inches above where it bifurcates. Questions fired from the roving instructors. What nerves supply the larynx? Show me the manubrium of the sternum, boy. The right bronchus begins opposite which thoracic disk? Wrong. Free the pulmonary veins from the what? What is it that you're going to separate from the thoracic wall? It's like unhooking the hoses before removing the motor, and the lungs are out and lying between the knees of our subject, spongy, the bronchi twiggy roots. We try to inflate them with a bicycle pump but have no luck. Study them. Interlobar fissures. Groove for the first rib. Is there an eparterial bronchus in the right lung? Did she smoke? Yes. Right.

Radiology lecture. "When you look at the chest radiologically, you are basically looking at arteries," says Dr. T. He tells us that a skilled radiologist can tell whether the X-rayed subject is a blonde or a brunette. Slide. Skeleton. Chest. "Here's a brunette who wears braids. The coiled hair in pigtails massed along the shoulders is dense enough to stop the rays." He says, "I'm not orally fixated, but all sorts of interesting clinical conditions can be observed in the boobs. Who likes boobs? Who likes blondes? Is this a man or a woman? Right. The areola shadow. Terrific. You can take your boards next week. Okay, now a rapid tour over the bronchial tree. Note that the right diaphragm is slightly higher than the left. This—slide—happens to be a publisher of some magazine, *Time* or *Life*. I don't recall who, but he had emphysema. You'll see this is supernormal, which is what an editor of one of those magazines should be, I suppose."

Finish posterior mediastinum, begin ventral shoulder and axilla. Amputate at midthigh, popliteal fossa, anterior and lateral leg and dorsum of foot. To the arm and elbow, hand, plantar foot. It is beginning to grate, like Ravel's *Bolero*. Our lady is an "only" to us—like the *only* in only twenty kilotons, not a full-scale thermonuclear explosion; or only 1,279 deaths from malnutrition; or the overall death rate for the three hundred cases was 0.33 percent, there being only one death. She is 65 percent oxygen, 18 percent carbon, 10 percent hydrogen, 3 percent nitrogen, 1.5 percent calcium, 1 percent phosphorus, and 1.5 percent other. Or she was, and if that was all, then it makes no sense.

RESOLVED, That the depredation of morals consequent upon the disinterment of bodies and the annihilation of the bitter feelings and sentiments that usually follow a long familiarity with the horrid dissection room, renders it no doubtful question whether medical colleges are not productive of more mischief than benefit to the country.

—citizens' resolution, Painesville, Ohio, 1845

To the dorsal forearm and hand, the joints of the lower extremity, and she is a mess, limbs severed and sawed. Some clown has positioned a loose leg between her thighs, the toes pointed toward her head. I feel a light touch on my shoulder and turn, to see a bony white hand dangling bits of skin and stringy veins and nerves, clutching at me, and I swat at it in panic, knocking it to the floor, and someone says, "Hey, cut the shit," and everyone laughs, then grimaces as a student raises a disconnected leg with its curled toenails and yellowed sole, holds it in front of his mouth, and screws up his face in a fiendish expression, pretending to take a bite. Near the windows, a woman in baggy PJs holds high an amputated hand, its middle finger rigid, extended, the others folded down, and someone yells, "Right on, Freda," and someone else says, "You mean right up," and another remarks, "Yeah, up hers." Someone says, "The fist would fit better," to which is added, "How do you know?" And Freda says "Fuck you," and everyone cheers.

Against the hacksaws' rasp, it is the Bruins and the Rangers, getting shit-faced, balling, the party at Mammy-Jammer's, Ralph Nader looking for volunteers for six weeks—100,000 doctors have quit smoking—beer. And there's the little mother right in there, you extensor pollicis brevis you, and someone singing, "Come to me, my melanoma baby," reciting mnemonics to identify the carpal bones: "Never Lower Tilly's Pants; Mother Might Come Home." Did you hear the one about the doctor examining the teenage girl? He puts the stethoscope on her chest and says, "Big breaths," and she says, "Yeth thir, and I'm only thirteen." How was that belly dancer show? Abdominal. "Hello, Doctor. I'm terribly embarrassed, but did I leave my panties in your examining room?" "No," he says. "Oh, come to think of it, maybe it was at the dentist's," she replies. This guy runs into a doctor's crowded waiting room and he's yelling, "Doc, Doc, my cock, my cock." "Just a minute, sir," says the nurse, aghast. "Please use a more delicate term." "Okay," says the guy, "my finger, my finger." "That's better," she says. "What's wrong with it?" "I can't piss through it," he screams. Hey, there's this guy lying in a sack at the hospital and he's really pissed about all the tests and crap . . .

An argument breaks out at the next table over who should have the patella, extricated with great difficulty, for a key chain or a charm bracelet. "Send it to Joe Namath," says someone, grumbling, as he fights his way through bands of cartilage and fiber and tissue to get at a knee joint. "Look what happened to the fat ballet dancer," says another, pushing a severed foot against the table so that the toes bend into a grotesque position. "I don't think I'm going to be anything when I grow up," says a woman ruefully. "I should have majored in arts and letters."

Dr. M. grabs up a wrist from a table and tells us that plenty of tendons cross it; it's a busy street. Look, see the beautiful tendinous arch here. Here's the hamate, and the hamate has a hook in it. See? Three muscles form the boundary of the snuffbox. See? This isn't just some stuff hung on a cadaver. It's hung on your shoulders. Get in there! Do some plumbing or carpentry or whatever your trade is. What do you tell students about the hand? Nothing. You scare them, that's what you do. There are only three specialists alive I'd trust to operate on my hands, and none of them are in this city. Warning. If we've anything left of the hand when we're through dissecting, then we haven't done it. Look. See the hook of the hamate. See the pisiform. It's beautiful.

We are into the peritoneum and abdominal topography. Mobilize the intestines. Begin abdominal circulation. The stomach, portal system, spleen. The inner sanctum. Liver, biliary tract, pancreas, and duodenum. Spermatic cord and testis. Identify the ejaculatory tract, cut into the mons pubis, identify the clitoris, the twigs of posterior labial veins. Slice open a penis that looks like a cold, blackened frankfurter, and who'd want to screw after all this? Dr. T. lectures on liver trauma, which is rising. "This one—slide—is from an accident right on our own expressway. This fellow—slide—did well enough to go on to jail."

We remove the large intestine and take it to a sink, fix it to a spigot, and turn on the water. It bulges, bursts, and sprays us. "What's the matter, didn't you ever stuff sausages before?" asks Dr. M. One student has draped a length of bowel around his neck. "Welcome to the Aloha Restaurant," he says, bowing. Gallbladder slit open, green inside—it has two small stones. Liver removed, cold calf's. "Best thing to do," says Dr. M., "is to get a pound or two at the market and dissect at home for practice." Ours is overly large and heavy and slices cleanly with a scalpel. Stomach opened. Chalky material inside, ridges prominent, like tripe. Intestines like Christmas tree tinsel, limp, once full and fat. A student with a lump of red latex hidden in his hand walks over to a friend, coughs into his hand, and startles him with mock blood. We find a semihard amber-colored piece of something stuck into a kidney and no one can identify it. "Hey, guys," says someone, "Dr. S. is walking around and he's got a book that gives the cause of death of all the cadavers, and he's asking questions." Dr. S.

asks us and we tell him atherosclerosis. He shakes his head, disgusted. "You're going to make great allergists," he says, and walks away. A student activist suggests putting a cadaver on every committee, and someone else feels it is such a nice day, we ought to take the bodies out on the lawn, where the secretaries are sunning themselves only a few feet away, and finish out there, where it is now spring. Resurrection time. In here, there is none, at least none that we can see, only Dr. M. saying, "Get your face into that anus. Get your finger into that rectum or you'll put your foot in it. Get in there if you're going to get anything out of this course. One finger in the rectum, two in the vagina, and remember you're not making a social call." Into the hardened vagina and beyond with knife and fingers probing, seeking more than what that old gang of mine, if they could see me now, used to sing: "When much to her surprise, her belly began to rise and out of her cunt came a little runt with his ass between his eyes." I unravel her sex, a grand tour, passing again through the mysterious and forbidden gateway I had traveled through once years before, before memory, and many times since, remembered, in an opposite direction, on different missions. We are tracing farther inward, but we find nothing but what we are supposed to find, and often not even that. I am disappointed. Dr. M. says, "Why anatomy? Ask it. Well, it's like this. It's nice to know what you're doing. Some goddamned idiot will suture a medial nerve to a tendon and it's good-bye Broadway, hello Skowhegan. That's all there is."

Lecture by Dr. S. "The professional anatomist is not merely someone who dissects cadavers. His field of interest is a broad one that involves the scrutiny of the structure of organisms at a number of levels of magnification. In the basic research laboratories, he uses an electron microscope to study, in detail, subcellular organelles and macromolecules, going deeper than his knife can take him. His sophisticated equipment has a resolution of between five to ten angstrom units and the magnification is around 250,000 times. This deep-seeking is essential if we are to understand how various systems function and mesh, how normal and pathological processes occur in cells and organs."

She is a heap, the hint of a human form. Only the neck and the head are left, a broken plaster bust; the rest is crammed into buckets and bags. Ruins of the dead. Our bodies lull us into a false sense of security. They're but passing travelers on a one-way trip from here to there, wherever that might be.

"We might as well face it," says Dr. T. "We're going to have to do the muscles of facial expression." We hiss. In the lab, we expose the depressor anguli oris ("When it contracts, you get a grin"), the buccinator ("Dizzy Gillespie had a fantastic bux"), the masseter ("When you clench your jaw"). Her features are now rubble, and with this last bit of her individuality ruined, she looks like every other cadaver in the room. In the lecture hall, Dr. T. concludes with four slides of a pretty woman's smile, a pleasant ending, but at the same time it cannot hide, after what we have seen, what lies beneath that lovely face, behind that blemish-free skin and those capped white teeth, a grinning skull no different from what we have left in the lab. It is like the plush nightclub when all the lights are on and the cleaning ladies are at work, and what shows are the snags in the rug, the nicks in the furniture, the paint streaks on the wall. It is being where the dirty dishes are stacked in a fancy restaurant, or sitting next to the waitresses' station, where their complaints and mocking remarks about the customers are overheard. In one sense, I am pleased with this view of reality that makes all men brothers. In another, I am sorry I have seen it, for it leaves me with a sense of loss: a sexual chase ended; the bright promise of a lunar landing no more; anticipation that is more exciting than the act, and it can never again be the same, to enjoy the morbid thrill I have associated with closeness to the dead human body, the ultimate in expectation.

Scalp, removal of the brain, cranial and spinal meninges. Orbit. Ear. Parasagittal section of skull, nose, and parasinal sinuses. "You can look for it, but you won't find the back of the mind," says Dr. M., "even though you're supposed to be putting all this stuff there."

We dissect the eyelids, and there is nothing inside, so we study the cavities and the diagrams in the atlas. Two of us hold the head on a block while one saws the top of the scalp. Bone dust and the smell of a woodworking shop. The top is pried off and we stand ready to catch the brain should it fall out. It does not, but droops liquidly. It is soft and pulpy, badly preserved, and we dump it into the bucket, this most magnificent achievement of biological evolution, a computer turned to jelly. The inside of the skull is smooth, mother-of-pearl. A student holds up his half head by the backbone and remarks it would be great in a torchlight parade to the stadium. At another table, someone has a firmer brain, and he skins off a portion of the cerebellum and asks, "How do you like it, rare?"

It is over at last, and I know nothing, really, of death, only bones and bodies, the symbols of death, and about all I have done is join an exclusive club that will never forget these long days, that has overcome a built-in aversion to corpses by simply treating them as machinery. Understanding of death may come when we stand on the brink of the grave, or it may not, but that is not important. What is more material is the dying, the relentless process by which we pass into extinction, often as patients, alone and helpless and despairing. The laboratory is rewarding in a practical sense, for I have seen my inner physical self in the mirror of a cadaver. It has stamped out a fear. But it has not taught me or these physicians-to-be anything about dying, just as it has taught us nothing substantial about death. It may even have stood in the way of any future enlightenment, for the anatomy lab and its methodology can easily deflect from humankind's ideal, which is empathy. It would have been better if the cadavers we had dissected had been identified, if we had been told something about their lives, and if we had had access to Dr. S.'s book detailing the causes of death. Then they would have been human beings, and the hardening process that goes on in the gross lab would not be transferred as easily to living people and to patients later on. Simplistic and naïve, perhaps. I tend to think not. Tempered and distorted by their gross lab experience, and somewhat arrogant now that they have reduced what once lived to a pile of offal, some newly minted physicians often will treat their patients in the same cold, businesslike way they treated the cadavers. They will regard death and dying merely as inevitable and will avoid the subject because it focuses on their inability to guarantee immortality. When they do face it, reluctantly, they will subject the dying patient to long and costly medical and mechanical procedures to prolong life, sometimes needlessly.

Moreover, the cadaver itself, at least as a tangible reminder that life is a terminal illness, will probably soon be gone, a relic of the past superseded by modern technology. Harvard Med and other medical schools are already devoting less time to gross anatomy than they did, and software that now enables students to dissect and move the body parts of computerized cadavers has, for all of its virtual reality, taken students further away from not only the reality of death but from the patient who suffers it. When Oliver Wendell Holmes compared the mesentery to shirt ruffles, and a sweat gland to a fairy's intestine, he was not lecturing as a disengaged scientist or as a mere mouther of elegant phraseology, but as a physician who could truly see beyond what the dissecting knife reveals. There is a stronger, although similar, message in the observation of the seventeenth-century anatomist Bernard le Bovier de Fontanelle. "We anatomists," he said, "are like the porters in Paris, who are acquainted with the narrowest and most distant streets, but who know nothing of what takes place in the houses."

6 | *Young Veritas*

NEARLY A CENTURY AND A HALF BEFORE THERE WAS A HARVARD Medical School, its venerable ancestor, Harvard College, was founded in a ramshackle farmhouse in the middle of a cow pasture in New Towne. It was 1636, and the town—which would be renamed Cambridge in tribute to the more than one hundred Massachusetts Bay Colony residents who had attended Cambridge University in England—was a dirty little village; Boston, across the Charles River and known as Shawmut by the Indians, had been home to the first Colonial governor, John Winthrop, for only six years. There was probably only one table fork in use—the one brought to America and given to Winthrop as "a wondrous gift." Public morals were under the watch and ward of Bible-brandishing Puritan ministers, simple men who founded the Congregational Church, which would steer the religion and politics of New England for years to come, and who, in their zeal to purify their Church of the policies and pomp of popery and the Church of England, railed on in two-hour homilies, trashed vestments and ceremony, and generally killed or numbed what little pleasure there was in the early settlers' hard life. Jamestown, Virginia, the first permanent English settlement in America, was not yet thirty years old, and the Mayflower settlement in Plymouth, peopled now with some twenty thousand immigrants from the British Isles, only sixteen. William Shakespeare had been dead only twenty years, Michelangelo seventy-two. The Thirty Years War was in its French phase, the Manchu were invading China, and Galileo was living in strict seclusion in Florence; three years earlier, he had appeared before the Inquisition to renounce his belief that the earth moved about the sun, and he was now completing his *Dialogues on the New Science.*

In Boston, on the three-peaked hill called Trimontaine, which would become Beacon Hill, the country's first grand jury was gnashing its teeth over Anne Hutchinson, a midwife and religious zealot who had been charged with antinomianism for preaching that faith alone, not the moral law, guarantees salvation, and, worse, that "the authority of private judgment was superior to that of the church." Hutchinson's other fault was that she was an eloquent woman, for while religious discussion governed the life of the colony, and although women were allowed to attend meetings at which Scripture was discussed, they could not speak. Hutchinson had insisted on the right to participate equally in such discussions, and when denied, she held meetings for women at her own house. It was too much for the misogynist moralists. Unwilling to tolerate her heretical spin on theology and her contention that the colony's efforts to enforce conformity to the established religious system violated any inherent rights of Christians, the magistrates banished her from the colony. In their minds, the quest for religious freedom that had launched the *Mayflower* was over. Hutchinson fared well for a time. Moving south, she met Roger Williams, the clergyman from Plymouth, also exiled by the court for his criticisms of the authorities, who settled her and her followers in what would become Rhode Island. Fearful, however, that Boston's unforgiving magistrates would pursue her, Hutchinson fled to the wilds of New York State, where hostile Indians spared the Colonial authorities from having to take action that was not, given the wrath of Puritan clergymen scorned in those days, unacceptable—she and her family, except for one daughter, were brutally murdered.

Eager to ensure that there would be no repetition of Hutchinson's heresy, and that there would always be a large dose of old England in the colonies, the Great and General

Court of Massachusetts high on the hill had allocated four hundred pounds "towards a schoale or colledge." It would be the first institution of higher education in America, but not, as Harvard romantics tend to forget, in the Americas: That honor belongs to the University of Mexico, founded in 1551. There was no charter, no mention of degrees. The school was to be a Congregational seminary for men whose aim was "the education of the English and Indian youth in knowledge and godliness," mainly with a view to their entering the Protestant ministry.

Nine students enrolled in the first class, their minds and morals shaped by rigorous instruction and vigorous floggings, all dispensed by the professor in charge, the mercurial Puritan schoolmaster Nathaniel Eaton (who, it was said, favored tree limbs over hickory sticks to make his point). As a scholar, he was among the hundred or so university-trained colonists who recognized the value of an education, especially reading, which assured that the ubiquitous Bible would be well thumbed. For the Puritans, religious orthodoxy may have been as stern as the rockbound coast they had settled, but it was also an intellectual goad. Early on, the General Court had decreed that every town of fifty families hire a schoolmaster to teach reading and writing to children and servants and that every town of one hundred establish a secondary Latin School, which boys would enter at age eight or nine.

Eaton had the benefit of such an education in England, where he attended Trinity College at Cambridge. But if he learned anything from Marcus Aurelius's sensitive and humble meditations, he soon lost it. A scholarly beacon he may have been, but as a human being he was an absolute disgrace. Apparently succumbing to the wild life of a Sabbath-breaker, he dropped out of Trinity, then saw the light for a time and studied theology, either to make amends or to acquire the garb of respectability. At twenty-seven, with no college degree but with a solid background in church teaching, Latin, Greek, and Hebrew, he became master at the new college, but without the dignified title of president. The impression he soon left on his students is summed up in what one of his charges wrote of him years later. Eaton was, this abused youngster said of his tormenter, "fitten to have been an officer in the Inquisition, or master of a house of correction than an instructor of Christian youth."

Three years after the school's founding, its name was, thankfully, Harvard, not Eaton, after Reverend John Harvard, a young English pastor and butcher's son who hailed from a district in London known more for its bordellos, prisons, and alehouses than for its educational facilities. A graduate of Cambridge University's Emmanuel College, Harvard donated half his estate of eight hundred pounds and his library of four hundred books to the institution in a deathbed will written a few days before tuberculosis killed him at age thirty.

In 1642, the first graduates were awarded A.B. degrees—no matter that the paper was illegal because the authorities had not yet agreed on how to charter the school or on who actually had the authority to graduate students. The process that would eventually confer a degree respected around the world had begun. Indeed, a member of the first class was one Henry Saltonstall, who would go on to earn an M.D. degree at Padua—there were no hospitals in Boston at the time, and no medical schools anywhere in the colonies—and would be the first member of the only family in America to have almost a dozen successive generations graduate from the same college, Harvard.

Fueled by John Harvard's gift, and what it raised from private donations, tolls from a Boston ferry service, the sale of livestock and wheat, and contributions from abroad, the college expanded its physical plant and its courses of instruction. Under Henry Dunster enrollment increased, but though Harvard was emphasizing liberal arts and a more general education, most of its graduates were still entering the ministry, and its masters and professors were still conservative lawmakers and ministers, its students their sons.

Among the ministers who would exert enormous influence over the school and the Boston community was Increase Mather, father of Cotton, and the zealous pastor of the Old North Church. The author of such spooky treatises as *Cases of Conscience Concerning Evil Spirits,* Increase was a convincing sermonizer who savored lines like "excess in wickedness doth bring untimely death," and a key player in the Salem witchcraft trials. A graduate of Harvard's class of 1656, Increase became president of the college thirty years later, and most accounts of his tenure agree that while he encouraged scientific study, he was vehement in his defense of the institution's Congregationalist bent. Men with relatively broader minds removed him, an action that dashed the hopes of his son, Cotton, the divine who had hoped to succeed him.

Cut from the same cassock, Cotton was a staunch Puritan who directed the full fury of his fanaticism at the Salem witches and shared his father's austere beliefs and his disgust for the "hideous clamors for liberty of conscience." He was, nonetheless, influenced by the growing scientific spirit of the day, notably by the discoveries of Isaac Newton. He also studied a bit of medicine, although a glance at his only medical treatise, *The Angel of Bethesda,* makes it easy to understand why Harvard Medical School hasn't an endowed chair in his honor: In it, he took a page from the Swiss medieval alchemist, Paracelsus, recommending a mixture of dung and wine for whatever ailed a body. (Paracelsus's concoction, stirred up with a dash of gold powder and a jigger of antimony, was a bit more appealing to the eye, although its alleged effect as an anti-aging elixir was as extravagant as the mixologist's real name, Theophrastus Bombastus von Hohenheim.)

Mather was a mere dabbler (but so, too, were virtually all of the physicians practicing in Boston at the time), but he was instrumental in halting a smallpox epidemic that ravaged the city in 1721. From his black servant, Onesimus, he learned that in Africa, smallpox had been controlled by extracting pus from the blisters of people suffering from mild forms of the disease and slipping it into the bloodstream of healthy people through incisions in their skin. The practice apparently didn't begin in Africa. When smallpox epidemics struck China in the twelfth century B.C., physicians cut pieces from smallpox scabs and pustules and inserted them into the nostrils of healthy children—left nostril for boys, right for girls.

Convinced that inoculation could save lives—it was effective but dangerous because the light sort of smallpox induced was still contagious—Mather promoted it from his pulpit with the same fervor of one of his soul-saving sermons. Eventually, inoculation became standard practice, to be replaced some seventy-five years later when Dr. Benjamin Waterhouse, a member of Harvard Medical School's first faculty, would introduce a far safer preventive to the United States, vaccination with cowpox.

In Mather's day, Boston's doctors were a conservative, mostly ill-trained lot. Before, during, and for years after the American Revolution, only a handful of privileged Yankee physicians—men fluent in the classics and Latin who also had the money to travel to Europe to study "physic"—had any formal training. More often than not, physicians were men with little schooling other than what they could glean from their overseas-trained mentors, or from others who had apprenticed. In all the thirteen colonies, some 3,500 "doctors" plied their trade, and less than 400 had legitimate medical degrees. Where today medical science is a restless, continuing, curiosity-driven quest for new knowledge, in the days of the colonies it was, with only a few notable exceptions among the formally trained, a rather lazy profession practiced by uncertain, even inept, men who could only sop up what they had learned from others equally unskilled and pass it on.

Undoubtedly, the apprentice system, which finds its modern-day counterpart in the clinical training of interns and residents, turned out a few good doctors. Experience and learning by example are, after all, still the best, and cheapest, teachers. Paracelsus, the consummate dabbler, knew it. "Not even a dog-killer," he wrote, "can learn his trade from books, but only from experience. And how much more is this true of the physician!" But all the experience and apprenticeship in the medical world of the day did little to improve the education and caliber of physicians, nor did they result in any dramatic application to the bedside of whatever discoveries were made. To be fair, as the social historian J. C. Furnas sees it, nowhere else in the world was medicine then any better, and the skills and traditions that hundreds of American doctors of the 1700s brought home from Edinburgh or Paris as basis for founding medical schools and training apprentices "were on much the same level of competence—10 percent knowledge, 40 percent pseudoscientific surmise, 50 percent bedside manner—as that of their august preceptors across the water."[1] The simple fact was that without a clue to the biochemical, environmental, and behavioral causes and effects of most diseases, it was virtually impossible for a physician to offer a credible diagnosis, prognosis, and effective treatment. Although, for example, doctors were aware that "something" in smallpox pustules was causing the disease—convincing George Washington to order the Continental army inoculated, a move that spared it from that scourge—germs and viruses had not yet been identified. There were no thermometers, stethoscopes, or hypodermic syringes. The standard practices, no matter the ailment, were elementary: Open a wrist vein and draw off a pint or two of blood; force a strong emetic down a patient's throat to induce vomiting; administer a purgative to cleanse the bowels. Washington, on his deathbed at age sixty-seven, was bled three times and—a quart was drained from him on the third try— given massive doses of calomel to cleanse his bowels and a tartar emetic to make him vomit. Blistering poultices finished off the weakened old hero.

In the medicine chests of the day were remedies like "Jesuit's bark," now known as quinine, which was used for fever; laudanum, powdered opium dissolved in alcohol, for the endemic dysentery; and all manner of local plants and shrubs, from which crude pharmaceuticals were made, and which often only hastened the course of a fatal disease. To relieve pain, doctors poured brandy or rum down the throats of patients, and occasionally, they administered opium. Surgery was just as basic, limited to surface tumors and to the extremities. In a sense, it was retrograde evolution, considering what prehistoric physicians were able to accomplish with their crude yet impressive trephinations—the surgical opening of a skull to repair head and brain injuries—and what Hindu surgeons five hundred years before Christ managed when they removed bladder stones by deftly cutting through the perineal tract. No Colonial doctor in his right mind would have even considered slicing into a live human belly, let alone a head, to tinker with an organ. They usually attacked only what they could see, which was in most cases a gangrenous or shattered leg. The standard procedure was quick and, usually, dirty: simply to hack off injured limbs, a haphazard process that resulted in enormous loss of blood and massive infections, which killed most patients.

Hospitals, thriving in other parts of the world, were virtually nonexistent in the colonies. Milan had opened its renowned hospital in 1445, and before the Reformation there were seventy-seven in Scotland alone. One can go even further back in the history of hospitals, to 4000 B.C., when temples of the god Saturn were used to house the sick and to educate physicians. But neither Boston nor Cambridge, which would become synonymous with scientific and medical excellence, had a general hospital until 1811, when Massachusetts General Hospital was founded. There was a rough and not always ready military hospital in Boston during the Revolution, along with a crowded, filthy almshouse to care for the impoverished sick. There were also a few private smallpox hospitals stuck out on islands in Boston Harbor, as well as several quarantine hospitals—detention centers known popularly as pesthouses—where immigrants with contagious diseases were isolated.

Farther south, in Philadelphia, the largest town in the colonies, there was one reputable haven for the sick, the Pennsylvania Hospital. Founded by Benjamin Franklin and a civic-minded pesthouse doctor, Thomas Bond, it opened in 1752, thirteen years before the College of Philadelphia (now the University of Pennsylvania) upstaged Harvard to start the young nation's first medical school. Staffed for the most part by physicians whose office walls were papered with degrees from the major European universities, the place reinforced the physician's role as a healer, but also as a royal entrepreneur. Indeed, Dr. Howard W. Haggard, a medical historian and professor of physiology at Yale some sixty years ago, had this blunt characterization of the eighteenth-century doctors:

> The better physicians, better usually because of some marked felicity of personality, occupied high social positions and were influential men. . . . Most of them were addicted to affectations which would be looked upon today as smacking strongly of charlatanism: dashing, gaudy carriages, powdered wigs, satin breeches, gold-headed canes, and muffs to protect the hands and preserve the "tactus eruditis" were the order of the day, as were also a pompous mien and an air

of infallibility. It was a time when art and personality and show rather than science ruled medical practice.[2]

America's first medical schools may not have barred the posturers and the social climbers from medicine (no more than they can today), but they at least were going to try to make it difficult for them to fake their way through a consult. In 1765, the College of Philadelphia was the first in the colonies to offer medical education, with the establishment of a chair in the theory and practice of medicine. It was held by Edinburgh-trained Dr. John Morgan, an early critic of the apprentice system who was keenly aware that a solid medical education required elements that medical students today take for granted: affiliation with a university and a teaching hospital, qualified professors, strict entrance requirements, libraries, and laboratories. Three years later, a medical department was opened at King's College in New York, later to become Columbia University's College of Physicians and Surgeons.

At Harvard, meanwhile, a group of students had formed a clandestine organization called the Anatomical Club, which met secretly to dissect cats and dogs, as well as human cadavers whenever they could be snatched from graves or diverted from funerals by fake mourners, who then substituted logs for the body in the coffin. Among the club's founders was John Warren, whose older physician brother, Joseph, was a general in the Continental army and the man who, before his death at the Battle of Bunker Hill, sent Paul Revere to warn Middlesex villages that the British were marching on Concord. An apprentice physician when the war broke out, John Warren, who graduated from Harvard in 1771, joined the army as a military doctor, and he soon demonstrated surgical skill that, considering the ham-handedness of his colleagues, might be characterized as deft: He managed to do a successful amputa-

tion at the shoulder joint when others were slashing and saw-
ing long bone, and he even sweated his way through an
operation on a dermoid cyst of the ovary. When the war was
over, he began giving lectures in anatomy at the military hospital and for the newly formed Boston Medical Society. So popular were they that Warren suggested starting up a medical
school, an idea that had already crossed the minds of Harvard
Corporation members, who, although not overjoyed that
Young Veritas was trailing the College of Philadelphia and
King's College, couldn't come up with the money to finance
their august vision of a Harvard Medical School. About all
they had in the way of start-up money was a thousand pounds
that had been bequeathed by a Harvard College graduate,
Ezekiel Hersey, of the South Shore town of Hingham, a doctor who had earned his medical credentials through the apprentice system. Unfortunately, Hersey had willed that only
the interest from the money (which had been reduced to a
trickle because of the "depreciation of the late paper cur-
rency") be used for a medical school, and that only to support
a single professor of anatomy and physic whenever such a position could be established. The Pennsylvanians and the New
Yorkers had a bit more (though not much) going for them in
the way of faculty, and Harvard, image-conscious even in its
abecedarian years, could not bear to do with less than its rivals.

Harvard's dons appreciated the notion that charity began
at home and stayed there, and they knew well how to set a
spare, cold Yankee table for the guests. They managed to
scrounge up eighty pounds for medical books and scientific
apparatus and decided on a proprietary arrangement whereby
fees collected from medical students would be paid directly to
the faculty in lieu of salaries. To make the start-up easier on
the Harvard Corporation's buttoned pockets, there would be
no new construction, either for classrooms or living space;
classes would be held in a dingy basement room in Harvard

Hall or the Yard in Cambridge; and instructors, most of whom would come from Boston, would have to cross over to Cambridge by ferry or ride horseback over nine miles of dirt road. To ensure a steady and speedy flow of students—which would presumably guarantee the future health of the colonists and the financial health of the faculty—neither degrees nor entrance examinations would be required; the only requisite for admission, it appeared, was the ability to pay fees of four to seven dollars. Warren drew up a curriculum that was as tight as the overseers' fists: six gut courses of lectures, an oral examination (not surprising, given that few of the early medical school students could actually write) after two years, and six months of apprenticeship with one of Boston's finest. Graduates would not receive a doctoral degree, only a bachelor of medicine.

Plans for the new school were approved on September 19, 1782, and two months later—in a logical choice, given his prior experience with amputations and stolen cadavers—the Harvard Corporation chose John Warren as its first professor of anatomy and surgery. Benjamin Waterhouse, an unpopular, pretentious outlander from Newport, Rhode Island, and probably the best-educated physician in New England, was appointed professor of the theory and practice of physic; Aaron Dexter, a Harvard graduate and a physician with a practice in Boston, was named professor of chemistry and materia medica.

The first faculty may have been distinguished, but what the Medical Institution of Harvard College (as it was first known) had under the rafters of its basement room was nothing to brag about: one primitive microscope that had been donated to the college a few years earlier and had been collecting dust on a display shelf, one copy each of *Dr. Mead's Treatise of Poisons and de Morbis Biblicis* and *Albinus's Twelve Tables of the Human Bones,* a donated human skeleton, and one set of human veins and arteries pumped up with wax.

Despite grandiose plans for the curriculum, the workload for the three pioneering faculty would be as taxing as lancing a boil: There were but two students in the first class, one of whom, John Fleet, went on to become an assistant in anatomy and surgery at Harvard and the first recording secretary and librarian of the Massachusetts Medical Society; and since there were no written exams, there were no papers to grade. Education flowed exclusively from the podium (an arrangement that suited the "pomposity of style" preferred by Waterhouse and an interminable succession of Harvard professors), with little chance of much student arrogance and incisive questioning, since the school's entrance requirements didn't include college training. The rules that were to govern Dr. Waterhouse's one-man department were that he "should teach the students by directing and superintending, as much as may be, their private studies; lecturing of the diseases of the human body . . . and, whenever the professors be desired by any other gentlemen of the Faculty to visit their patients in difficult and uncommon cases, they shall use all their endeavors to introduce with them their pupils who are properly qualified." Waterhouse probably had the toughest job, because trying to teach clinical medicine without a hospital and patients—the almshouse was a cross between a charnel house and a lunatic asylum, hardly a place that would provide the knowledge that American medicine needed to keep pace with what was going on in Europe's centers of learning—was like trying to teach someone to swim without water.

Anatomy and chemistry were also taught through lectures and demonstrations, and students, always passive spectators in the era of amphitheater medicine, had no opportunity personally to ransack the human body and perform their own chemical experiments as they would routinely do years later. In anatomy, they would listen to Warren, who not only lectured enthusiastically to make the "driest bone in the human body," as Oliver Wendell Holmes would observe later, "a subject of animated and agreeable description" but had to serve as procurer of cadavers. In the absence of a citizenry enlightened enough to donate its remains, about all Warren could do to obtain his specimens was continue to connive with town officials to have bodies snatched from graves, or from time to time take advantage of the Act of Dueling Law, which was ostensibly designed to discourage dueling but also permitted the bodies of slain duelists to be turned over to the anatomists. Some of the victors, too, probably ended up on Warren's table: Authorities often charged the winner with murder, hanged him, and sneaked the body over to the school for dissection.

Occasionally, students did the procuring. A member of the second graduating class described one body hunt: "An old lady, both large and interestingly muscular, was buried in the graveyard of Christ Church. The beadle informed friends at the college, and he agreed to dig a shallow grave and leave a shovel near it. Thirty students descended on the cemetery at night and carried off the prize in a large sack." Intervention by Governor John Hancock, who was also president of the Harvard Board of Overseers, prevented a march on the medical school by irate townspeople and quashed any idea of expelling the students and disciplining Warren.[3]

Chemistry, then in its infancy, got equal time with anatomy in the basement classroom, although the gaseous atmosphere in the early lab was often more remarkable than the scientific demonstrations, which were not always successful. "This experiment is one of remarkable brilliancy," Dexter once assured his students as he confidently touched a powder with a drop of igniter fluid and backed off in anticipation of a sudden burst of flame. Nothing. "Smile, gentlemen, smile," Dexter apologized. "The experiment has failed, but the principle, gentlemen, remains firm as the everlasting hills."[4]

Over the next few years, the medical faculty and student body grew, but expansion brought a new student problem. In one lecture he delivered at the end of a medical course, "Cautions to Young Persons Concerning Health," a highly miffed Waterhouse described the "evil tendency" to use tobacco, especially cigars, and the abuse of "ardent and vinous spirits in general." The student body was deteriorating, Waterhouse warned, adding that six times as much liquor was being consumed on campus annually than the students' fathers had downed. "Unruly wine and ardent spirits," he chided, "have supplanted sober cider," noting that never in his twenty-three years of experience had he seen "so many hectical habits and consumptive affections as of late."

But worse, requirements for medical students had not toughened, and the curriculum remained a showcase for the experts who favored charges with sharp eyes and ears but shut mouths. Scientific investigation, which would become a hallmark of Harvard Med, was virtually nonexistent and would long be overshadowed by European research: While Harvard Med struggled in mediocrity, in Italy Luigi Galvani was inducing muscular contractions in dead frogs' legs with electricity; in France, Philippe Pinel had blamed mental illness on an organic cause; and in Germany, the poet-anatomist Johann Wolfgang von Goethe discovered the intermaxillary bone in the upper jaw. Indeed, a half-century before Harvard Med even came into being, the Englishman William Harvey had identified the heart as the pump that forced blood through the body, and the Italian Gasparo Aselli had discovered the lymphatic system.

Soon, however, one of Harvard Med's own would have his name on something noteworthy, and although it would be old hat in Europe, it was new to America. Through contacts in England, Waterhouse obtained a publication printed in 1798 by the physician Edward Jenner, reporting a successful vaccination against smallpox. While protection could be achieved by inoculating healthy people with matter from small-pox pustules, as was done in Cotton Mather's day, the person inoculated most often contracted a mild case of the disease, from which he or she fully recovered in a few weeks. However, uninoculated people who came in contact with those experi-encing the mild form of smallpox were themselves exposed to severe smallpox, from which they were totally unprotected, and brief epidemics often flared up because of the inoculations. Jenner had discovered that an inoculation with matter from cowpox, a mild disease caused by a virus similar to that which caused smallpox, conferred immunity to human smallpox. Vac-cinating a person with cowpox material also wiped out the contagious nature of the old method of inoculation.

Waterhouse was enthused, but his Harvard colleagues were skeptical, and several condemned vaccination as a whim that would soon be discredited. Waterhouse took his case to the American Academy of Arts and Sciences, presided over by John Adams, who was also President of the United States at the time. The wisdom of the technique was questioned, so Waterhouse, determined to lay the matter to rest once and for all, proposed a unique approach: He would vaccinate his own children (two sons, ages five and three, and a year-old daughter) with cow-pox vaccine sent him by Jenner, then inoculate them with smallpox virus. Without the hobbles of today's ethics commit-tees, experimental protocols, and informed consent, Water-house proceeded. No signs of smallpox developed. Two years later, Waterhouse repeated the experiment on nineteen chil-dren; none came down with the disease.

Elated, Waterhouse sent a copy of his pamphlet *A Prospect for Exterminating the Smallpox* to President Thomas Jefferson, along with some inoculant. Jefferson vaccinated his family, ser-vants, and presumably himself, then sent Waterhouse a letter expressing his indebtedness. Jenner sent an autographed silver snuffbox with a pair of lancets.

Waterhouse's achievements may have impressed London and Monticello, but among the powers in the grubby basement medical school, it was but one more reason to dislike him. For although the founders of the school were willing to keep the lamp of knowledge burning, most of them weren't especially comfortable around someone like Waterhouse, who believed he alone was the lamp. A graduate of the University of Leyden and brainier than most of his colleagues (John Warren, for example, had earned the right to practice after passing an exam given him by a Salem practitioner), Waterhouse was argumentative and imperious. He marched smartly about Cambridge, according to Oliver Wendell Holmes, "with a look of questioning sagacity and an utterance of oracular gravity," forcing the citizens to listen to his learned talk when they were well and to send for one of the other doctors when they were sick. Even worse, though, Waterhouse was a Quaker, which meant, according to the prejudice of the day, that he had been a misguided troublemaker from birth, and a foreigner to boot, coming as he did from a place proper Bostonians regarded as a colony of escaped convicts and madmen, Rhode Island. Then there was the monopoly hold he had on cowpox vaccine (Waterhouse grew his own strain and picked up 25 percent of the profits from its use by doctors), and a transparent offer to donate some to the Massachusetts Medical Society for use among the poor. The gift was never officially recognized, a snub that provoked Waterhouse to publish a scathing attack on the prestigious society's own integrity, which must have given him pleasure but that also confirmed his colleagues' low estimation of him.

The fact that smallpox vaccination was becoming routine also presented problems for Waterhouse. Newspaper cartoonists who reflected the public's concern were not kind to him and Jenner, or to the preventive technique: Vaccinated patients were depicted sprouting horns and miniature cows, caricatures that would persist for another hundred years. In 1911, George Bernard Shaw would speak for the opposition at an Irish anti-vaccination league meeting, saying that the local government's methods of inoculating children "with casual dirt moistened with an undefined pathogenic substance obtained from calves [is] really nothing short of attempted murder."[5]

What finally did Waterhouse in was his endorsement of efforts by another group to form a rival medical school in Boston. Furious, his colleagues—Warren, his son, John Collins Warren, and Aaron Dexter among them—called for his expulsion. In 1812, while fund-raising for the planned Massachusetts General on the Charles in Boston was under way, Waterhouse, age fifty-eight, was sent packing. But while Harvard stripped him of his faculty robes, Waterhouse still had the right connections, among them President Madison, who appointed him inspector of military posts. He died in 1846, two weeks before another significant medical advance associated with Harvard would be recorded, the first public demonstration, at MGH, of the use of ether during surgery.

By now, the school had literally moved up in the world of medicine. It had abandoned its basement quarters and now had anatomy rooms over an apothecary shop in downtown Boston, with classrooms nearby in a building up on stilts on the mudflats of the Charles, next to MGH. The hospital, "for the reception of lunatics and other sick persons," had opened to patients in 1821 and was providing desperately needed clinical training for the medical students, a liaison that would prompt a former Harvard Med dean to admit that Harvard Medical School without MGH would have been about as effective as the bridge at Avignon, or one half of the Longfellow Bridge between Cambridge and Boston. No matter that checking into a surgical ward was a grim experience. "Almost every week at the hospital," one observer stated solemnly, "deep groans of distress or sharp cries of agony penetrated into the innermost recesses of the building, and were often distinctly audible through the neighborhood."[6]

Scenarios like that would end with ether anesthesia, the first significant all-American contribution to medical science. It debuted on October 16, 1846, when Dr. John Collins Warren, then a professor of anatomy and surgery at Harvard, stood quietly over a patient in MGH's surgical theater and solemnly announced to students and physicians, "There is a gentleman who claims he has discovered that the inhalation of a certain agent will produce insensibility to pain during surgical operations, with safety to the patient. I have always considered this an important desideratum in operative surgery, and after due consideration I decided to permit him to try the experiment."

The patient before him was suffering from a superficial vascular tumor in his lower jaw, and the gentleman who had made the claim was a dentist, William G. T. Morton, who had used ether while extracting and filling teeth. With the patient muttering in a semiconscious state, Warren made a small incision, removed the tumor in five minutes, and, perhaps astonished by the patient's calm, announced somberly to the awestruck gallery, "Gentlemen, this is no humbug." It was not. The patient hadn't budged during the operation, murmuring when he came out of it that though there was some pain—somewhat akin, he said, to having had his skin scraped with a hoe—it was not severe. The revolutionary technique prompted Oliver Wendell Holmes, who coined the word *anesthesia* and would become dean of the medical school the next year, to exult: "The fierce extremity of suffering has been steeped in the waters of forgetfulness, and the deepest furrow in the knotted brow of agony has been smoothed forever."

By the time the Civil War erupted, Harvard Med had more than a dozen faculty and a thousand graduates on its rolls. Legislation now enabled licensed physicians to acquire unclaimed bodies for dissection. (That privilege wouldn't come to the outland until later. The Ohio Anatomy Law took effect in 1881.)

German microscopes had become standard equipment in anatomy labs; diagnosis, now aided by the doctor's most powerful tool, the stethoscope, was becoming more scientific, and doctors everywhere in the United States were taking case histories, recording symptoms and their severity, keeping records of treatment, and doing postmortems. Ether, which had spurred a dramatic increase in the number of operations, was now being used during childbirth, as well, although not without opposition from clergy, who embraced the biblical notion that women must bear children in sorrow. When the British obstetrician James Young Simpson, who was the first to use chloroform during labor, was attacked by Scottish clergy, his response was also biblical, from the passage in Genesis that deals with easing Adam's labor pains: "And the Lord caused a deep sleep to fall upon Adam, and he slept: and he took one of his ribs, and closed up the flesh instead thereof. And the rib, which the Lord God had taken from man, made he a woman, and brought her unto the man."

But ether, for all its benefits, had in a sense been going it alone. Surgery was successful but still dangerous because of infection that too often caused the patients to die. That would change with the advent of "Listerism." Joseph Lister, an English physician, had surmised correctly that germs were the cause of the putrefaction in compound fractures, and he soon discovered that because they could be killed with carbolic acid, amputation, the usual procedure when complicating infections stymied the surgeons, was no longer necessary. Lister cleaned wound sites with soap and water and a carbolic-acid solution, dressed them with carbolized bandages, used other antiseptics such as bichloride of mercury and boric acid, and invented sterile catgut sutures and a machine that sprayed a mist of antiseptic into the deadly air of operating rooms. Sterilized instruments and operating rooms followed, and surgery was headed into the new age of antisepsis and asepsis.

Cleanliness was not, however, an easy sell. Carbolic acid may have been popular, but sloppy operating room practices overrode its effectiveness. Attendance at one of the Saturday morning operating clinics at MGH during the 1800s confirmed that. One surgeon reported:

> After the patient had been etherized and wheeled in, a brief resume of his history was given, and the operating surgeon would ask each of the visitors in turn to step up and examine the patient. The operative field was cleaned up in the most perfunctory manner [and] a few towels were wrung out and draped around the field. The operating surgeon was usually garbed in a black Prince Albert coat, kept hanging in a closet for the occasion and showing numerous evidences of previous operations in the way of dried blood, wound secretions, etc. Preparation of the hands was done in careless fashion, especially by the older surgeons. . . . No special choice was exercised in the order of operations—opening an infected case might just as well as not precede a clean operation.[7]

Such crudities in hospital and laboratory alike would not deter expansion, and Harvard Med's collection of teaching hospitals in Boston grew quickly: Children's Hospital, "to care for the little waifs who crowd our poorer streets"; the Free Hospital for Women, for "treatment of poor women afflicted with the diseases peculiar to their sex"; and the Boston Lying-

In, for women who were "married, recently widowed and known to be of good character" (unrespectable poor apparently went to the House of Industry down the road) were soon on the Boston scene. And Harvard's fund-raisers were still taking anything they could get: The Free Hospital's first donations included a dozen sheets and pillow slips, a demijohn of whiskey, a mop, twenty-five Bibles, nine gallons of oysters, a ton of coal, four boxes of matches, three washtubs, an ice pick, twelve two-cent stamps, and a doormat.[8]

But while Harvard's constellation of hospitals was expanding and offering students more access to patients, the school itself was, like others in the United States, still a shabby diploma mill turning out doctors generally not much better than the three hundred quacks practicing in Boston, who, the *Boston Surgical and Medical Journal* bristled, constituted a "phalanx of infamous knaves who fatten themselves in their hiding places without knowing or caring to know anything more about medicine than they do of the revolutions of the new planet Neptune." These "great spiders," the *Journal* continued, "compete successfully with men distinguished for their high moral and professional attainments."[9] Yet, four years after the Civil War, Harvard's own phalanges were still gaining admission on practically zero requirements, with ability to pay the fee the sole ticket for entrance. More than half the students could barely write, and only 20 percent had a college degree. There was but one endowed professor, and the proprietary arrangement that permitted faculty to collect fees from their students and divvy up the proceeds at the end of the year was still in place. To qualify for a degree, all a student needed was his apprenticeship—if he was lucky, he didn't draw a licensed version of a "great spider"—and two four-month terms of lectures, only one of which had to be at Harvard, with the second lecture series exactly the same as the first. Thus, a student could attend the same lecture series twice—paying twice for the same lecture; a formal "final examination" was administered to candidates for the degree, a test that was more of an afterthought, which succeeded only in sending more infamous knaves to visit the sick of the Commonwealth. As Walter Bradford Cannon described it:

> Nine professors representing nine different important subjects sat each at a table in the examination room. Nine students were admitted to the room in a group, and each sat down with a professor. At the end of ten minutes a bell rang and each student moved along to the next table. This process continued until [at] the end of ninety minutes all had been examined, whereupon they all filed out.
>
> Each professor had a card, white on one side and marked with a black spot on the other. In order to secure the individual professional judgments, uninfluenced by conference, the Dean immediately called out separately the names of the students in the group; and after each name the professors simultaneously held up their cards—the white side meaning approval, the black spot disapproval. If five professors displayed the white side of the card, that is, if the student had passed five of the nine subjects on which he had been examined, he was granted the degree of Doctor of Medicine. Thus, a young man could go forth from this School quite ignorant of four of the nine branches of medicine which he was supposed to use in his practice.[10]

Such was the appalling state of affairs in 1869 when Charles William Eliot, a thirty-five-year-old educator, chemist, and mathematician, became Harvard University's twenty-second president. A Harvard College graduate, Eliot had taught analytical chemistry there and at MIT and had spent several years in Germany and England studying science and educational methods. Liberal and farsighted, he would make drastic changes in Harvard's management practices, curricula, and goals.

But it was Harvard Medical School, this embarrassing appendage to an institution on its way to becoming the premier place of higher learning in the United States, that undoubtedly gave Eliot many sleepless nights. For Harvard Med was not only in grave need of therapy but was, in fact, in worse shape than any other part of the university; it was a collection of poorly organized departments managed exclusively by a few members of Boston's snootiest families, a clubby government unto itself that ran its own financial affairs independent of the university, and even held its own private commencements. It had not required more than a glance at the Harvard Med dossier to convince Eliot that the school's educational direction was "notoriously lax" and the school itself "a sort of trading corporation as well as a body of teachers."

Eliot plunged in, serious reform in mind. He called for stiffer entrance exams, a baccalaureate-degree requirement, fewer students, a curriculum that ran over three years instead of the two four-month years, careful grading of courses, abolition of the fee system that paid faculty, and, of seminal importance, more use of clinics and laboratories. As a chemist who had studied the impact of science on medical practice abroad and who had taught lab science, Eliot saw medicine as an experimental science as well as a clinical calling, and he was determined to place more emphasis on research in both medical education, which he viewed as graduate training, and practice. It might have been easier to reform Lady Sneerwell's School for Scandal.

Where Eliot's road to change wasn't rocky, it was barricaded by Brahmins, a formidable lot indeed. For one, there was Holmes, who had stepped down as dean sixteen years before but was still teaching anatomy and physiology. Educated at Harvard College, the Massachusetts Medical College, and in London and Paris, Holmes had acquired a reputation as the student's patient friend. So gifted a teacher was he that he was assigned the one o'clock lecture time because no one else could hold the attention of tired and restless students in their fifth hour of classes. There was also the literary Holmes, the man who took on the U.S. Board of Navy Commissioners for its decision to scuttle the forty-four-gun frigate *Constitution*, Boston-built and the most famous ship in the service. Holmes penned his celebrated "Old Ironsides," whose stirring line castigating the government for planning to "tear her tattered ensign down" triggered a national uproar and enough patriotism and money to get the ship restored and permanently berthed in Boston, where it sits as the oldest commissioned vessel in the U.S. Navy. When he wrote his daring novel *The Guardian Angel,* the story of an errant preacher and a fifteen-year-old girl, clerics were outraged. In materia medica, too, Holmes sometimes marched to a different beat. A few years before he became dean, he read a paper before the Society for the Advancement of Medical Knowledge; in it, he reviewed reports of puerperal fever (the bacterial infection, accompanied by blood poisoning—which is also known as childbed fever and occurs in women after childbirth). Because the evidence led ineluctably to the conclusion that midwives and doctors passed the disease from infected patients to the uninfected, Holmes recommended standards of hygiene for medical personnel. He was not taken seriously, even by one of his colleagues, Harvard's preeminent professor of obstetrics, Walter Channing, who sternly countered the finding in another paper. Curiously, three years later, the Hungarian physician Ignaz Semmelweis would be credited with discovering the same mechanism of contagion. Holmes recouped later: While physiologists were still doing anatomy with only their hands, he introduced the microscope into medical school teaching of the subject.

Holmes's views on medical education and the meaning of good doctoring had been shaped by the training he received in clinical medicine in Europe, and he felt there was more to the practice of medicine than devotion to science and research. "The young man knows the rules," he told one group of graduates, "but the old man knows the exceptions. The young man knows his patient, but the old man knows his patient's family, dead and alive, up and down the generations."[11] In an introductory lecture he delivered to a Harvard Medical School class two years before Eliot's arrival, he was more forceful. "The most essential part of a student's education," he said, "is obtained not in a lecture room but at the bedside. Nothing seen there is lost. The rhythms of disease are learned by frequent repetition. . . . A medical school is not a science school, except just so far as medicine itself is a science. On the natural history side, medicine is a science; on the curative side, chiefly an art."[12]

Holmes alone would have been enough for Eliot to deal with, but there was another major curmudgeon in the young president's life, Henry Jacob Bigelow. The Boston-born son of a respected physician, Bigelow had entered Harvard College at age thirteen, graduated from the medical school, and studied in Paris under doctors who stressed clinical methods and pooh-poohed emerging German research as little more than a fad. Thoroughly grounded in all aspects of practical surgery and with ambition flaming, he returned to Boston determined to confront "the crushing incubus of a notion that judgment and experience come only with age," and he set up a successful practice. Two years later, at age twenty-eight, he was a surgeon at MGH. His colleagues and students called him the "most brilliant operator" in all New England, and for good reason. Bigelow had been blessed with the surgeon's two greatest gifts.

One was a faculty for instant decision. ("When you have a cut to make, make it!" he would tell his students, brandishing the longest amputating knife he could find. "Long, or at least competent, incisions give no more pain than short ones. They heal as quickly, and more than that, they do their intended work without need of repetition."[13]) Bigelow's other gift was exceptionally adroit and graceful hands, which he fine-tuned by endless dissection of not only cadavers but door locks. He extracted and took apart so many bolts, tumblers, catches, springs, and levers and carefully studied so many keys and keyholes, that he could pick any lock in fourteen seconds; he could also slip a dislocated femur back into its hip socket with one hand and open a windpipe with a single stroke of the scalpel. He was an inventor and modifier of surgical instruments and operating chairs; he made plaster of Paris casts of his grip and had the handles of his surgical instruments manufactured to conform.

When Eliot arrived, as president, auspiciously the same year construction of the Suez Canal ended (although that project was considerably less daunting than revamping Harvard Med), Bigelow had been on the faculty for twenty years, a senior professor of surgery, and an overpowering presence at the school, at MGH, and in the medical politics of Boston. The consummate surgeon-practitioner, Bigelow held a philosophy of how good doctors came to be that was as firm as the casts of his hands—and guaranteed to clash with Eliot's. He believed fervently that "physicians are born, not trained, and that same applies more strongly to surgeons," and, like Holmes, that medicine was predominantly an art, not a science. The changes Eliot was advocating, he felt, placed too much emphasis on secondary and less applicable knowledge, which students would not need in practice and were sure to forget.

Bigelow expressed his sentiments this way: "Is the average

medical student to be educated as a pioneer, an explorer on the outskirts of medical science?" This is a question that no doubt had merit then and is perhaps pondered more often today by the many students who are pulled between a desire to serve personally and selflessly and to follow the removed, equally rewarding calling of "big science." His answer: "He is to cure disease, and until he can do this with all the collected actual and accepted knowledge and wisdom of his day and generation, he cannot spend his time profitably in experiments and exploration."[14]

In another shot at science, Bigelow protested, "Recorded phenomena stored away by the physiological inquisitor on dusty shelves are mostly of little present value, perhaps to be confuted next year."[15] He was not opposed to progress, he argued, even though for nearly ten years he adamantly refused to accept the idea of antisepsis (it was either from luck or by virtue of his surgical skill that his patients escaped infection). Progress would come, he believed, from a continuing sequence of odd discoveries, some by intent, others by serendipity, such as the discovery of ether.

Eliot, the aloof chemist, listened unswayed. He formally placed a proposal for stiffening entrance requirements before the Harvard Corporation, a move that enraged Bigelow. "The Corporation!" he thundered at the new president. "Who are the Corporation? Why, Mr. Crowninshield carries a horse-chestnut in his pocket to keep off rheumatism! Is the new medical school to be directed by a man who carries a horse-chestnut in his pocket to cure rheumatism?"[16] Holmes complained that Eliot was coming to too many faculty meetings and kept them going till too many midnights; Bigelow groused that Eliot's demand for written exams to be taken by students was ridiculous, because most of them couldn't write.

And so it went until 1871, when Eliot's "New Plan of Instruction" was hammered into shape at last—in, of all places, the living room of a still-grumbling Bigelow. Ten years later, Bigelow retired and moved to the outskirts of Boston, where, according to a friend, he took up horticulture, "trying to make plants grow on the top of a hill in New England which the Lord intended should grow in a swamp in the tropics. The curious part of it is that he seems to succeed." He died in 1890, shortly after he convinced himself that an increasing contraction in the outlet of his stomach would soon do him in. The postmortem confirmed his diagnosis.

Harvard Med now had new rules. Applicants had to come in with a background in natural history, chemistry, physics, and the German and French languages—all acquired while undergraduates. A certificate of good moral character was also required. There would be three full years of study, and examinations—on paper. No one would get a degree until he had passed an examination in all departments.

At the Harvard commencement of 1909, three years after the medical school dedicated its Great White Quadrangle, the present-day temple of learning nestled among several of the school's teaching hospitals (MGH remains some distance away, on the Charles), Eliot retired. He received two honorary degrees, one of which read, "Not in buildings alone, but also in the instruction and research within its walls he found the Harvard Medical School brick and left it marble."

7 | "The Beginning of an Evil"

THE DRASTIC REFORMS THAT ELIOT INTRODUCED—BEFORE THE century was out, they would include a bachelor's degree requirement for admission and a mandatory fourth year of training—dramatically improved Harvard Med and helped shape the future of American medical education. But in one crucial aspect of its mission to improve the quality of physicians, it still lagged: the acceptance of women and minorities into the ranks of those who could become good doctors. The widely held myth was that these petitioners lacked the competence, dedication, and intelligence to deal with the sick.

It was not only the medical school that was remiss in this regard. Not until 1870 would the first black graduate from Harvard College; he was Richard Theodore Greener, who went on to become dean of the Howard Law School and U.S. Consul at Vladivostok during the Russo-Japanese War. W. E. B. Du Bois, the fiery activist and one of the founders of the NAACP, was the first African-American to receive a Ph.D. from Harvard, and that did not come until 1895.

While a trickle of blacks managed to gain admission to the medical school in the years after the Civil War, women had a far longer wait: The first women would enter Harvard Med only at the end of World War II, graduating 167 years after the school was founded and 100 years after women had been granted medical degrees elsewhere in the United States. It would be even longer for the first African-American woman to come out of Harvard Med a physician: Mildred Jefferson, who graduated in 1951.

The scarcity of nonwhites and women in the classrooms, along with the undercurrent of insensitivity to these groups in case presentations, reflected the institution's own indifference and contributed little to the professional, social, and moral development of a generation of physicians, as well as making Harvard Med's goal of turning out the best doctors a hollow mockery. As Harvard professor Leon Eisenberg, who would chair a Harvard Med commission on relations with the black community, observed, "To the tens of millions of medically disadvantaged people in this country, Harvard's claim that it trains the leaders in American medicine is a source of condemnation; we have been training the leaders of a grossly inequitable system."

The medical school barriers would eventually fall in the 1960s, toppled more by pressure from the women's movement, the civil rights movement that engulfed the United States after Martin Luther King, Jr.'s assassination, and socially conscious medical students supported by a few faculty than by any sudden realization on the part of the Harvard Corporation that medicine was an equal-opportunity employer.

The battle began in November of 1850, a vexing month for the dean of Harvard Medical School, Oliver Wendell Holmes, and the administrators. Two letters were on Holmes's desk, and as he perused them, he knew they were certain to trigger responses ranging from dyspepsia to apoplexy among members of the faculty and student body. The letters were applications from three "young men of color," and a persistent woman, all cheekily seeking admission to lectures that were, and had been since the school's founding sixty-eight years earlier, staunchly white and male-only. It was to be Harvard Medical School's first full-blown encounter with affirmative action.

Holmes turned first to the matter of the blacks. The women's issue had, for all intents and purposes, been dealt with a few years earlier when the university's hierarchy, the president and fellows, responded speedily to the musings of a faculty member who had simply wondered aloud—probably after hearing a rumor that a woman was planning to apply—whether a female might be admitted to medical lectures and allowed to take the examinations for a degree. There was one massive collective fit. Never! the dons had said at that time; there was absolutely no need to change the medical school's rules, which implicitly excluded women, and that was that. Shortly thereafter, a woman did formally apply. She was the same one, Harriot Kezia Hunt, who now had a new petition on Holmes's desk. Even though Holmes had supported her first request, arguing that times were changing and this young woman was "full of zeal for science," she had been turned down quickly in faculty cable-ese: "Inexpedient to reconsider."

The request on behalf of the blacks was not as personal. It had actually come in a letter from the Massachusetts branch of an agency that had been established in 1817, the American Colonialization Society, to help freed Negro slaves emigrate to Africa; a tract of land purchased by the society near Cape Mesurado became the republic of Liberia in 1847. The time seemed right, for civil rights was in the air. The former slave and ardent abolitionist Frederick Douglass had not long before delivered an impassioned antislavery speech off the New England coast, on Nantucket Island, and Boston's blacks were running a major station on the Underground Railroad, hiding fugitive slaves under their roofs prior to finding them safe havens throughout the North and in Canada. The Congregationalists, who had been the founding fathers of Harvard, were also active, demanding social justice for blacks.

Holmes called a faculty meeting to discuss the petition. The letters of application, along with letters of support from society officers, were read and debated. There were warnings about "intermixing" and "personal proximity." The students would find acceptance of Negroes "injurious." But the school had little recourse but to admit the blacks, since they had already paid for tickets to classes with the help of the society, and it would be difficult to deny them the right to attend. Reluctantly, the school approved the three students, Daniel Laing and Isaac H. Snowden of Boston and Martin Delany of Pittsburgh. They never made it past the first semester.

Within weeks of the blacks' admission, an angry group of medical students sent ominous letters to Holmes and the faculty, threatening, among other things, the necessity of some effort "on the part of those opposed to prevent this inexpedient action" and requesting the "opportunity to make such arrangements for the future as shall be most agreeable to their feelings in the event of negroes being allowed again to become members of the school." The dissident students followed their notes up with a resolution that was more direct. The admission of blacks, they said self-righteously, was "highly detrimental to the interests and welfare of the institution of which we are members, calculated alike to lower its reputation in this and other parts of the country, to lessen the value of a diploma from it, and to diminish the number of its students." They ranted on that they could not be identified as fellow students "with blacks, whose company we would not keep in the streets, and whose society as associates we would not tolerate in our houses." They predicted that admitting the blacks would be the "beginning of an evil, which, if not checked, will increase, and that the number of respectable white students will, in future, be in an inverse ratio to that of blacks." Spare us, they pleaded, from having to be in such company "or of compelling us to complete our medical studies elsewhere."[1]

Another group of students did disagree, and they signed a counterpetition proclaiming that they would consider it "an evil if, in the present state of public feeling, a medical college in Boston could refuse to this unfortunate class any privileges of education, which is in the power of the profession to bestow."[2]

But the support went unheeded. After agreeing on the one

hand that it had no authority to revoke the blacks' tickets, the faculty caved in to pressure. The students could finish out the semester, but that was all. "This Faculty," the Colonization Society was informed, "deem it inexpedient, after the present course, to admit colored students to attendance on the medical lectures."[3]

While Holmes was overseeing the monumental Faculty flip-flop over the blacks, he was also pondering the application of Ms. Hunt. He may have been irritated because the matter had ostensibly been closed by the earlier decisions of the president and fellows to uphold the school as a male bastion, and he was aware that it would touch off another round of dissent, which his precise nature did not relish.

Holmes had been so cordial to Ms. Hunt when she first approached the school that she sent him a note thanking him for the "gentlemanly kindnesses" he had shown her. He had supported her at that time, and he apparently saw no reason to change his attitude now. On the broader question of whether women should be allowed to become doctors, he was even more forceful. Years later, on the one hundredth anniversary of the founding of the medical school, he would express a view of female physicians that few of his day shared. In a typical flight of poesy that undoubtedly drew more than a few withering looks from his colleagues, whose own pronouncements were generally as stimulating as a mouthful of sand and dust, he declared, "I have always felt that [nursing] was rather a vocation of women than general medical and especially surgical practice. Yet I myself followed a course of lectures given by the younger Madame LaChapelle in Paris, and if here and there an intrepid woman insists on taking by storm the fortress of medical education, I would have the gate flung open to her as if it were that of the citadel of Orleans and she were Joan of Arc returning from the field of victory."[4]

Here and there an intrepid woman. Holmes's remark, even

though it reflected his consistent willingness to flout Harvard chauvinism, grossly understated the role women had carved out for themselves in medicine almost from the dawn of recorded history. He did well to invoke Madame LaChapelle. The renowned *sage-femme* wrote a noteworthy treatise on obstetrics after analyzing some forty thousand labor cases, a work that significantly influenced the practice of her specialty. But forget those who had gone before. The faculty might argue that Pallas Athena, goddess of storms and battle, who also taught the care and feeding of newborns and to whom Greek mythology traces the healing arts, didn't really exist, so female medical school candidates should draw no conclusions from her. But there were other role models, among them the professional midwives of the Old Testament and the courts of ancient China; the *wiese Frauen*, practitioners of herbal medicine who sucked the poison from the wounds of Teuton warriors; Trotula, student in the Middle Ages at the famed medical school of Salerno, who wrote extensively on gynecology and emphasized, among other things, the preservation of the perineum intact during labor; and Saint Hildegarde, the "Sybil of the Rhine," born in Bockelheim in 1098, expert diagnostician and healer of goiter and scrofula. There was Anne Marie Victoire Boivin, pupil of LaChapelle, inventor of the pelvimeter, recipient of an honorary M.D. degree from the University of Marburg, head of La Maternité in Paris, and the Dr. Benjamin Spock of her day.

The faculty now struggling with Ms. Hunt's application might also have conveniently forgotten that when Harvard Medical School was founded, not only had Italy's famed medical school, at Salerno, been teaching a level of medicine hundreds of years before (and which made Harvard's at the time look like faith healing) but it was so advanced in its educational thinking that it had admitted women from its very inception;

and that even the master surgeons of England had, in 1389, recognized women physicians.

But there were other examples nearer to home and more recent. Only the year before Ms. Hunt's current application, Elizabeth Blackwell, a friend and follower of the ardent abolitionist Harriet Beecher Stowe, had become the first woman to graduate from an American medical school, the Geneva Medical College in Geneva, New York, and several other women had followed suit. The year before that, the first American medical school for women, the New England Female Medical College, had been founded just down the road from Cambridge. In a few years, it would not only be churning out women doctors but would break two rules and award the M.D. degree to the first African-American woman graduate of a U.S. medical school, Rebecca Lee.

Worse yet, in Seneca Falls, New York, the first national women's rights convention had also sent out some signals that were enough to ignite borborygmi among the Harvard dons—especially suffragist firebrand Elizabeth Cady Stanton's stirring declaration: "We hold these truths to be self-evident, that all men and women are created equal." And only a few miles to the west, in Worcester, the first national convention of women's suffrage was loading up for another volley.

Hunt, fresh from the Seneca convention, and still pumped up over the rousing speech she had delivered on the need for women physicians, now had all the fight and fortitude—and even the credentials—necessary to back up her application. She was not exactly a medical novice. A schoolteacher, she had apprenticed—the requirement for all would-be doctors of the day, even for the chosen ones at Harvard—with Dr. and Mrs. Richard Mott of Boston, a pair of organic alchemists from England whose treatments and cures relied heavily on a pharmacy of medicines, essences, fomentations, tinctures, poultices, distillations, waters, coagulations, infusions, compresses, and decoctions made from enough vegetables, roots, herbs, oils, flowers, and gums to rival the ingredients the three weird sisters of Macbeth brewed up in their boiling cauldron. Mrs. Mott had written a popular handbook and patients were flocking to her and her husband—enough to convince Boston's defensive medical establishment that the Motts were nothing but medieval quacksalvers who were, not incidentally, cutting into traditional Back Bay business.

With an admitted disdain for established medicine, which she once referred to as "worse than useless," Hunt had added self-education to her apprenticeship, and in 1835, after Dr. Mott died and Mrs. Mott returned to England, she set up a practice. Still determined to be accepted by organized medicine even though some of its doctrines and doctors troubled her, and unfazed by her earlier rejection by Harvard, Ms. Hunt, forty-five years old, had fired off her emotional letter to the medical faculty.

Swayed, perhaps, by the writer's fervor, by Holmes's support, and the new realities of the day (although some have suggested that her age and matronly appearance, which made her less of a distraction for the young male students, made her more acceptable), the faculty approved her application. She would be admitted to the lectures, "provided that the admission be not deemed inconsistent with the Statutes," which probably meant that attendance did not imply that a medical degree would be conferred on a woman.

Degree or no, things were looking up for Miss Hunt. But it wasn't to be. Unlike the black students who had gotten at least a taste of a Harvard education before getting the boot, she never took a seat. And it had little to do with her penchant for bilberry infusions for dropsy and pennyroyal tea for suppression of the menses. Something else had crossed Holmes's desk—"a remonstrance," as he put it—from male students who felt that a woman's presence would interfere with their studies. So much for the matron factor. Apparently a woman to Harvard men, any woman, was someone with too many moving parts to be trusted. On the "advice" of the faculty, Hunt withdrew her application before the term began.

It would be sixteen years before women tried again. A disgruntled Hunt was still practicing in Boston, the honorary degree she received from the Female Medical College of Pennsylvania a few years later carrying as much weight with the Boston medical establishment as a copy of Cotton Mather's *The Angel of Bethesda*. Holmes was no longer dean, but he was busy lecturing on the use of the microscope, serializing "medicated novels" for the *Atlantic Monthly*, giving public addresses, and supping with his transcendentalist crowd at the Saturday Club. It was just as well that he had a breather, because in just three years' time, he would become deeply embroiled in a much larger "unpleasantness"—a clean sweep of the Harvard Medical School by the new, reform-minded president.

This time, there were two applicants, and now it appeared that both faculty and students might be ill-advised to turn these ladies down. Lucy E. Sewall and Anita E. Tyng already had medical degrees, from the female medical colleges of Boston and Pennsylvania respectively, and Dr. Sewall was a founder of the New England Hospital for Women and Children. Both women had been practicing in Boston for some time and were on the staff of the hospital. Their rationale was that they needed additional medical education to sharpen their skills, and what better place to acquire it than Harvard? They wrote to the dean:

> Finding that our diplomas, though legally sufficient, are not always considered satisfactory by male physicians, we are anxious to put our qualifications beyond

dispute, and therefore appeal to you, the Faculty of Harvard Medical School, as to the highest medical authority in the state, to give us the opportunity of doing so.

We request you Gentlemen kindly furnish us with particulars of the conditions on which you would allow us to graduate at your school, and we hereby declare ourselves ready, on sufficient notice, to comply with any such conditions, whether of study or examination, as it may seem proper to you to prescribe.

Trusting confidently that in the interests alike of justice and of medical science you will not refuse us this opportunity of proving our title to the degree we have received, and our fitness for the duties we have assumed, we subscribe ourselves, Gentlemen, your obedient servants.[5]

Rejection came anyway. Again, the only credentials the women lacked were anatomic, and the only cure a sex-change operation. The school had no provision, the obstinate faculty informed Miss Sewall and Miss Tyng, for training them for medicine, or, in fact, "for the education of women in any department of the University." Harvard's conception of a good doctor, and a good student of other disciplines, still did not include women; its faculty had yet to shed the innate puritanical distrust of women in high places that had been left it by the icy faculty-ministers who had lorded it over Colonial Harvard.

After the Sewall-Tyng affair, there were a few lively discussions about admitting women, and five or six professors of medicine not only agreed to open their lectures to them if authorized by the Harvard Corporation but also went so far as to express the belief that such a move would "be no disadvantage to the school." Somebody in the Harvard Corporation also tried a bold end run, asking the faculty if there was "any serious objection" to passing an amendment resolving that: ". . . until otherwise ordered, any Professor in the Medical College may admit to the lectures and recitations, besides matriculated students, any other person whom he may see fit and whose admittance will not in his judgment prejudice the interests of his regular classes; persons thus admitted to pay the regular fees, and to comply with such conditions as the Medical Faculty judge necessary for the interests of the Medical College."[6]

In a note accompanying the proposed resolution, the writer added, deliberately or inadvertently, the kiss of death. "It is of course evident," he admitted, "that this would allow women to attend part of the lectures in the College." The faculty took a rain check.

In 1872, the determined women tried another approach, one calculated to play on faculty heartstrings. The petitioners, officers of Boston's female medical college, came at Harvard like widows and orphans in need of shelter and guidance. One later account of their move, written by a faculty member, reeks of Brahmin good breeding: "The New England Female Medical College accosted Harvard in a manner that Harvard seemed to consider as almost indelicate. The Female Medical College, looking for a wider scope and a firmer base, suggested, in fact, that it be adopted by the University. Harvard did not accede to this solicitation and thus the New England Female Medical College cast about for another lord and master, transferred its affections to Boston University, and today lives happily in the fond embrace of that institution."[7] Next case.

In fairness, if it is any comfort, Harvard wasn't alone in its attitude. At about the time the New England Female Medical College "accosted" Harvard, Queen Victoria was writing to her prime minister, William E. Gladstone, suggesting that Sir William Jenner, the queen's physician, could confirm her view in the current debate that allowing "young girls and young men to enter the dissecting room together" was an "awful" idea. American doctors were also reading, and undoubtedly cheering, a recent article in the *Transactions of the American Medical Association,* the gist of which was that the "woman question" in regard to medicine was only one of the forms in which the *"pestis muliebris,"* the woman's plague, was vexing the world.

Nonetheless, the ladies of Boston were giving it another try. In 1878, on the assumption that money does indeed talk to academics and lesser mortals alike, especially at fund-raising time, they tried bribery. This time, Harvard's response was a bit slower in coming. Actually, the profferer was one woman, Miss Marion Hovey, described as a "blue-stocking of the Boston Back Bay variety."

Miss Hovey applied for admission to the high-ticket lectures and was prepared, she informed the president and fellows, to sweeten the petition with ten thousand dollars if Harvard would but grant the "advantage" of a medical education to women on equal terms with men. She argued that women graduates of the Boston University Medical School were already practicing in Boston, that many were not well prepared and that Harvard could help them, that Boston's talent pool ought to be expanded, and that Harvard's stubbornness just wasn't fair. Women, she implied, were at the end of their tether.

Miss Hovey's offer prompted what Harvard historians have called a "searching study of the matter," one that was rivaled, perhaps, only by a heated debate going on at the time over whether a woman physician would be called doctor or doctoress, and another over the propriety of women being allowed to dissect nude male bodies. The board of overseers formed committees. Financial officers salivated at the prospect of some easy money. Experts examined how women were being educated in medical schools in Europe and across the United States. They were not especially impressed. The Massachusetts Medical Society was polled; most of the respondents agreed that women should be educated as physicians, either equally or separate. A majority report was hammered out, and, *mirabile visu*, it recommended acceptance of the gift. But this was Harvard, and the majority did not necessarily override cooler heads. Drs. Henry Beecher and Mark Altschule, two Harvard historians who examined Harvard's contributions to medical education and the practice of medicine, offered this convoluted explanation of what happened: "[The minority report] agreed with the majority that medical education should be provided for women, possibly in a separate school, which might or might not be created by Harvard. [It] opposed, in general, the report of the majority as being untimely and of dubious value, a threat to the well-being of the School. That is to say, Harvard should not then accept the responsibility for educating women in medicine."[8] It did not.

With the minority now in control, it appeared doubtful that any woman would ever trouble the school again. Enter Marie Zakrzewska, a Prussian midwife who had come to the United States for a bona fide medical education. She had befriended Elizabeth Blackwell, who helped her get into medical school at Western Reserve College, where she received her M.D. degree.

Dr. Zak, as her friends knew her, had opened the New England Hospital for Women and Children, and in 1881, she took the ball from Marion Hovey, also choosing the palm-greasing method to bring the boys at Harvard around. Her offer upped the ante to fifty thousand dollars if Harvard would open the "fortress of medical education" to women. The offer went to the board of overseers, and again a study committee was appointed. This time, the majority advised against taking the money, and a minority favored it. In what may have been inspired by a combination of pangs of conscience and fiscal needs, the overseers astonished everyone by accepting, again, the minority report.

Dr. Zak was cheered. But only for a time. The wrath and clout of the faculty rolled out like thunder. The dons decided that nothing should be done without the "advice and full concurrence of the Faculty," that the money offered was not enough to do what Dr. Zak said it would do, and that, indeed, the cash hadn't even been raised yet. It would take two world wars to budge the stonewalling Harvard faculty.

World War I had forced England, France, and Germany to rely on female physicians at home and in battle zones. In the United States, medical educators were predicting that if the war dragged on, there would be an urgent need for properly trained women doctors to take up the slack as potential male applicants entered the service and doctors shipped out. Even the American Medical Association, not known for its interest in any rights that did not concern the male physician, had begun to admit women to its membership; and in what must have galled Harvard, archrival Johns Hopkins Medical School had been accepting women students for some years, not out of any commitment to fairness but because of the $500,000 that came with the deal.

Harvard began to come around, but as gingerly as patrolling the trenches. Perhaps it was recalling the past so that it would not be condemned to repeat it, but, on the other hand, Harvard had never really lost enough of its past to recall. Indeed, Somerset Maugham's description of how a professor of gynecology opened a lecture still summed up most faculty thinking about females: "Gentlemen, woman is an animal that micturates once a day, defecates once a week, menstruates once a month, parturates once a year and copulates whenever she has the opportunity." If that was not sufficient, the faculty could still fall back on the authoritative pronouncement of one of its own, Holmes's nemesis in the matter of childbed fever, Walter Channing. "It is obvious," he intoned, "that we cannot instruct women as we do men in the science of medicine. We cannot carry them into the dissecting room and the hospital. Many of our more delicate feelings, much of our refined sensibility, must be subdued, before we can submit to the sort of discipline required in the study of medicine. In females, they must be destroyed.'"[9] Nevertheless, the President's Report for the war years noted that women's claims for "the best opportunity to study medicine is a just one, and no hindrance should be given to all properly qualified persons to enter upon such studies. *Many women are particularly well-qualified for medical laboratory and research work.*" [Emphasis added][10] Harvard then seized upon a grand compromise that was nearly as condescending as the last line of the President's Report. It would allow Harvard doctors to train women in a course of medicine—but the program would be under the auspices of Radcliffe College, Harvard's female arm. It was a case of adoption without benefit of the family name. Undeterred by becoming mere mistresses of the Harvard faculty, a number of women applied. But as quickly as the plan was conceived, it was scrapped, mainly because most of the women who had applied were already students at other medical schools, and Harvard felt it was just "not proper" to consider these.

After the war, the medical school appeared to lighten up a bit more. Perhaps the fears of a doctor shortage during the war heightened awareness of what might occur in future emergencies; perhaps it was a new spirit of liberalism. More than likely, it was simply appreciation of the fact that Harvard had fallen far behind the pack in educating women. Whatever the impetus, Harvard began offering courses at the medical school for increasing numbers of Radcliffe women working toward advanced degrees in the medical sciences. In 1919, the medical school offered a plum: It named Dr. Alice Hamilton an assistant professor of industrial medicine, the first woman appointed to a faculty position at the school.

Again, however, Harvard had proceeded cautiously. As though it was reassuring its old guard that the appointment had nothing whatsoever to do with equality, the school imposed three requirements that Hamilton had to accept if she wanted the new post: She could not enter the Harvard Club, she could not participate in the commencement academic procession, and, as if she needed further proof that the playing field was not level, she was not to expect "professorial privilege" in securing football tickets. The conservatives were to be soothed further, because Dr. Hamilton was never advanced in rank. But more important to the diehard faculty was the assurance that the *medicine* in Hamilton's title was not to be confused with its use in the coveted M.D. degree. Those initials still stood for male doctor.

And so it went until World War II, when events pushed the woman's issue to the point of no return. Plagued by intern and resident shortages, forced to rely on female doctors trained elsewhere to staff its hospitals, and aware that many very competent women were already taking courses at the medical school toward their advanced science degrees, Harvard finally began to cave in. In 1943, the faculty recommended to the president and fellows that women be admitted, but advised that action be held off for a year to "give further consideration to this problem." If the writers of the memo were looking for time to kill the whole idea, it didn't work. The next year, a more tolerant faculty, in an overwhelming vote, urged again that the Harvard Corporation authorize the admission of women. It was over at last, and in September of 1945, Harvard admitted its first class of women. As one old grad put it, "Harvard had dug the grave in which finally will be buried a curious medical antipathy."

School would not be easy for the twelve pioneering

women. There was still simmering opposition to their presence. Just before they began classes, an article in the *Alumni Bulletin* called attention to the negatives.

> The opponents maintain that while women have considerable ability, each place taken in the Harvard Medical School by a woman represents a lost opportunity to a potential male physician, which is later wasted if, a few years after her graduation, the woman abandons medicine to raise her family. This, they argue, constitutes a net loss in educational investment. With the per capita investment in educational plant, equipment, and personnel so much greater in medicine than in any of the other professions, we should not invest it in a student who cannot carry forward the work for which she is trained. Who is right? Only time and the Overseers will tell us; progress thrives on constant change and medicine has remained one of the few fields of endeavor still largely closed to women.[11]

Some suggested that the women were at Harvard to pursue husbands rather than careers. And a Boston newspaper, heralding the first female class, reflected more on its appearance than on its brainpower: "As you look them over, they seem girls with better than average good looks, their streaming bobs and feather cuts dot the close-cropped heads of men in the Harvard classroom, the laboratories and the school library where famous men laid the cornerstones of illustrious careers."

Doris Rubin Bennett, who died of leukemia a few months after I interviewed her for this book, was a member of that first class. She recalled that when she was preparing for her own groundbreaking interview back in 1945, her mentor told her to "get the bows out of your hair, don't wear saddle shoes, and look really nice." She took his advice. "So, I put on a gray pin-striped suit, a big hat, high heels, really elegant. But before I went in to see the dean, my mentor said, 'Be sure you come and see me first. I have to check you out.' When I got in, the dean took one look at me and told me I was in. I don't recall that he asked me much."

Bennett became a clinical instructor in pediatrics at Harvard Med, an achievement that, she joked, classified her as a national historic monument. In 1984, she told an Alumni Day gathering what it was like to be a female student at Harvard Med in those days. There were the not-always-good-natured hazings, the deans who were always too busy for the women. She described how those in charge of housing flatly refused to allow the women to live in Vanderbilt Hall, the male sanctuary. One story concerned the anatomy professor, a courtly classics scholar, who insisted that women, as in the days of the Greeks and Romans, should be kept barefoot and pregnant; another was about the physiology professor who urged the women students to go to the burlesque houses of bawdy Scollay Square to watch and learn as stripper Sally Keith demonstrated "hitherto undescribed movements of pectoral and gluteal muscles." She recalled the outpatient-department instructor who prevented her and another woman student from entering a room to examine a patient with syphilitic lesions because the man would be embarrassed by their presence.

"At that moment," she said, "we became charter members of the as-yet-unfounded women's liberation movement. We demanded our rights. We had paid the same tuition as our classmates. Our instructor had a whispered conversation with the head nurse, who invited the two of us to enter the room, cautioning us to be very still. We tiptoed in, where we saw the patient stretched out on an exam table, covered from head to toe with a laparotomy sheet. Only the primary lesion protruded. The plan fell flat because my friend and I broke up completely and fled from the room laughing."

In her address, Bennett paid homage to the women who chose to structure their lives around practicing medicine and motherhood, saying she felt that fitted the ideal of the caring doctor. "These lady doctors are not just as good as their male counterparts," she said. "They're better. Women are governed by a biological imperative. No matter how willing husbands are to share homemaking and child rearing, only the woman can bear and nurse the children. This ability somehow seems to impart to women the need and desire to nurture, to care for the weak and helpless. What better quality for a good doctor?"

If women physicians are to be the antidote for the sometimes callous disregard that their male counterparts show for the patient, and if compassion is more noticeable when a woman doctor is at the bedside—notions supported by a spate of current data—Harvard Medical School was not about to rush out and prove it. Dr. Bennett's pioneering class was but a stream that did not immediately open any floodgates: By 1969, only 164 women had graduated from HMS—better than none, one might argue, but certainly nowhere near the number of men who walked out with M.D. degrees over those twenty years. Moreover, even though they were now being admitted, acceptance was another matter. Dr. Anna Stein Kadish, who got her M.D. degree from Harvard in 1967, a year when women comprised 7.9 percent of the class, recalls that her daughter's birth certificate read: "Occupation of father: medical student; occupation of mother: housewife (medical student)."

Neither did Harvard seem overly eager, before 1969, to right the imbalance in its minority admissions, an area whose record was far worse than for women. Between 1952 and 1972, HMS graduated twelve black physicians and eighteen other minorities; in the 1968 first-year class, only two were enrolled. Again, Harvard was not alone in keeping the doors barely ajar to women and minorities. In 1969, women accounted for only 7 percent of medical school admissions nationwide, and the percentage of women faculty members was even lower. Between 1968 and 1969, there were only 266 blacks out of nearly 10,000 first-year students in all U.S. medical schools, around 2.7 percent of the total enrollment. The picture becomes bleaker still when one considers that half of the black students were attending all-black medical schools, Meharry and Howard, making black enrollment in all other U.S. medical schools 133, or 1.4 percent—this at a time when blacks made up 11 percent of the country's population. Native Americans, mainland Puerto Ricans, and Mexican Americans got even shorter shrift: There were only twenty-six.[12]

Some at Harvard maintain that the school had long wanted to enroll more blacks—and, indeed, a token one or two were occasionally aboard, with three in 1927 considered an enormous breakthrough—but that their scarcity was due more to a lack of qualified applicants than to bigotry. It is an old argument used to defend "honest prejudice," and probably true, but only so far as it goes. It begs the question of why Harvard, as a beacon of liberal education and innovative programs, did not take steps sooner to provide for minority students who were, perhaps, not intellectually equal to the white applicants but who had qualities and talents that would still make them good physicians; or why, for example, it did not tailor programs that would accept the deficiencies and hone the proper skills. Special handling—what some at Harvard might have disdainfully characterized as itself a kind of racism—was required not only for moral reasons but for the evolution of medical education, and, since an *A* average alone does not define a good doctor, for the very fact that medical practice requires men and women who are devoted to people as well as to their own egos, to providing health care to the impoverished in neighborhoods that had been denied it and that were not especially big draws for Harvard's white cream of medicine.

The realization that training minority medical students, either to serve their own communities or pursue research and academic careers, was not strictly the business of "the other" medical schools was forced upon Harvard amid the national struggle for civil rights in the late 1960s. At the time, there were but five blacks working for their medical degrees out of some six hundred and the atmosphere was growing peevish. The school's prime gadflies—Jonathan Beckwith, Leon Eisenberg, and an assortment of angry students among them—were abuzz. Militant students intruded into the puritan simplicity of University Hall in the Yard, holding it by force until a distraught and frustrated President Nathan Pusey summoned the police to evict them. Ad hoc faculty committees hammered out proposals calling for scholarships for blacks, vigorous recruitment of minorities, and faculty changes. Debates were acrimonious. There were demands for an immediate goal of fifteen blacks a year, as well as counterarguments that the school would never find fifteen who met Harvard's lofty standards. Others opposed quotas, preferring "substantial numbers." Dean Robert Ebert, responding to a petition from some three hundred medical students, appointed a committee to explore ways the school might contribute to solving Boston's black community problems and how best to resolve the thorny issue of maintaining high standards while opening the school's doors to minorities. Dr. Eisenberg has recalled the discussion the committee's report evoked:

> The two major issues—maintaining "standards" and identifying criteria for "disadvantage"—that were raised remain with us today. All agreed that it would be a disservice to the students if we were to lower

standards for competence for graduation, but there was no explicit address to the question: competence for what?

On the other hand, some of the very same speakers wanted us to admit "the truly disadvantaged" and argued against "creaming" the pool of black talent. There was and is something a bit quaint about that worry on the part of a faculty that has always creamed the pool of white talent.[13]

Dean Ebert had made no secret of his positive view of affirmative action, a stance that did not ingratiate him with the few fogyish members left on the faculty. He was not a Harvard graduate, a tradition that had been broken in the early 1900s when Dr. Henry Christian, "an outsider," as one account described him, was named dean, a clear signal that Harvard Med was at least trying to start drawing water without a hand pump. A Rhodes Scholar at Oxford in the late thirties, Ebert had earned a doctorate in philosophy, then his M.D. degree from the University of Chicago in 1942. He became a professor of medicine there and, later, at Case Western Reserve. A respiratory disease specialist, he accepted a Harvard appointment as the Jackson Professor of Clinical Medicine and head of Harvard's Department of Medicine at MGH.

The year Ebert was made dean, 1965, the paucity of women and minority medical students was a concern, but not a major one. American medical schools were in a precarious position for other reasons: Graduates were opting to specialize rather than practice general medicine, the nation was heaving through a physician shortage, science seemed to be shoving bedside medicine aside, and, more troubling, the delivery of quality health care was spotty, with many neighborhoods, notably the poor black and Hispanic ones, underserved.

Ebert was clearly the right man for the tough years ahead, a breed of physician not always easily found, a blend of the thoughtful, sensitive clinician interested in the welfare of the community, a man well versed in the broader aspects of health care, and a skilled educator and researcher. He was, in short, a good doctor. While his clinical interest was primarily in tuberculosis, he had engaged in basic research that was aimed at a better understanding of the infection and the effects of drugs on the metabolism of the tubercle bacillus. Indeed, a speech he would give before the National Tuberculosis Association the year he assumed the deanship at Harvard—and which got him a mention in the reference volume *Familiar Medical Quotations*—seemed to show him as a doctor who could deftly straddle the fence separating practice and science. "I have never been convinced," he said, "that the physician concerned with the science of medicine was any less concerned for his patient than his less scientifically oriented counterpart of a generation ago. There are probably as many 'kindly old specialists' as there are 'kindly old family physicians.' "

Ebert had gone to Harvard full of ideas about how to improve the delivery system, notably through the HMO concept, the health maintenance organization. "When I was at Case Western," he would later recall, "the meat packers' union decided to start a prepaid group practice. The term *HMO* hadn't been invented yet. They visited me, brought in a bunch of advisers, and we talked about using the hospital for patients. It was intriguing, and seemed to make a lot of sense. So I arranged a meeting between hospital executives and the advisers, and it kind of fell apart for two reasons. One was that the private practitioners were afraid of it, probably because it looked as though it was going to be too successful. The other thing was that they had just gone through a great period of curriculum change and they didn't want to get into anything else new. And also, they probably wondered what people outside academia would think about our joining forces with what were then considered radical organizations.

"I was disappointed because I didn't feel those were very good reasons. A number of us, Ben Spock among the group, went to Washington to meet with Jack Kennedy, who was promoting Medicare and needed some doctors who felt it was a good idea. Well, when we got back, it was in the papers, and we were accused of bringing Western Reserve's name into this, and we were told that we couldn't do anything that would compromise the university, even as individuals.

"Well, when I got to Harvard, I figured, you know, Harvard is conservative, but it certainly never cared what anybody else thought. They don't. The upshot was that we founded the Harvard Community Health Plan for the local community, a pioneering HMO."

Ebert would not, however, be very long into his deanship before other concerns would surface. "When I started that summer of '65," he would say later, "I figured, well, this is going to be a breeze. But then the school year began and things heated up, to put it mildly. And maybe, on reflection, I made myself too available. I got too involved, but I feel that what I did was the right thing."

Ebert was fully aware that while the process of renewal and reform at the medical school is not always dramatic and swift, it is at least continuous. He sounded the alarm in a memorable annual report to the president and fellows of the university for the academic year 1968–1969. "These are revolutionary times," he warned, in words that struck a chord that, remarkably, is still being played more than twenty years later, and which is applied today, by other speakers with but slight variations on the theme, to the current state of American medicine. "The currents of discord and disaffection that are sweeping through virtually every institution have not failed to leave an imprint on medical education. Critics of the social order, among whom are many medical students, see a reflection of much that is wrong with modern life in the shortcomings of American medicine: its materialism, its inefficient organization, its toleration of a double standard of care for rich and poor, and its too rigid adherence to beliefs and practices of the past. Those to whom 'commitment' and 'involvement' represent the highest good demand that the medical school demonstrate its vitality and contemporary relevance as an institution by subordinating theoretical preoccupations to practical action, to become, in fact, an agent of social change."

As Ebert saw it, medical education at Harvard was a continually changing tide that had to be observed from a broad perspective. The earliest manifestations of protest had occurred a decade before the current wave struck, when students began to demand a more active role in both the planning and implementation of their education. Teaching, they claimed, was too impersonal, too passive, and bad. Lectures and other means of mass communication were unpalatable. The students demanded a more intimate, more active exchange, more seminars and fewer lectures, more tutorial-type relationships in research, and fewer laboratory exercises. The content of the curriculum was criticized, the relevance of basic science in the "new" era of medicine, an era, as Ebert put it, "of pragmatism concerned more with the practical application of scientific knowledge and less with an effort to extend it." Students were determined to work with and to serve people directly and intimately. Psychiatry, it appeared then, offered the greatest opportunity for person-to-person contact and, indeed, more than a quarter of each graduating class was entering the field. Then, service orientation shifted conspicuously away from the individual. The emphasis, no less intense, was now on social groups, particularly the poor and oppressed.

Ebert was not unhappy with shifting tides. "The boldness

with which students state their demands and their defiance of authority is disturbing to many of their elders," he declared. "In contrast to the preceding generation of students who adapted themselves to the system, these students are determined to change the system and are impatient with delay. Although the faculty frequently shares the same goals, they seldom approach them in the same way, giving rise sometimes to conflict and suspicion. There are, unfortunately, no easy solutions and no magic formulas, but steadily perspectives are enlarging, and productive work is being done."

Ebert's words and his oft-stated commitment to both the education of minority students and to Harvard's high standards of education were not taken lightly. Eventually, it was decided to increase the number of minority places by fifteen, and class size was expanded from 125 to 140 to accommodate the new students. Some 135 applications from black premeds, six times the usual number, were received for the class of 1973. Harvard enrolled sixteen, and the School of Dental Medicine took three. That class was still top-heavy with science majors—most of the students, in fact, had science preparation considerably in excess of the minimum requirements—but this time, a majority had indicated career goals in practice or community service, with a strong concern for the delivery of health care, rather than in science. Affirmative action and all of what it could mean for both students and the people they would care for—action that had been denied the three "young men of color" whose application had landed on the desk of Oliver Wendell Holmes more than one hundred years earlier—had come, at last, to the Harvard Medical School.

But, as was the case with the first women's class, life would not go smoothly for the black students. The excitement of admission soon wore off as the realities of a demanding curriculum set in, and some students, perhaps not as well-grounded as their more privileged colleagues, found it a tough grind.

Moreover, although attitudes toward the minority students were generally favorable, there were some rumblings—although no incidents, thankfully, like the one involving an early black student at the school, Louis Wright, who in the 1900s was forbidden to attend a pregnant woman in the Boston Lying-In Hospital and deliver babies because of his race. "I paid my tuition," Wright told his detractors angrily. "I want what the catalogue calls for, obstetrics at the Lying-In."[14] He won his case.

But there were signs of suspicion and doubt. While the expanded class was hitting the books and the wards, some faculty were still uncomfortable with the decision to admit blacks. Were these students good enough? Could they be trusted in the hospitals? Wouldn't it have been better if they had been rejected upon application by the simple device of initials—NHM, "not Harvard material"—scrawled by screeners across the paperwork? It was fine, went the argument, that the new candidates had the potential for becoming good doctors. But there was unease over what some professors and administrators saw as the too-relaxed standards of admission and education that had brought them in. In their book, *Medicine at Harvard*, written at the time, Drs. Altschule and Beecher commented on the special problems faced by faculty and black students:

> There is a conviction on the part of some members of the Faculty that blacks are handled too gingerly. As one man put it, instructors toss "snowballs" to the black students—easy questions it is hoped they can answer. If this is true, it will last only a very few years. Clearly, some blacks have difficulty in adjusting to the School in the first and second years. Many have a good deal of self-doubt and insecurity. By the third year, however, they usually have developed enough self-

esteem and security to carry on better work. Some believe that the blacks have more emotional disturbances in general than whites, but data are not yet available to establish or reject that view.

At [this] time, it is not what has been done for them that needs attention, but what has not yet been done. Quite commonly, they wanted and expected special treatment; they wanted their needs to be recognized by Harvard Medical School, especially their poor preparation, but their problems remain and are various. Blacks seem to have more financial difficulties than do whites. Whites often create environments that lead to cliquishness on the part of blacks.[15]

The two professors went on to say that during Dean Ebert's tenure, sociologic deprivation had become a qualification for admission:

The view was held that since some men were unqualified through no fault of their own but solely as a result of societal inequities, their deficiencies could not be held against them. Hence, less than optimally qualified students were not only accepted—they were recruited. Perhaps as a result, for the first time in history, Harvard students failed the National Board Examinations in significant numbers. The quality of the school was sacrificed in order to make it an instrument of societal reform. This change has not, however, demonstrably improved society. In this respect, Harvard was no longer a leader but had become a weathervane [sic] . . .

While such concerns were being aired, an article in the prestigious *New England Journal of Medicine* by Dr. Bernard

Davis, a senior faculty member and a renowned biochemist, further inflamed the minority students. Incurring wrath was not new for Davis: He had also been speaking out against what he felt were the unfounded claims of some scientists, Harvard's among them, that genetic tampering posed a major threat to humankind. In his article, Davis argued:

It would be a rare person today who would question the value of stretching the criteria for admission, and of trying to make up for earlier educational disadvantages, to help disadvantaged groups. But how far faculties should also stretch the criteria for passing students is another matter. If a board licensing airline pilots allowed extraneous considerations to interfere with objectivity it would be considered criminal. The temptation to award medical diplomas on a charitable basis raises the same question, even though the consequences of fatal error in the two professions are not equally visible and dramatic.

Many faculty members have wondered whether the stretching of standards in their schools in recent years has not exceeded what is reasonable. The problem is illustrated by a distinguished school that recently waived its National Board requirement and awarded a diploma to a student who had been unable to pass Part I in five tries. The award of this degree was virtually inevitable, after five years of investment by the school and the student. But we must look at the erosion of internal standards, and the postponement of decision, that allowed this situation to develop.

Medical faculties can derive deep satisfaction from their success in recruiting and helping many able students from groups that were formerly excluded. But it has also become apparent that patience and sympathy cannot overcome the inability of some students to handle the material. It is cruel to admit students who have a very low probability of measuring up to reasonable standards. It is even crueler to abandon those standards and allow the trusting patients to pay for our irresponsibility.[16]

Woodrow Myers, who went on to become commissioner of New York City's Department of Health and Hospitals, was among the furious black students at Harvard Med around that time. "We were compared to airline pilots who had flunked landing," he recalled at a recent Alumni Day observance. "In comments to the press [Davis] said that lower standards applied to minority students at Harvard Medical School affected the school's quality and would lead to poor medical care in hospitals across the country. To maintain and enhance our access to this wonderful profession, we have to remember that there are still people who, in the 1990s, believe what was said about us in 1976. In spite of whatever success we have achieved, we must remember that the struggle for equality, the struggle for equal access, the struggle to carve a role in the medical establishment has not ended, and that throughout our lifetimes will remain a major challenge." Another student wrote, "Those of us whose skin is black or who have Spanish surnames have lost some public confidence and this has adversely affected our doctor/patient relationship. Now, in addition to the normal issues we must deal with, one more has been added—the irrelevant issue of one's ethnic heritage."[17]

Dr. Davis countered all allegations that he was attacking the competence of all minority students by arguing forcefully that he supported the true goals of affirmative action and that he had merely criticized an excessive lowering of standards. Indeed, when it came to the extremes of quotas or a completely color-blind policy, Davis had suggested a compromise:

a reasonable stretching of academic standards, but not a numerical quota, since that "would remove the possibility of controlling the degree of stretch."

The brouhaha soon died down, and the arguments over standards and quotas was on its way to becoming purely academic. In a few years, the U.S. Supreme Court, by virtue of its decision in the celebrated Bakke case, would rule in favor of affirmative action in medical schools. Allan Bakke, white, had been denied admission to the University of California medical school, which had admitted black candidates with weaker academic credentials. Charging racial discrimination, Bakke appealed, and in 1978, he won a high-court ruling, which agreed he had been illegally denied admission. It also stated, however, that medical schools were entitled to consider race as a factor in admissions. It was essentially the same as Davis's compromise, but, as Davis pointed out, based on rather different reasoning.

Ebert retired in 1977 at the age of sixty-three. As president of the Milbank Fund for the next nine years, he supported special projects in medicine and health, and he later served as special adviser to the president of the Robert Wood Johnson Foundation. Of all that he accomplished as dean—including the development of the Harvard Community Health Plan and the Harvard-MIT Health Sciences and Technology (HST) Program at the medical school—he is proudest of the role he played in the decision to recruit minority students actively during 1968 and 1969. At seventy-eight, he recalled for me the roily affirmative-action days.

"Aside from the student disorders and demands, there were some members of the faculty, distinguished members, who felt that HMS had always been number one in the nation and that it was in danger of slipping because minorities were coming in and standards were being lowered. Merit was the key, they said. But you know, admission committees have to look at a lot of different dimensions, and it all boiled down to the question of whether they wanted some diversity for a change. We always claimed we weren't prejudiced, you know, but look, we had maybe ten minorities, and I recognized there was definitely a problem.

"Yes, we did relax our standards. But without question, it was the right thing to do. Other schools couldn't now say, Well, Harvard hasn't done it yet. The low scores on National Boards? How well you do as a school on National Board exams is a ridiculous yardstick. What you really want to know is what happens to these people when they get out. Many have had distinguished careers and been of great service to their communities. The purpose of medical education is not to pass the National Boards with the highest scores, but to send out physicians who answer the needs of our society for excellent care and quality research. A good doctor has nothing to do with how well he or she did on a test."

Harvard Medical School has been able to maintain a minority presence close to 20 percent—in 1992, fifty-two minority students, almost 22 percent of the acceptees, were offered admission, the highest number ever accepted. Women at Harvard have fared better. They represent about 45 percent of the class these days, similar to other medical schools.

But while both groups have a better showing in the classroom, they're still not as visible on the other side of the desk. Minorities and women alike—and not only at Harvard—run into barriers when it comes to obtaining a faculty post and getting promoted to full professorships and department chairs.

"It is shocking how little progress has been made at the faculty level," Dr. Eisenberg has said. "Over the past decade, representation for all minorities at HMS has remained at about 3 percent for professors, 1 to 1.5 percent for associate professors and about 2.5 percent for assistant professors." The lack of minority faculty translates into a lack of mentors, a problem that could easily be alleviated if the school hired from among the three to four hundred minority physicians it has trained, says Harvard neurobiologist Edward Kravitz, who was involved in the affirmative-action struggles. "We have our own pool. If they're good enough to graduate from Harvard, then they're good enough to be hired by Harvard."[18]

Women, too, might make the same observation about their own lot at Harvard Med. They have also been shut out of faculty rooms, and while the situation has improved, relatively few have broken through the glass ceiling and into the upper rooms of full professors and department chairs. Nine years before Alice Hamilton became the first female faculty member at HMS, the "outsider" dean, Henry Christian, was scribbling a note to Harvard University president Abbott Lawrence Lowell. Christian was no Ebert, let alone Oliver Wendell Holmes. The topic was an instructor with the unisex name Dr. Willey Denis, whom Christian had just discovered was a woman. The tone of Christian's note made it clear that he hadn't heard of Holmes's Madame LaChapelle and couldn't care less if he had. "The feeling in the faculty," he wrote, "is strongly against appointing a woman to be in a teaching position. It seems satisfactory to change the title from Research Assistant to Technical Assistant and to omit the name from the roster of instructors and simply have her name appear upon the payroll as do other technical assistants, stenographers, etc."

In one respect, times have changed. Since 1968, the percentage of women faculty in U.S. medical schools has grown from 13.3 percent to around 20. At Harvard, according to Terri Rutter of the *Harvard Medical Alumni Bulletin,* from 1987 to 1991 the number of full professors at the school doubled, from eleven to twenty-two. Moreover, the increases are just as significant in the lower rungs: In 1987, there were 60 female associate professors, 110 in 1991; 185 assistant professors in 1987, 236 in 1991; and 1,050 women entered training status in 1987, compared with 1,506 in 1991. "Numbers, however, do not guarantee success," Rutter says. "Issues such as promotion into higher rank, gender bias and sexual harrassment, and general disparities between men and women in academia, and society, have prompted the school to establish methods to confront these problems."

HMS officials point out that the goal for hiring and promoting women at the medical school is to hire at a percentage rate comparable to the percentage of women nationally who are available at that academic level. At this time, at the levels of instructor and professor, the percentages for 1991–1992 are close: 7.8 percent women in the pool of professors, 6.7 percent hiring of actual HMS professional appointments; for instructors, the pool is 40.4 percent, with 44.5 percent hiring. Dr. Eleanor Shore, dean for faculty affairs, points out that discrepancies occur between the levels of instructor and assistant professor, the point where people begin their research. It is also the time when women who choose to have children usually begin to take time off. As a result, they don't fill these ranks as quickly as men. Ten years ago at Harvard Med, there was but one child among eleven female professors; today, twenty-two female professors have twenty-seven children among them.

"The brain doesn't go dead after an absence," Shore, who compares women leaving to have children to men leaving to go off to war, has observed. When men return, they do so in full confidence and with the school's support. When women return, they often encounter what others call "disparate impact." Rutter explains that when search committees review CVs, they naturally tend to be more attracted to the familiar: a record of progression and productivity that they recognize as important to a career in academic medicine. "The CVs of women who have taken time away from research to have children," Rutter says, "may not reflect the same consistent level of productivity as the men applying for the same position. As a consequence, the man may get the position because his track record is more in line with what the interviewers expect."[19]

How long will it take for women to crack academic medicine's glass ceiling? Clyde Evans, HMS associate dean for clinical affairs, has said that simple logistics indicate that true parity in numbers will take a while because the ratio of women to men in academic medicine has been unbalanced for so long. Nationwide, only 10 percent of women faculty are full professors, compared with 32 percent for men. Obviously, the low number of women reaching full rank explains the relatively few women who have chairs: There are about eighty, 4 percent of the total; some 14 percent of associate deans are women, and 26 percent of assistant deans.[20]

Medical schools are, however, readily admitting more women, and in a few years they will, without doubt, comprise 50 percent of the classes, at least in the West and Northeast, where they apply and are admitted more often than in the southern and central regions. But though the general acceptance rate for women is still lower than for men, it is sure to change, and, equally important, the reasons behind their absence today are not the ones that held them back in the days of Holmes and his bigoted faculty. According to the Association of American Medical Colleges, one reason may be that women have slightly lower scores on the MCAT. Another factor may be that women applicants, on average, are slightly older than men, and younger applicants have a higher acceptance rate. Still, for the 1991–1992 entering class, as for previous years, the acceptance rate of women thirty-five years and older is generally higher than that of men. Moreover, many of these women have had experience in another health career or in community service, an important ingredient that often separates the caring physician from the one who simply goes through the motions.

8 "I Heard Your Cry"

PATRICIA DONOHOE WAS *MS.* MAGAZINE'S WOMAN OF THE Year in 1987, one of thirteen "who turned the beauty of their dreams into action." She came from a relatively poor background in the Boston area, where her dream of becoming a doctor was modulated by the dictum of her neighborhood: Don't even think about it until you become a good scholar. She did become one, and an equally good athlete, and was admitted to Columbia University College of Physicians and Surgeons, graduating in 1964 with a research prize to go along with her M.D. degree. After surgical residency at the New England Medical Center, which is operated by the Tufts University School of Medicine, she took her pediatric surgery training at Harvard-affiliated Boston's Children's Hospital and MGH. She and her husband are the parents of two daughters and a son.

When I meet her, she is in one of her many spaces at MGH. She has a lab where she and her team have pioneered research on a natural but rare fetal-growth inhibitor, Müllerian inhibiting substance (MIS), which is instrumental in determining gender and has a promising inhibitory effect on certain animal tumors. She has another lab, where she and her colleagues have detected the molecular signals that beam from Y chromosomes and direct male gonadal differentiation. She is also found regularly in operating rooms, tediously repairing congenital defects of the esophagus and trachea that cause food to seep into the airways and obstruct breathing, cracking open tiny chests to remove tumors deep within, and deftly reconstructing urinary tracts in day-old infants; she also spends time in conference rooms, fielding reports on grant applications and research progress, and in classrooms and clinics, where she teaches medical students, residents, postdocs, and senior staff.

Today, she is roaming her warren of examining rooms with Shawn Nasseri, who is now beginning his second year of medical school. She chats with her young patients and their mothers, examines the kids, offers a prognosis here, a bit of follow-up advice and reassurance there. The things she says on these minirounds are a blend of medical jargon for the medical student's benefit and momisms.

"Atta boy," she tells a four-year-old from whose side she took out a large bluish mass when he was a year old. "Roll over on your tummy, okay, Michael? You're awful good, Michael. Who's your teacher? Do you love her?" To Shawn, who takes careful mental notes, she says, "We weren't sure what it was. He was at an age where it was risky to do an arteriogram, so we did an MRI. Gave us good resolution. That's a great boon to kids, because if you go around sticking needles into their arteries, you can have a lot of complications." To Michael's mom, "No, no signs of recurrence." To a five-year-old girl in the next room, "Hey, sweetie, see your X rays? You're lookin' better today, don't ya?" To Shawn, "By the book we shouldn't have been able to deal with this. It was rather complex surgery." To the mom as they leave, "My love to your husband." A Cambodian teenager is next. A week before, Donohoe had done a thoracotomy on him, opening his chest wall to remove a cystic mass, a painful operation. "How about lifting up your shirt? Let's see how things are going," Donohoe says. The youth does so easily, without even a wince. "Arm up high; reach up the wall." The youth complies, stretching as though the operation had never occurred. "Dynamite," says Donohoe. "Terrific. You're all right. You're all right."

A twelve-year-old is last. His operation was a complete urinary-tract reconstruction.

"How ya doin', Craig?" The boy smiles.

"Some leakage," Donohoe says to Shawn. "Entire tract was dysfunctional. A little bit of a diverticulum here before it goes into the prostatic. . . . Bladder looks quite nice. We made a U here and then the skin graft; it had ballooned a bit, but I think we can trim that—"

The mother interrupts. "God, I hope so," she says.

Donohoe tousles the boy's hair. "Tell me, Craig," she says, "when you wet, are you losing a whole bladderful?"

Craig doesn't understand the question, so she rephrases. "If you empty your bladder and then go about your business, are you leaking?"

"Yes," says Craig.

"It's become a social thing," says the mother. "The odor. His friends give him a hard time."

"Is he a good scholar?" Donohoe asks.

"He blacks out on math," says Craig's mother. "They'll keep him back. It's not the ability. He just daydreams a lot. His mind is always somewhere else."

"Let's look into a tutor," says Donohoe firmly. "I think I can help you work that out. We'll fix it for you, Craig."

Later, I repeat the question the skeptical first-year medical student put to her at the Orientation Day clinic—about how she could spend so much time with one patient. She has a simple answer: "The amount of time you spend depends on the amount of time they need."

Shawn Nasseri figures Donohoe is the paradigm of the Harvard physician, someone he'd like very much to emulate. "Just look at her. She's a well-respected researcher and teacher, a full professor at Harvard Med, a surgeon, a counselor. She's the ultimate. That patient with enuresis? Not doing well in school. Who's the first person to say he might need a tutor? She has leverage with the parents. They're going to listen to her."

He sighs deeply. Hard times and debt are already on his mind. "So if I want to become a Pat Donohoe working in Boston, where there's very specific surgery, I have to understand that with surgery training, the subspecialty training, and the research training, I'm looking at fourteen years."

Shawn is from Kansas. "A Persian from Kansas who wants to be a poet and a doctor." He is telling me this while we sit in Donohoe's office while she goes to get her deli sandwich. He is an exuberant, genuinely compassionate young man with dark hair and eyes and a round face, a talker on fast forward, which fits with the breakneck curriculum he follows. "But then, maybe that's cultural. I grew up with Dr. Zhivago, the movie, the book, and I always wanted to be Zhivago, a poet for the soul and a physician for the heart." He laughs self-consciously at the rhetoric. "But you know, there's no one more revered in my culture than the physician. Teachers may be politically active and so you can't trust them. You can't trust the clergy because they're always political. So who's the person who's always going to help you no matter who you are? Dr. Zhivago. If not medicine, you'd better be an engineer if you're Persian."

Shawn and an older brother came to the United States with their parents, both teachers, when Shawn was six. They had left Iran before the revolution that deposed the Shah and put the Ayatollah Khomeini in power, but for a time, life wasn't much better for them in Kansas. Two things are burned into Shawn's memory: the poverty level they lived at and under and the prejudice directed against Iranians. "I remember we couldn't even buy a hoe for our vegetable garden because we didn't have the money, and I remember getting beat up a lot in school, which I eventually reversed by working out with weights." Eventually, the Nasseris' situation improved, and Shawn's brother graduated from the University of Kansas Medical School while Shawn was entering Harvard Med.

Shawn had started out as an engineering major at Kansas and worked summers at the Los Alamos National Laboratory, doing nuclear physics. But then Dr. Zhivago consumed him. He began reading a lot of poetry, landed a spot as a teaching assistant for a class on poetry in the oral tradition, and started writing his own. He also realized that he wanted to work with people and not behind a computer screen for the rest of his life. "During my most excruciating decision-making about medical school, family, and finances," he wrote in a personal essay for a scholarship application, "one moment of every day stood out. While crossing between the chemistry and biology buildings on a glass sky-bridge, I would stop to watch the children playing innocently below in a playground run by the developmental psychology department. Regardless of what difficulties I faced or what decision I agonized through, every time I stopped to watch those children I would smile. I now had a reason to write." And a reason to become a doctor.

"You know, working in theoretical physics doesn't give you a lot of personal interaction except in management," he tells me. "I could have been working on weapons systems and SDI or propulsion systems, and that's fascinating, but there's not a lot of involvement with people. So I got involved with this pulmonary physiologist who was looking into what happens in lactic acidosis and the release of blood elements that mediate damage and injury. It all relates to people like long-term athletes, who sometimes don't get enough oxygen to their muscles, and how you might treat that. We were working with goats, doing actual surgery. Well, I developed a sort of rapport with them, because goats are very social animals, and I started to realize the implications of the science we were doing.

"So I got started in physiology and got really turned on by it because it's basically about everything that works in the body. Very few medical students know what physiology really means. Anatomy is easy for them. If it's about what's there, it's anatomy. If it's about how it works, it's physiology. When it's about things that go wrong, it's pathophysiology."

While still an undergrad, Shawn also started working in free health-care clinics, learning how to take temperatures, blood pressures, and to draw blood. He graduated in three years and got into Harvard Med, "carrying the golden banner into battle." That meant he wanted to pursue primary care, become the family doc, take care of everyone and everything, physical, mental, social, and dental. That first year, he went from being a layman to someone pretending he knew about medicine. It was a time of transition, with a lot of book learning. He sopped up highlights of science. But he also learned and did things that Pat Donohoe could not in her day. When she was going through medical school, education was strictly divided into the preclinical and clinical years, with patients barely seen by students until the third and fourth years. With so little early contact with ailing people and so little attention paid to their environment, even when patients were finally allowed into the curriculums, empathy took a backseat, ethical dilemmas were best dealt with in electives like Philosophy 102, and the matrix of medicine and societal issues that is the bedrock of modern health care was generally left to rump sessions conducted by community activists and a few radicalized faculty. All of that had changed by the time Shawn arrived. He would see patients in the first two years, and quickly learn to take histories and perform physical examinations at the bedside. He would be required to immerse himself not only in the biological sciences and studies of human systems but also in social medicine, health-care policy, behavioral science, and preventive medicine and nutrition. And always, emphasis would be on the patient-doctor relationship, in classes and, ideally, on the wards, where, among other doctoring skills, the essential quality of empathy is best taught by example. If Shawn and his classmates are to practice American medicine in the next century, they will have to understand even more than their predecessors that in every single case of organic disease there is a complex interaction between the disease process and the intellectual and emotional processes, that disease affects and is affected by events that are sometimes as formless as a wraith, as elusive as the back of the mind. And they will need to heed the often-ignored words of a late Harvard professor of medicine, Francis W. Peabody, whose name adorns one of the student academic society's rooms. "The good physician," he said, "knows his patients through and through. . . . Time, sympathy and understanding must be lavishly dispensed, but the reward is to be found in that personal bond which forms the greatest satisfaction in the practice of medicine. One of the essential qualities of the clinician is interest in humanity, for the secret of the care of the patient is in caring for the patient."[1]

In his first year, Shawn heard the word *gestalt* a lot. "They say it at least six hundred times. 'This is the gestalt of biochem, the gestalt of anatomy. We don't need you to learn every single pathway,' they say. We learn the highlights of the major organs, because it's been proven that if you learn six hundred structures in the arm, you'll retain only ten. Like fingers—five and five."

He is not much different now in this second year, and he talks excitedly about how much he still loves it all, the free time to pursue clinic and research, the teaching philosophy, the tutorials in which real medical cases are analyzed, the faculty, which is more often than not on the cutting edge of research and patient care, the diversity of the student body. " 'Feel comfortable to adjust here,' they tell us. My brother's medical school experience was very different. There were one hundred and seventy people competing for the same grades. Fifty percent were not as bright as the top twenty, and they despised the ones at the top because they were the bright ones. People walked around talking about how much they studied, how many hours a day. They intimidated the others. 'Okay,' they'd say, 'you studied physiology. Did you know this?' At Harvard, I learned this: The brightest students teach the others. And the others help the bright students learn how to teach. Because I got my degree in physiology, there were times during our physiology and biochem block when I'd say, Oh yeah, this is my old friend congestive heart failure, and my friends would ask me about it. I learned so much just from talking to them and having them ask things like, 'How come someone gets blue in their third finger?' Your friends ask much more piercing questions than any exam can."

At this stage in his education, it is the exposure to hospitalized, ailing people that provides him with an intense emotional high, and observing Donohoe, who has managed to blend good science with the art of humane medicine. "There are a lot of technology types among our students, and they're going to cure Hodgkin's disease and things like that. But there are a lot of other ways to heal. A lot of us really love to work with patients. I love kids. How can you not help but want to help kids? Many times, after seeing patients, I go home and write poetry, and cry, even, because they were such tragedies. I wrote a poem about one five-year-old girl who had a tremendously malfunctioning genitourinary system. It was fused—no rectum, no vagina, no bladder." Five years ago, Dr. Donohoe did a staged operation on the child, twenty hours long, and put her back together. "Then the little girl gets one or two units of blood and gets infected with HIV. So here's this little girl, wonderful, sweet, a real trooper, who's gone through so much surgery, has three holes in her abdomen—one to drain urine, one to drain feces, and the other one I couldn't even figure out at the time—and she waddles in to see the doctor because she has some bone problems, too, and they're now trying to make her continent so she can go to school. It re-minded me of *Macbeth*, everything was done, and then it was undone."

He wrote this about her, titling it, "I Heard Your Cry":

Through all the suffering
you smiled bravely—

recovering from every
intervention against
your frail body
with the resilience
capable only in
our children.

And yet
after endless
procedures
were finally done,

we cried at the
tragedy of
what was undone
through the cruel
workings of
a new disease

which would
remain relentless
on a steady
plunge towards

fulfilling your shadow—
in the loneliest
of ways—

thru tormenting
agonizing days

of never-ending
suffering. . . .

As we can only
watch through
the window of
our own mortality . . .

senseless but in tears
at our own inability
to heal your pain
through even the
touch of

my
crippled
hand.

In his essay for the scholarship (which he did not win),
Shawn wrote:

Sometime during my first year of medical school,
when the novelty of being a medical student had worn
away, I began to realize what a unique position students hold in medicine, especially in hospitals. On the
one hand we are the complete novices who spend all
our time trying to learn the diagnosis, the prognosis,
and the intervention for every disease. However, we
are also the "privileged" observers who become part

of the care of patients as they are scanned, poked, bled, cut, and dehumanized as disease "cases." And yet we stand as outsiders to the system who are oftentimes shocked and saddened by what we see. We wonder at the irony of the treatment and the disease, the chemo-therapy and the leukemia, the torture and the child.

So many times after I have encountered a child with leukemia, a young man with AIDS, an elderly lady with epilepsy, or a newborn with "birth defects," I have lingered in the hallway or the lecture hall to write from my vantage as observer and participant. For me, the medicine and its consequences are my duty, but the poetry is the bridge from my soul to the human being with the illness. Only through the poetry can I maintain an equilibrium between my role as phy-sician and my identity as a person.

In the next year, Nasseri will need his poetry even more to get him through.

9 | *Science Is Easy, Humanity Hard*

PAT DONOHOE SAYS THE AMOUNT OF TIME YOU SPEND WITH patients depends on the amount of time they need, but her sensitivity, and that of Shawn Nasseri and Francis W. Peabody and a precious few others at Harvard Med and its teaching hospitals, is not easy to infuse in medical students who do not have the seeds of it to begin with. "This psychosocial stuff is unrealistically rigorous and academic," wrote one student in an assessment of efforts to teach humanism at the school. "It is jammed down a person's throat, with a lot of politically correct language and ideas. They are trying to make it more scientific than it is. There was an idea that you could teach the students to be compassionate. I rejected that at the very beginning as being insulting and counterproductive." Other students carried on about a "party line" on humanism and sensitivity that they had to toe or they would wind up in trouble.

Harvard Med psychiatrist Susan Block, who collected those disheartening comments, laughs it off. "There was some truth in it because it *is* my party line that compassion is important with patients. But that idea of a party line makes it look like it's optional, and it's a way of devaluing. You might be a Republican or a Democrat, but you can't be anticompassionate. Is it a party line that you're supposed to be a competent doctor?"

At Harvard Med, many doctors and faculty also don't care much for the "party line." Teaching compassion requires enormous resources and commitment, things that go far beyond a lecture course on the character of an ideal doctor-patient relationship or a sort of clinic at Brigham after Orientation

187

ceremonies. They'll try to teach it, spooky and mystical as it appears, because they know they're expected to, and they'll do it if the basic science faculty doesn't have to give anything up. But the focus is, and always has been, teaching medical students to look at disease as something to be diagnosed, treated, and researched.

Block believes that if empathy is to be taught, it has to be embedded in every aspect of the curriculum and that it has to continue into the third and fourth years, when students are less under the control of the medical school. And that, despite the professed and glimmering objectives of medical school faculty, does not always happen. Almost as soon as they hit the wards, Harvard Med students learn three things: (a) good role models are as hard to find as primary care doctors; (b) students will be rewarded for their ability to recall minutiae, which, in the grand scheme of things, as one Harvard-trained doctor puts it, makes no difference to the patient's outcome; and (c) shock of shocks, the hospitals are indifferent to their being there and are not always nice places to work. Moreover, university hospitals are high-tech intensive, and while they may be good settings for students who want to learn to care for patients, they are not necessarily the best places to learn how to care about these people.

Brent Forester is doing hard time as a resident in internal medicine at MGH when I first meet him. He has an undergraduate degree in psychology and plans to make a switch to a career in psychiatry. He knows all too well how the constraints of time can be the enemy of caring. "It's assumed, when you apply to medical school, that when the admission committee asks why you want to be a doctor, people will always say it's because they want to help people. And that's what it is to be a good doctor—someone who really cares about a patient as a person, someone who obviously has the skill and the knowledge to practice from the scientific point of view but who cares about the patient and his relationship to his or her family and the world around them. Unfortunately, doctors become so specialized that they know only a lot about a small part of medicine. They're really not true doctors. You hear people joking around here all the time, saying, 'Okay, we've got a cardiologist on this, but, hey, where's the doctor? Has anybody seen a doctor?' It's all so intense now, so much material to master, and, yeah, physically exhausting when you're dealing with life-and-death issues. People come and go. On a given day, you're taking care of an average of ten patients, and when you're on call—now I'm in the coronary-care unit, on call every third night—you might pick up six new ones.

"It sounds terrible, I know, but to be empathic takes so much out of you that you don't always do it. In medical school, we had a course in which we learned how doctors need to care about more than the patients' medical problems. From day one, they're very into telling you that to be a good doctor you don't need just the skills and the knowledge but you also need to be able to listen to other people and to share. It was a structured thing. They really can't teach you that. You've just got to pick it up. And I think, too, you have to be born with it.

"Some people walk in and out of a room and spend three minutes with a patient, and that's it. Nurses spend more time; medical students do. When I'm on the wards, I supervise one or two students a month, and I notice that they take care of two to three patients at a time, when we're taking care of fifteen and can't possibly spend much time with them. These students really are extremely empathic, they really care for more beyond the medical, and they tell me how a family feels about such and such. It's helpful to me, and the patients love it because they feel the medical students are their true doctors, as opposed to those of us who come in and out every day. I spend no time in outpatient clinics; I only take care of inpatients who are very sick. This is a very warped perspective. And that's the thing I don't really like about internship, not being able to spend time with patients, which is really what I like to do."

In fairness, teaching compassion is more difficult than teaching pathophysiology and the expression of mutations. It was far easier back in the mid 1860s, when Oliver Wendell Holmes was dean and when the practice of medicine was an art that did not treat patients as mere proving grounds. Whenever Holmes wanted to bring tears and tingles to fresh young graduates and impress upon them what their education had really been all about, he had only to say, "Go, then, to meet your chosen science, who waits for you like a bride adorned with her ancestral jewels and crowned with fresh gathered garlands! Disease is calling you from his bed of anguish, Death is looking for you to smooth his pillow, posterity is expecting you, impatient to be laid in his cradle!" Today, if such oratory finds its way into a lecture at Harvard Med, it comes from the mouth of a second-year student who's written a parody of the old gent for the annual class show.

Inserting humanitarian values into a medical curriculum— in the view of not a few Harvard faculty more the duty of a Sunday school than a medical school—is even more difficult when the school is Harvard, given the institution's inextricable link to discovery and the procreation of discoverers, as well as a faculty that comprises the world's largest biomedical and educational community. Many at the school still maintain that its responsibility to the patient is to turn out more clinical researchers, doctors who work with patients, yes, but with more of an eye toward measuring their responses to, say, a new drug or treatment. As useful and commendable as that may be, it still amounts to the application of new technology to human beings.

There is another barrier. The premier medical schools prefer to train one-note specialists along with the researchers, which means that only a fifth of the current crop of students plans careers as family doctors, general internists, and general pediatricians, the physicians who are not only better listeners but are the fulcrum of any health-reform program worth mentioning. Unfortunately, general practice doesn't pay as well as the specialties: an average of sixty thousand dollars less a year, not too appealing to most students who want to rid themselves of huge tuition loans and start a practice.

It may also be that the humanistic attitudes Harvard and other medical educators say they are trying to inculcate in their students are not only hard to teach across the board but impossible to teach, or, more important, lastingly impress. Some students will never cultivate empathy, no matter how hard they, or their teachers, try; there will always be health professionals who are comfortable with the medical insiders' joke about what constitutes a difficult patient—the one who, when you ask, "How are you?" tells you. The ones who have it were probably born with brains blessed with the neurons and circuitry that enable them to feel another's pain, or perhaps grew up in an environment where compassion was valued. Some psychiatrists suggest that the determinants have something to do with the relationship of a child to its mother, around the nursing period; something begins to develop in such a close two-person system that may, in fact, be the foundation for later empathy, the capacity to develop concern.

With such arguments, it's not surprising that there is no required Empathy 101 in the Harvard Med curriculum, and one faculty member who doesn't believe it would do much good even if it was there is Dr. George Bradshaw Murray, a number of the Society of Jesus, an associate professor of psychiatry at the Harvard Medical School, director of the Psychiatric Consultation Service at Massachusetts General Hospital, a neurophysiologist and specialist in partial seizures, and a philosopher.

Murray is also the school's spike-haired expert on the Thompson submachine gun, a member of the National Rifle Association, and a fervent defender of the right of fun-gunners to spray junked cars with assault rifles. Meat-fodder with Don Shula when they played football together at John Carroll University, he is known to the students who love him as Friar Tuck, the Raja of Fahja, the Pharaoh of Feck, and the Nabob of Numma. He's not exactly the popular image of a Harvard faculty member, or of a Jesuit priest—he was ordained in 1965, seven years before he got his M.D. degree from Creighton University—let alone a role model for the medical students who will encounter him soon enough and who may be trying to ease a little low-tech empathy into their science-oriented doctor training.

"I do not have any scientific evidence that courses don't help," he says, "but I don't see where in the hell they do for all the time one puts into it. Anyway, I don't think that contemporary medicine is really that wholesome to engender caring and nobility among new docs. You're really treating the doctors and the faculty, and the government, with a lot of this. It gives the impression they're doin' something, and it makes them feel good. Do courses make anybody change their views? What you do is take this guy out and clean his clock and tell him that's what he can expect next time he drives drunk. But, oh no, they say, that's punitive. That's 1880. Classroom time for caring? That's like saying, Now here's how we disassemble the atomic bomb, or Here's how we discuss cancer with a patient. That's all verbal. It's like taking pharmacology. You go through the alphablockers and the beta-blockers and the fahja-blockers and you've had no clinical experience, and you wonder about a beta for this, or is it a baba over there? And the kids say, 'Hey, they should teach us which one.' Even if they did, they wouldn't understand it. And all this feckless—that means without feck—take a course, take a numma, doodadoodadoo, and all that Kübler-Ross—death has been very good to her—is great for a certain class of people, but they're the ones who already cathect."

So, is there any hope? Murray rolls back in his chair and recalls a time at a bedside when he was a medical student.

"There was this resident standin' at the head of the bed, and he's presentin' the case to us. And while he's doin' that, he's tappin' on the patient's forehead with the end of his pencil. Like, he'd give the numbers—the creatinine is this, tap; the BUN is that, tap; the numma is this, tap, tap. Well, the chief finally says, 'Say, Frank, come on outside.' Well, all we heard out there was blah, blah, blah, 'Frank, you're pissin' me off,' fahjanumma, blah blah, and 'Tappin' the guy on the head!' When he came back in, I noticed he didn't tap the guy anymore, and I never forgot that."

He also never forgot Tom Hackett (the late chief of psychiatry at MGH), who used to sit down with his patients. When this new crop of students follows him about on consultation psychiatry rounds, they'll see him do just that (with exceptions—"I don't sit on any woman's bed"). "Hackett'd say, 'If you're going to stand and talk to a patient for two point five minutes, you can sit for two point five minutes.' He was right. Because that two point five minutes you're sittin' there translates into the psychological time, in the patient's mind, of five minutes. You've just doubled your caring time with the patient."

But then, Murray will inform his bright-eyed charges, doctors can overdo it—like when they fake familiarity. Thinking about that in front of his students, Murray looks as though he's going to retch. The form that breeds contempt in him, he tells them, is the habit some caregivers have of calling patients by their first names. "I say, Not unless you're asked, pal. 'Well, Ralph,' some of these docs and nurses say, and this Ralph is eighty-seven. 'So, Ralph, you got any pains?' 'Yeah,' Ralph ought to be sayin', 'I have one, and it's you.' That sort of thing tends to infantilize people."

If undue familiarity does that to patients, another attitude, more common among psychiatrists and medical social workers than other health-care specialists, dismisses them. This one does not make Murray especially joyous, either. "That's when you're calling a patient your client. Look, kids, *client* comes from the Latin, *cliens, clientis,* meaning 'to lean on,' and *patient* from *pati,* meaning roughly 'I suffer,' 'I allow.' You lean on a lawyer's wisdom and you're his client. When you put yourself in the hands of a doctor, you're suffering, you're allowing, and it's not a doctor-client relationship. The biggest pragmatic difference between a client and a patient is you never do a rectal exam on a client. That's not in the relationship, and if it is, you're into somethin' else."

Murray also wants his students to understand that the patient is not only the one who feels the pain; he or she is also an instructive music book. To read it satisfactorily requires that they pay attention to an inner music, the tone of the patient's voice, the body movements, the winces, the facial tics, the grimaces, and the smiles, all of which, if the student is observant, will reveal the patient's inner state.

"Can you teach caring to medical students?" he asks me before I ask. "Well, if you want to teach it, it has to be done in a way so that the person *wants* to do it rather than just holding it as a strategy. Look at the mathematician. I believe that for him, the coming out right—two plus two equals four—and the insight are sources of tickle, even though he doesn't hyperventilate, start to sweat, and have urinary inconti-

nence. The point is wanting to care. There used to be a tradition of professionalism, or volunteerism, in medicine. Now we
have this new alphabet system, HMOs, BCOs, and M.B.A.'s
running the insurance companies for which we now work,
things that spell acquisitiveness, and the mercantilization of
medicine, and the denobilization of it. They talk about managed care today. It's not managed *care*. It's managed money.
Doctors are asking why they should get up at three A.M. to
see a patient. Some years ago, I had a patient whom I used
to see every other day in the hospital for a month. My bill
was three hundred and fifty dollars. I sent it in, and I got back
a check for seven dollars and fifty cents. Are you shittin' me?
That was a mercantile transaction, not one that had anything
to do with my caring.

"If those people, Medicaid, had asked me for a freebie, I
would have said sure. That would have allowed me to do noble
fahjah. This has all come up with Clinton and his wife. They
want the physicians to do caring stuff, but they don't realize
physicians have done that for years. Of course, you don't ad-
vertise it. You hit a four-bagger for the Yankees, are you goin'
to roll into the dugout, saying, 'Ja see where I put that one,
guys?' They'd say, 'Siddown, ya bum.' Look, it doesn't pay to
be noble in medicine these days, period, and you're not going
to get paid for being caring, period; it doesn't pay because
nobody gives a shit. They say, 'Ring the guy who's on call at
the HMO this morning; don't bother me.'"

Ned Cassem, MGH's chief of psychiatry, also has an S.J. after
his name. He and Murray are among only eight Jesuit psychiatrists in the United States and a dozen or so Jesuit physicians
in other fields. Neither man advertises his religious connection,
nor is it hidden. Murray prefers to say that he doesn't do
spiritual direction or unspiritual direction.

Cassem, who received his M.D. degree from Harvard in

1966, has done a good deal of what is known in the field as grief work—dealing with the emotions of dying patients and their families. He told me once that while being a priest as well as a psychiatrist has helped him deal with the terminally ill in ways that other caretakers perhaps might not, he has always tried to walk a fine line, because he has felt put upon by the accusations and suspicions of his psychiatric colleagues, to the effect that anyone who has any kind of sincere and deep religious conviction is hiding his or her head in the sand and just has to be running away from problems.

Years ago, I accompanied him on rounds at Youville Hospital in Cambridge, a chronic disease and rehabilitation facility near Harvard Square that had been founded for the incurably ill in 1895 by the Sisters of Charity. The place was not unknown to me. As a kid growing up in the neighborhood, I would go on Sunday walks with my mother past the brick walls and iron gates—it was then called the Holy Ghost Hospital—and as we hurried by, she would urge me to bless myself and say a prayer for a peaceful death for those inside. Later, one of my mother's brothers, pain-racked by a fast-spreading cancer, would die there, comforted by caretakers who, like Cassem, were keenly aware that the terminally ill need to talk with someone who does not rely on superficial conversation or play other games of avoidance. So, nights and days, seven days a week, Cassem and a dedicated group of doctors, medical students, nurses, and divinity students from seven graduate schools of theology listened to patients' fears, their anger, and their bargaining; they dealt with the patients' depression and, if it all worked out the way it was supposed to, sat quietly with the dying as they finally accepted the inevitable.

For Cassem—who eventually became an assistant in psychiatry at MGH and moved into the chief's post when Tom Hackett died—such work is a case of give-and-take. He has helped countless patients face death, and he learns from them; they are what keep him going, even after a heart attack some years ago, and that is what he tries to get across to his students in the psychiatry course he teaches. Without doubt, he will probably have more influence on students' attitudes toward patients than all the patient-doctor courses they will be subjected to over the next few years. He will, to paraphrase an Italian proverb, work more wonders on them than a churchful of saints.

"When I ran the seminars at Youville," he recalled, "I noticed something interesting happening. I'd go to the hospital at six in the evening, tired, drained, wondering what it would be like not only to go through a seminar but then to have to go through four hours of supervision. It'd be just like putting in another day's work. And I found that when I left there at midnight, I'd feel enormously refreshed, exhilarated, far less fatigued than when I set foot in the hospital, and that after having come here from seeing very sick, mentally ill patients all day long, working with them almost exclusively on an individual basis.

"The question that I always entertain and sometimes put to dying patients is about what kind of human resources they have that allow them to face, to confront, wasting neurological diseases, quadriplegia, debilitation, the humiliating circumstances of death, and I'll often come away from those intensive interviews having dealt with an individual who's absolutely phenomenal, someone who in the midst of feces and saliva and bad odors and weakness and all the devastating aspects of being ill still preserves a dramatic human quality about him, sometimes a sense of humor, and other times dignity and real reflectiveness, some real bits of human wisdom, a flair for describing what life is like . . . and I'm really edified. These people inspire me, and you really do learn that resources of the human spirit are enormous."

At the heart of it all—helping patients to cope and caretakers to learn from the patient's struggle—is the ability to communicate—the patient with the physician and, because that is impossible if the doctor is not receptive or tuned in, the doctor with the patient. Both can find it difficult—the patient, perhaps, because he or she cannot bear to face an invasive treatment; the doctor because something inside has been lost, or because he lacks something that might never have been there to begin with. "And you know," says Cassem, "you can't fake it. People sense that right away. You can't just tick off the essentials of a diagnosis on a checklist. Say you're looking for aortic stenosis. You ordinarily have to have angina, dyspnea, and syncope. So you say, 'Do you have chest pain? Are you short of breath? Do you have fainting spells?' But it's not that simple. Those things are just part of it. You have to hear the patients, put yourself in their shoes. What are they going through? What have they been through?

"We had this young guy named Mark who had a first round of chemotherapy for a lymphosarcoma. He went to a hematologist, who started percussing his chest. The doctor goes down one side, and that's okay; then he goes down the other, and wow, he gets a dullness, and he says, 'Shit.' He knew it was a recurrent pleural effusion and that remission was over; the cancer was back. The hematologist says, 'Excuse me, Mark, for my language.' The patient looks at him and says, 'That's okay, Doc, it's nice to know you care.' Mark wasn't listening for any eloquent dialogue. Maybe he was looking for some moisture in the doctor's eyes at that crucial moment. He knows from the hematologist's response that this poor guy is really upset, and the patient feels closer. And that is what's going to get mileage later when the exalted skill no longer will buy any more time. From that point, what's left is the relationship."

But a relationship is quite often what students and doctors

do not want. Many do not even know how to establish one. "Some resist learning what one can learn about compassionate care," says Cassem, "because the empathic process involves unpleasant things, like terror, disability, life foreshortened. They may have the medical equipment, but many—perhaps when they have a patient with a lot of abdominal symptoms and they suspect ovarian cancer—will say, 'I hope she doesn't ask, because I don't have any answers and it makes me feel helpless.' But you have to be willing to let her say whatever it is she wants to say. Some others will just be silent, or they'll change the subject. That's when they say, 'Oh, don't worry about it.' It's not that they're mean. It's just because they're unwilling to take the next step. For instance, you're dealing with a man on borrowed time and he says, 'I was thinking about buying a new car.' You can reply, 'Well, whatever you say.' Or you can be brave and ask him, 'Exactly what do you mean by that?' He's implying he'll be dead and he wants to tell you about it. But there's always that specter of not wanting to hear it, that feeling you don't want to open Pandora's box. But you know, you're not opening the box when someone brings the topic up; it's already open."

The problem, says Cassem, is that caretakers are stuck with their own equipment. Or they may feel there is a magic formula for dealing with sticky situations, an emotional checklist that parallels the physical one. "I don't think anybody is good at it. It's just something you have to have, and I don't know what it is. I think I know how it has to be modified, though— by listening very carefully to what a person is saying and by detecting things from the tone of the voice, the music, the emotional state. Doctors do it in different ways. I grew up with family doctors who were role models. Then when I got into medical school, there were the residents who were brash in a cheerful kind of way, and the patients got a charge out of it. We had this attending physician who used to ask patients about syphilis all the time. He used to tell us, 'Boys, remember the ditty, *Every little breeze seems to whisper Louise,*' Louise being lues, which is syphilis. Well, we'd go in to see some really sick guy, and after the genitals were exposed, the doctor would say, 'Say, that looks like a formidable weapon you've got there. Ever have an infection down there?' The point is, the patient didn't mind and it got the relationship going, but it wasn't my style. You develop your own. Over the years, I tried anything to get in touch with the individual. You just have to be brave enough to get in touch. You have to get the fear of a connection out of your system."

But compassion means to suffer with, and that can take a lot out of the caretaker if he or she allows it to. Students are generally unaware of the burden when they invariably write in their application essays that they want to be Marcus Welby and Albert Schweitzer rolled up in one, gentle and available, and ready to heal the world. "It'll drain you; you'll run out. And you have to think about your own reserves," Cassem warns them. Which is why George Murray is a competitive gunner ("it relieves the tension, gets all the angries out") and why Cassem scuba dives in Florida and the Caribbean, where there are no beepers and telephones and where the fish do not talk.

Don Lipsitt, Harvard Med's expert on factitious disorders and hypochondriasis and the chief of psychiatry at Mount Auburn Hospital in Cambridge, is on rounds. The students with him are planning careers in nonpsychiatric subspecialties, but they are here now to learn something about the diagnosis and treatment of the major psychiatric disorders seen in a general hospital.

They stop at the bedside of a woman, and as Lipsitt begins his interview, tears well up in her eyes. She says she is feeling a bit anxious, that her mouth is dry. One of the students breaks away from the bed and goes immediately to the sink to get her a glass of water. Later, Lipsitt can't let the gesture pass without comment.

He tells the student, "One might say, 'Oh, there's a sensitive student who saw the patient was getting thirsty.' But the fact is, you missed the whole interaction. You just have to stay through it, stand it, listen to it all without feeling you have to do something about it. A lot of doctors do that, shutting off a patient as soon as they start talking about something other than their physical illness. Sometimes, they'll do it with a tissue. They'll take one out of the box on the desk and hand it to the patient as soon as he or she starts to cry. It's a basic message: Stop crying."

Some years ago, Lipsitt and a colleague made a brief film, *The Hidden Patient,* for general practitioners. Its aim was to hone interviewing skills and help the doctors deal with a patient's emotions. In the film, an overweight woman talks routinely about her dieting, but eventually, after some pointed questioning, she gets around to telling the psychiatrists what she never told her internist: She had had an abortion and was upset about it because she wanted the child and her boyfriend said no.

The woman's eyes fill as she says this, and she adds that her family is angry at her for her decision. The interviewer asks her how she deals with it, and her answer is, "I eat." There is more to the story. "I took the film to an AMA meeting," says Lipsitt, "and ran it in a booth on a continuous loop so doctors dropping by could pick it up easily. The response was fascinating. Doctors would come in with their wives, but as soon as the film got to the point where the woman starts looking sad, the doctors got up and left. The wives would stay."

Is there any hope for the students now passing through this school, the ones who will be those doctors one day? Interestingly, the student who criticized "the psychosocial stuff" went on to become quite compassionate with his patients. The way Susan Block sees it, the dramatic shift had something to do with anxiety, something that will afflict every student once they leave the womb of the medical school in their third year. "You might say that the more one hates a course, the more one will learn from it. It makes people anxious when they grapple with some of this social science and behavioral material. People get anxious when they have to think, say, about whether they're homophobic or not. If you're not making a student anxious, you're not helping them look at themselves, and a good curriculum will make the students the right amount of anxious. If they get too anxious, they'll just shut down and won't learn anything. But you have to make them uncomfortable to be effective, and one bit of evidence of a curriculum being successful is that it makes students anxious enough to be pissed off."

10 | *Hearing the Music*

MGH'S BULFINCH BUILDING IS A GRAY, GRIM, GRANITE EDIFICE fronted by eight towering Ionic columns, a reminder of the past intruding into the sprawling modern hospital complex that tries to smother it. Designed by America's first professional architect, Charles Bulfinch, and constructed of stone hammered into shape by inmates of the Massachusetts State Prison, it was completed in 1821. The designer's trademark classic style is evident, but the Bulfinch is, the purists say, a "classically defective" building, flawed by a huge square roof with chimneys at the corners, an arrangement that detracts from the impressive dome that rises above. MGH shrugs off such barbs, probably because of the National Landmark status that has been pinned on the amphitheater under the dome, where, on October 16, 1846, the first public demonstration of the use of ether anesthesia during an operation took place, thus marking a new era for surgery.

In a dimly lit conference room in the old building, five members of the first-year class gather for a ritual—waiting to see their first patients—that has been going on in Bulfinch since 1835, the year bedside teaching was first mentioned formally in a Harvard Med catalog as an opportunity for students. In that year, the lip service that Harvard had been paying to "practical instruction" out of the classroom gave way to a new policy that allowed medical students who attended the lectures in Theory and Practice to make regular medical visits at MGH.

The students who are waiting for patient assignments will not do much hands-on work during these next few months. That will come in their second year, when the principles of clinical medicine, including the techniques of examining patients, will be taught. In this segment of Patient/Doctor I, a full-year course for first-year medical students, they will learn how to take a patient's medical history and master basic communications skills, as well as being introduced to the social, ethical, and psychological aspects of the physician's role. In the process, they will try to appreciate not only how illnesses affect patients' lives but also what the implications of illness are for the caregiver.

Handing out the assignments is Dr. Laurence Ronan, who, when he is not teaching, is director of a new MGH residency program in medicine and pediatrics that is as much a departure for Harvard Med as Ronan himself is. A 1987 graduate of Harvard Med (he also graduated from Harvard College, and since he trained at a Harvard teaching hospital, he's known as a "Preparation H"), he is the rarest of all Harvard Med grads, a doctor who actually pursued a career in general practice. The residency program he directs emphasizes community-based primary care in immigrant and refugee neighborhoods of Boston, and it trains young doctors to care for patients through the entire life cycle, from the newborn to the elderly, some of whom have already turned one hundred. Outside the clinics they staff for a quarter of their time—the rest is in medicine and pediatric training at MGH—the seven residents in the program visit the elderly and disabled in their homes, the terminally ill in hospices, and the homeless living in shelters.

Ronan's class for first-year students meets in Bulfinch once a week for two hours, an all-too-brief time, although a forceful reminder that patients are the reason the students are here, no matter whether the form of healing and treating they have chosen is direct or indirect, at the bedside or in the lab. Some have a true sense, as Ronan says, of wanting to be part of the medical culture, an openness to experience, and they will take to it easily. They will be comfortable with the patients they will soon see, ask them the right questions in the right way, and pose leading questions and interpret the answers. They will learn how to hear the inner music that George Murray spoke of, how to read the tone of a patient's voice, to hear clues to things unsaid. "Patients have an emotional agenda," Ronan explains. "They may want to share innermost secrets and they may want the caretaker to discover them. They might talk about their high blood pressure, but in fact it's that they want to talk, say, about a son in jail. There's a whole emotional world out there beyond what we know about a patient. We're trying to get our students to smoke that out." The students who are successful will also demand more, as does one young woman who complains to Ronan that she and her colleagues have twenty hours of science a week and have been granted only two weekly hours of a vital class like this. Shawn Nasseri is another of those who understand the value and the necessity of such early patient contact. "Shadowing doctors and visiting patients took on a different meaning," he says, "but not quite what I expected. I didn't get a beeper. What I got were many poignant learning experiences as doctor and patient, a little more awareness of who I am. I wouldn't trade it for any other year."

Others, among them, perhaps, students who have never experienced a seriously ill or dying relative or friend, or those who know that they will not be entering clinical practice, or those who are simply tone-deaf, will present their questions to patients in the form of a grocery list. The recitals will be obligatory, studied, as in a confessional, and the answers that are elicited will sometimes not be heard, only jotted down on a clipboard. They will not take as much time with, or pay much attention to, the indigent, perhaps because of what a medical ethicist might refer to as a moral lactic deficiency, a lack of the milk of human kindness. They will not, as someone once wrote in the *Journal of the American Medical Association* years ago, learn that a medical history is a "living document and not some inert words on paper to be added to the reams of dusty files in the record room." Medical students are all privileged observers, as Nasseri says, but some will invariably dismiss that gift and be more like moths hovering above the stage in a concert hall: They got admitted, but they don't appreciate the performance.

The students all have their assignments. In the past few months, they have listened to the advice of skilled interviewers—psychiatrists, pediatricians, internists, surgeons—who are their instructors. They have watched skits staging confrontations between doctors and the terminally ill, sat with the pretend patients who memorized a script and were paid for their acting ability, and questioned these actors about their illnesses, all of it recorded by a video camera and taking place under the watchful eyes of faculty sitting behind one-way mirrors and taking notes on their performance. They have role-played, either making believe they were doctors questioning patients or trying to be patients themselves. Depending on their degree of interest in direct patient care and in experimental theater, they either liked the fakery or hated it. Today, there will be no more classroom instruction in interviewing techniques, no surrogates; the patients will be real. Moreover, the students will be on their own, uncoached by anyone but a patient.

Ronan tells them little but their patient's name, age, and sex. The rest is up to them. "It's on different levels," he explains to me as they leave the room. "They go over a health history, smoking, drugs, alcohol, and they take a sexual history. Another level is aimed at developing a patient-doctor relationship, the shared intimacy with the person and how to deal with that. They have to learn to be concerned with those moments in a patient's life that I consider the most attractive part of general practice, the moments that really define one's life before it's over—the births, the raising of children, attempts to have mates, struggles to work with stress on the job, challenges that have to do with the patient's own illness or the illness of a partner, the disabilities. The key component in it all is just learning how to talk to a patient."

The student I accompany is twenty-one and ready to "smoke that out." We check in at the nursing station on a floor that has a lot of elderly patients. The student gives a male nurse behind the desk the patient's ID, and informs him in a somewhat apologetic voice that he's a first-year student and that the patient is expecting us. "Be my guest," says the nurse briskly. "Have a ball."

We find the room, and the student knocks softly on the door, opening it before he hears anybody answer. We enter. It is stuffy inside, and there is a vague smell of feces and urine hanging in the static air. The student carefully closes the door behind him, a simple gesture but an essential amenity of ward rounds, along with drawing the curtains and seeing to it that the lighting is not harsh and that the patient is comfortable before a question is asked.

The patient, Eddie Conroy, is seventy-two years old and is lying on his back in bed. He is not comfortable. He raises his head slowly as we approach, then struggles up on his elbow, his other hand reaching across his body to grasp the bed's rails. The student draws up a chair and sits down. I remember what George Murray said about that, about how sitting down when you're talking to a patient doubles the psychological time spent. The smoke-out begins.

"So, Mr. Conroy," says the student, looking up from a list on his clipboard, "can you tell me what brought you here?"

Conroy falls on his side with a sigh, and it is hard to tell whether he is exhausted or exasperated by the question that students—first-, second-, third-, and fourth-year—residents, nurses, aides, and janitors have been asking him regularly. "I . . . came in . . . in the . . . ambulance," he says with an effort. He interrupts himself as he speaks because he has a severe case of the hiccups.

"No, no, I mean, Mr. Conroy, like, what is your problem?"

Conroy cocks his head toward the first-year student and asks, "What . . . is . . . your . . . name, sir?"

"I'm Chris," says the student.

"Well, Chris, let . . . me tell . . . you. You . . . name it . . . and I've . . . had it." He lets out a huge gasp.

The student's face is stony and he does not move. This is going to be a challenge.

"Like, I mean, what are you being treated now for?" the student asks.

"Chris, I . . . have . . . the hiccups."

"Yes, Mr. Conroy, but what is your major problem?"

"I have . . . myas . . . thenia . . . gravis, sir."

Chris tries to write it down on his pad. "Myasth . . . ?" he says with a puzzled look.

"Myas . . . thenia . . . gravis," says Conroy, trying to shift his position to get a better look at the student.

"How does that affect you, Mr. Conroy?"

"It is . . . a muscle weakness. My face . . . my throat. I . . . thought . . . I was having . . . a stroke."

"Are you in pain?"

"No. No . . . pain."

I'm thinking again of George Murray, and he's saying, "Yeah, Doc, I have a pain, and it's you."

"What medications are you taking, Mr. Conroy?"

"I . . . don't know . . . for sure."

"Pain medication?

"No. No . . . pain. I take a antidepressant . . . a thing for my . . . stomach . . . some other things."

"You have stomach trouble, Mr. Conroy?"

"Yeah. They . . . took . . . out . . . cut me across . . . here."
Hospital-conditioned, he starts to undo his johnny. Chris
doesn't move off his chair, so Conroy forgets about it.

"Uh-huh," says Chris. "Are they treating you well here,
Mr. Conroy?"

"Beautiful. Marvelous. The nurses . . . are . . . wonderful.
There is . . . one . . . who reminds me . . . of my youngest . . .
daughter." His eyes start to fill.

"How many children do you have?" Chris asks, jotting.

"I . . . have five . . . daughters, sir."

"Are you married, Mr. Conroy?" Conroy stares at the student, then rolls back onto his pillow. "Yes, sure I . . . am married." He sighs, looking at the ceiling, an arm across his face.

"And your wife, Mr. Conroy?"

"My wife . . . is . . . in a . . . depression." A tear rolls
down his cheek. "She is . . . feeling . . . awful because . . . I am
in . . . here and she . . . can't . . . do anything . . . about that."

"And you feel bad about that?"

"Of course . . . I . . . do. We have a good . . . marriage."

"How long have you been in here, Mr. Conroy?"

"Four . . . teen months."

"Fourteen months? You've been in here for fourteen
months?"

"That is . . . right . . . sir. They told . . . me when I . . .
came in that . . . it would be . . . only . . . two . . . weeks."

"And what happened?"

"They don't . . . tell . . . me. Maybe . . . the myas . . .
thenia gravis."

"And you'd rather be home, then, Mr. Conroy?"

Conroy doesn't reply right away. Then he says, "But I . . .
can't. My wife . . . isn't cap . . . able of taking . . . care of . . . me."

"How are you paying for this hospitalization, Mr.
Conroy?"

"I am . . . not sure. I have . . . Medicare . . . and I'm trying to get . . . some Medicaid . . . and some other . . ."

"What did you do for work, Mr. Conroy?"

"Chris, I . . . was a . . . clockmaker."

"Did you go to college?"

Conroy rolls back up back up onto an elbow and shakes his head, grimacing in discomfort. "No . . . no college. I was . . . an apprentice . . . then . . . I became a . . . clockmaker."

"And what does your wife do, Mr. Conroy?"

"She is . . . a home . . . maker. She's at . . . home. She's in . . . a depress . . . ion. She cries . . . a lot."

"And how does she manage without you?"

"She has . . . one of . . . my daughters . . . moving back . . . in with her."

"Do you know what causes your hiccups, Mr. Conroy?"

"The . . . myasthe . . . nia gravis."

"What did you used to do when you were well, Mr. Conroy?"

"I worked. I was . . . a clockmaker."

"I mean, like, what did you do for relaxation?"

"I used . . . to go out with . . . my buddies. I played baseball . . . minor league for the . . . Red Sox farm . . . when I was . . . younger. The Boston . . . papers had me . . . in a local . . . hall of . . . fame."

"Did you smoke when you went out, Mr. Conroy? Drink?"

"No . . . I don't smoke. I had a . . . couple when . . . we went . . . out. But I'm not . . . a drinker."

"So you played baseball. Tell me about that, Mr. Conroy."

"I was . . . pretty good . . . but I was . . . a minor . . . leaguer. I was good . . . but not good . . . enough for the . . . majors . . . I don't think. I quit."

"Why did you quit?"

"I got . . . married. You might . . . say, Chris, that . . . I was . . . in . . . love."

"Uh-huh. What do you do here to pass your time, Mr. Conroy?"

"I read. Sit in the . . . wheel . . . chair."

"Watch TV?"

"Sometimes. But . . . you know, Chris, there is . . . so much . . . violence and . . . death . . . and I can't . . . handle all . . . that."

"What do you miss most?"

"Being . . . home. I miss . . . my family. Going out . . . with my . . . pals. Working with . . . my clocks. I was . . . a clockmaker, Chris."

"Well, Mr. Conroy, is there anything that you care to tell us, anything that I haven't asked you about?"

Conroy answers quickly, almost as though he had been waiting for the question. He struggles up higher in the bed, grabs the exercise bar dangling in front of him, and says, looking straight into the student's eyes, "Chris, let me . . . tell you . . . something. You could . . . be in the . . . bed in the . . . next room . . . someday, just like . . . me. And don't you . . . ever forget . . . that. It happened . . . so quick . . . to me. Don't . . . you ever . . . forget that."

"Well, thank you for the time, Mr. Conroy," Chris says, looking at his watch and extending his hand. "I hope you'll be home soon." Conroy shakes Chris's hand. "Thank you . . . sir," he says. "They told me . . . when I came . . . in that I'd . . . only be here . . . two weeks. I hope . . . so."

We go out into the corridor just as a third-year student is approaching the room. It is his turn to smoke Conroy out, or try to.

Back in the conference room, Chris and the other students debrief. Chris is first. He outlines what he asked and Conroy's replies. He asks for more information on Conroy's myasthenia gravis. "We don't think that's his problem," says Ronan flatly. "It might be some other neurological disorder." Chris wants to know where Conroy got the diagnosis. It might have been an option that someone suggested to him, Ronan says. Why has Conroy been in for far longer than the two weeks he was told originally? Don't know, have to ask around upstairs. What causes the hiccups? Could be a lot of things— disorder of the stomach or esophagus, bladder irritation, something that stimulates the hiccup centers in the brain's medulla oblongata. Chris mentions the baseball. Someone asks whether he might have raised it because it was a personal loss, suggesting that for some patients the last loss, in Conroy's case his now being unable to return home to family and friends, is a reminder of all the losses one has had. Perhaps, says someone, the past losses that are recalled are some unfulfilled goal.

What about his comment that he quit baseball to get married? Did that mean he regretted having to give up the sport for the woman he loved? Maybe. Did he have to get married, because she was pregnant? Interesting. Chris doesn't mention the clockmaking. He hadn't pursued it during the interview. But wasn't it Conroy's way of opening a door to a little more personal communication with the student? I'll buy that. Was he asking to be heard as something more than a case, someone infirm, a burned-out old guy? Very good. Was he asking the student to see him as he was, when he had a life? Excellent. Was he trying to tell Chris that he should not view the elderly, perhaps his own parents, as they appear in the hospital, in extremis, weak, acutely ill, chronically sick, not able to function, dependent, sitting in a wheelchair? Was he not trying to say he had had independent problems, that the life cycle is far broader than what it appears in a bed on the MGH geriatric ward? Very, very good. More questions, unasked. Did Chris decide not to pursue Conroy's occupation because he did not consider it relevant? Or was he fearful of becoming too caught up in this man's life, of perhaps opening what Ned Cassem referred to as a Pandora's Box that had already been opened?

Another student who is deescalating from his experience with an elderly cancer patient may have been in the same position. He tells the group he "lightened it up" when things got too emotional. Ronan advises him to fight that tendency. In similar situations, some students say things like "It doesn't hurt too much, does it?" or "It may not be as serious as you think." That typically happens during encounters between surrogate patients and medical students. One time, Ronan tells me, a person acting out the part of a patient whose mother was supposed to have died of stomach cancer asked the student if he, the patient, also had cancer. Instead of asking why the patient was asking, the student told him, "I really doubt it, but we'll run some tests to confirm that." The student should not have assumed that there was no cancer, Ronan says, because if there was, he'd have to extricate himself. "There is a danger," Ronan says, "in trying to minimize the negative. You have to hear about it. You have to face it. You are not doing yourself or your patient any service if you do not. You cannot comfort by denying the problem."

MGH's preeminent cardiologist, the late Paul Dudley White, physician to royalty and dictators, the man who introduced the electrocardiograph to the United States but was perhaps best known for nursing President Dwight Eisenhower back to health after a critical heart attack in 1955, peace marching, and taking the EKGs of whales, also knew the value of a probing medical history. "A doctor who cannot take one," he was fond of repeating, "and a patient who cannot give one are in danger of giving and receiving bad treatment."

But good history taking and a thorough medical examination—the way it used to be done before magnetic resonance imaging, positive emission tomography, and endoscopic retrograde cholangiopancreatography electrified the medical scene—also take time, and White came from a medical tradition, all but dead now, that produced physicians who were willing and able to take the time, whatever time was necessary, with a patient, touching, feeling, talking. Today, that personal time is eleven to fifteen minutes per patient, sometimes more, quite often less. In the pockets of their white coats, attending physicians and residents on rounds carry palm-top computers, punching in notes on a patient's condition, working out formulas for the right drug doses, calling up a disease's etiology, symptoms, signs, differential diagnosis, prognosis, and treatment. In their offices, physicians use informatics programs loaded with personal health histories to conjure up treatment options, as well as other programs that enable patients to participate in the decision-making process as they weight the risks and benefits of surgery, radiation, or chemotherapy.

Chris's interview with Ed Conroy took twenty-three minutes, without a physical exam, but Chris is a student with time to waste on such encounters, and he does not yet have to fret over the relationship of the number of patients he sees to his income, as he surely will if he enters private practice. When Chris becomes a resident, he will see a lot of patients like Conroy, but the emphasis will not be on lengthy communication and on getting to know the patients well, as virtually all medical students do when they are starting out, but on getting people in, getting it done, getting them out. If he is a surgical resident, he will soon realize that a lot of surgery must be done on the very day the patient comes in, leaving little time or inclination for much personal contact. Caring though he may be, the system in which he will work not only has scant time for communication but it does not always pay what the doctors want and/or need for the time that empathy takes. It pays for a list of accepted procedures, tests, and treatments, not for taking more time than the insurers feel is necessary, not for lingering too long with a hands-on diagnosis when one can be obtained simply by clicking a computer cursor through a data base of symptoms; it can be as easy these days as getting cash from an automatic teller. In the interest of cost cutting and compensation, conscientiousness is derailed.

The students now passing through Patient/Doctor I will not yet have to swap their consciences for the bottom line, nor will they have Paul Dudley White to turn to for guidance about the way it used to be done as they fumble through their first history-taking assignments. They will, of course, encounter a few physicians on the faculty and hospital staff who will write and present papers on the need for a return to the sacredness of the physical exam and establishing a relationship with the patient and who will bemoan the fact that today's medical students are too scientific and too wedded to high-tech tests and computer screens, to the exclusion of their eyes, ears, and hands. But most, when push comes to shove, will opt for megabytes and all the other "ram, bam, thank you, ma'am" accoutrements, for these are, after all, signs of advancement and will, it is hoped, improve the way health care is delivered and help knock down spiraling medical costs. No one in their right mind at Harvard, no matter what they sometimes say in nostalgic (and politic) moments and when they are posing for fake-and-shake photos with someone who's just given the school big bucks for "improving health care," would really like to see the emphasis in teaching medical students focused equally on actually practicing medicine and on elucidating the molecular mechanisms of disease.

If these Patient/Doctor I students are fortunate enough,

though, they will soon encounter a physician who, as a young MGH staffer, worked closely with Paul Dudley White. But it is not that privileged association that makes Allan Friedlich, a cardiologist and a clinical professor of medicine at Harvard, so special. It is because, in his own words, he is "somewhere between a rare bird and a dinosaur." He still takes an hour to do a history and exam of a new patient, thirty minutes for a longtime one. When Friedlich one-handedly takes your blood pressure, listening trancelike for signs of the systolic and diastolic rhythms for what seems an interminable period, it makes the lab tech who's speeding through it for all comers during a new pharmacy opening look like a preschooler playing doctor. When Friedlich is listening, his eyes fixed on the needle moving slowly down the graduated scale of the gauge, the room itself seems quieter than when the patient entered, and the hiss of air released from the sphygmomanometer and even the street noises melt away; it is as though the arterial beats that have wholly absorbed him have somehow found their way out of the earpiece and mesmerized all sound away. He looks beyond the numerical markers on the dial, as George Murray and the Patient/Doctor I students look beyond what a patient says, probing for another kind of music that lies beneath so many millimeters of mercury—signs of worry and fatigue and excitement, as well as those of relaxation. He has learned well what Oliver Wendell Holmes once said about stethoscopists: "Remember that their errors spring much oftener from the faults of their brains than of their ears."

Allan Friedlich is seeing an old patient, which is to say he is old in years and a regular. He is eighty-two, tall and straight as a basketball player, a retired financial consultant who, in his younger years, pitched for Harvard and later, in the early 1930s, for the New York Yankees. He has had a litany of heart and other problems, and when asked about his baseball career, he answers, "I could have been pretty damn good. I pitched a no-hit, no-run game against Yale, was five and two with the Yankees, and then got farmed out to Newark. I said to Joe McCarthy, 'For Christ's sake, what do I have to do to stay in this ball club?' And he says to me, 'I want twenty and five.' Then I got sick with peritonitis, and I got out. Too bad . . . I enjoyed it."

He's sitting in a chair aside Friedlich's desk, ready for the physician's own variation on the smoke-out.

"Okay, let's play catch-up. You're still on a no-salt-added diet?"

"Yup. My wife is helping with that."

"Eat out a lot?"

"Not a helluva lot."

"So it's a pretty good no-salt-added diet?"

"I'd say I was three-quarters good. I use a substitute."

"Like what? Potassium chloride?"

"I don't know what the hell it is. I don't use it much."

"You're on digoxin—Lanoxin? Oh point twenty-five? Little white one?"

"No, not little. Yes, they are. Beg your pardon."

"You've got a list of your medicines?"

"Damn right. I'm getting terribly efficient in my old age. Maybe it's my secretary who is, though. Goddamn it." (He fishes in his pocket for a scrap of paper.)

"That's okay. I'm going to walk you through it. Okay. Lanoxin, once a day."

"All of them are once a day."

"Now, your Lasix is forty milligrams now?"

"Dunno. Seems a lot."

"Is it round or oval?"

"Round, but I cheat on that one. Sometimes I take a half."

"How many days would you take a half?"

"Couple."

"So it's about twenty twice a week and forty the rest?"

"Yeah. Once in a while, I go without."

"Do you object because you have to pee too often?"

"Well, yes. I have to live in the can when I take it."

"Potassium—K-Dur once a day?"

"Yup."

"Blood pressure? Isinopril?"

"Uropril?"

"No, that's for your gout."

"Zantac?"

"That's for your stomach."

"As you can see, there's not much wrong with me."

"So you aren't on a blood-pressure medication any-more?"

"Well, I got six medicines."

"So you're off the Isinopril. The gout pill. That's a big one? Three hundred milligrams."

"I don't know whether it's for gout or for this damned osteomyelitis. I feel it once in a while. The toe that they lopped off? That seems okay. I have a little touch of it in the same toe on the left foot."

"Do you keep that padded?"

"I don't do a damned thing for it."

"I see. How much trouble does it give you?"

"Not much."

"Okay. The Zantac, you take one at night?"

"Yeah. When I remember. When I forget, I take it in the morning. I'm on six things, you know."

"Now, the Coumadin. What color is that?"

"I'd say it was a light purple."

"That's correct. Two milligrams?"

"Isn't that down there, for Christ's sake?"

"Yes, but you won't mind if I look for errors?"

"Not at all, pal. I take all six in the morning."
"Good for you."

Friedlich is also Ned Cassem's personal physician. "If you're sick," Cassem says, "you want competence intertwined with the relationship. Allan is such a distinguished clinician, but he seems like . . . he's my friend." Friedlich, who is seventy-six and still seeing patients, went from Des Moines to Dartmouth to Harvard Medical School, where he got his M.D. degree in 1943, something he had aspired to from the time he was six. "My role model was a pediatrician who went to those schools, and I was going to bust my ass to do the same, even though I had no money and the only college graduate in my 'family' was a black cook." He applied to Harvard Med one weekend when he decided to take what little fun cash he had to the Harvard-Dartmouth football game. "I had had enough to drink to make me figure that so long as I was in town, I might as well apply. I was so relaxed, so I called up and I had one interview with one dean, got accepted, and picked up a national scholarship in the bargain."

Friedlich likes to talk about the days when docs got up at 2:00 A.M. to do whatever they had to do that was right, about what that sort of schedule does to and for the caregiver, and about Paul Dudley White and caring physicians.

White, born in 1886 in Boston's Roxbury section, was of Colonial and Revolutionary stock, with a brother named Joseph Warren, after the patriot/physician who was killed at the battle of Bunker Hill and whose younger brother, John, helped found Harvard Medical School and MGH. White's father graduated from the medical school in 1880, and Paul Dudley would accompany him on house calls around Boston in a horse and buggy. White graduated from Harvard Medical School in 1911 and began a long association with MGH, during which time he devoted most of his professional life to the causes and treatment of heart disease; just before World War I, he went to England to continue his studies, and when he returned to Harvard, he brought with him the first electrocardiograph machine to be owned by the school. He eventually became a clinical professor of medicine at Harvard and chief of MGH's heart service. Those who remember the Eisenhower days will also vividly recall White's daily bulletins to the news media, after the President's coronary, detailing Ike's condition, down to his bowel habits. A man of calm disposition, he once said that he hesitated to tell off even the perpetual telephone-calling hypochondriacs because "once in a great while, sometimes after years of apprehension, a call is justified, and my reply may quiet the caller for months to come."

Friedlich was taking his MGH cardiac training when White was in charge, eventually joining the other young doctors who cared for White's patients while the man was traveling and becoming a household name. "He'd come in from time to time and review what we'd done," Friedlich says, "and he was wonderful with the patients. I've seen him on kissing acquaintance with men as well as women, and that's the sort of thing you can't teach in lectures to medical students. You get it from your role models. I never saw Dr. White angry at a patient. He could tolerate the most impossible people, and he saw a lot of those, the ones who'd sought him out from all over the world because they had to have the best. But he never talked about how he dealt with them. He just showed it. And that's how we got it; that's how we changed our behavior when we were straying.

"I recall an old Jewish woman, a patient of his, who had had a heart attack. I was taking care of her in the hospital for Dr. White and she told me she had to go to a grandson's bar mitzvah the next day, and I told her that was just out of the question. I said it was risky, that she needed to be protected in the hospital. Well, Dr. White came in to see her, and it was apparent that this trip meant so much to her. To my amazement, he said, 'Well, you know if someone came and took you by cab and if you just go and don't dance and then come right back, I think it would be all right.' He had enough stature to get away with that. None of us would have taken the chance."

Over the years, Friedlich began to emulate White's style, his calm, his thoroughness. "There's a science to being able to get a reliable history, to get all the facts that are needed to formulate a proper decision. If you know the people, you can do it better. If you can pick up small clues, you can do it better. There is just no substitute for hard digging, and sometimes what you have to do is let the patient tell his own story, and he'll tell you the facts. I'll never forget what happened to me once when I didn't listen. We had this complaining guy in here, and everything hurt. His neck hurt; he's a real complainer, and I had a low view of this kind of patient. Well, my assistant resident was hearing-impaired, and he took this guy very seriously as a person. He got some films, and we found out that the guy had widespread cancer metastasis. That taught me loud and clear that you cannot preconceive anything from a person's appearance or personality."

"Where do you have your prothrombin blood test?"

"A place out there on Longwood."

"Do they tell you afterward how much Coumadin to take? When to have it rechecked?"

"He doesn't say. Leaves that to me, which is probably a mistake. He sends me a copy of the damned thing, which is Greek. Didn't he send it to you?"

"No. And it worries me a little that you're sort of floating in this regard. That anticoagulant, you know, if you get too much, you'll bleed, which you ran into—you sure as hell did. If you don't get enough . . ."

"I'll get a stroke."

"Yes, sir! That's why I would like you to see to it more carefully."

"I'll get my wife to look after it for me."

"Okay. Have it a minimum of once a month. All we want is that it's regulated by someone who knows how to regulate it. Have you had any bleeding?"

"No."

"Have your stools been blackish?"

"No."

"Any trouble with speech or coordination?"

"Hah! Not if it wasn't due to alcohol."

"Weak spells? Couldn't use a hand? Couldn't write or speak?"

"A small stroke, you mean? No, thank God."

"Well, if you do, I want to know about it. That's not something you brush under the rug."

"There's something you haven't asked me about, though I know you will, damn it. I carry this nitroglycerine around. I only used it twice."

"Oh? What led you to use it?"

"Well, I was having a pain . . . here."

"In the chest. How often? Once a week? Once a month? Ten times a day?"

"Give me once a month on it."

"Where exactly do you feel it?"

"Could be anywhere."

"In different places?"

"Yeah."

"What kind of sensation is it?"

"I'll tell you what it is. Remember when they carted

me in with the heart attack? That's what this damned thing feels like."

"Sharp pain, or dull?"

"Dull."

"Pain or more like pressure? Burning?"

"Just pain, I guess."

"Can you say where it's more likely to occur?"

"In my diaphragm."

"Then it's more in your stomach area than your chest. Is it related to physical effort? Hurrying too fast? That bring it on? Meals? What?"

"I think it relates to whether I'm a good boy or not. When I go out and have a couple, two or three, I get it."

"Does it make you burp?"

"Occasionally."

"Does burping make you feel better?"

"I imagine."

"Okay. My suspicion is it is more related to your esophagus than angina. Does the nitro have any effect?"

"Well, it did seem to fix everything up."

"How long after you take the nitro do you feel better?"

"Three minutes."

"How's the breathing?"

"Pretty good. I was down in Florida for a few days, and I took mile walks. No problem."

"How about if you climb up one flight of stairs, normal speed?"

"No problem, but after two, I think . . ."

"What do you feel with two flights?"

"Just a little out of breath."

"Puffing, or sometimes a squeezing?"

"No, puffing. My other docs say my lungs are clear."

"How many pillows do you use?"

"Two."

"Do you wake up short of breath?"

"No."

"How about swelling of the ankles?"

"Unfortunately, they do."

"More or less than in the past?"

"I tell you, I think it's my fault. When I was taking Lasix every other day, the day I take it, my left ankle swells up. The day I don't take it, it doesn't swell."

"On the other hand, the day you take the Lasix might have gotten rid of enough fluid so that the next day your ankle wasn't swelling."

For Friedlich, the physical exam is also a science. "In a sense, it used to be more challenging to judge by listening to a patient. A lot rode on your ears and putting it all together. Now you can do these things much more directly because the science of the good physical exam has been greatly enhanced by the technology that has been used to explain some of the things we used to hear about but didn't know what they were. The mitral-valve prolapse? Used to be that we were just hearing what we called a pericardial click. Well, that's for the birds. We know from echocardiograms now that it's mitral-valve prolapse. But, you know, nothing is infallible. The echo has been a boon for allowing us to make decisions, but there have been a few circumstances where it can be very misleading, and if that doesn't fit in with what your ears tell you and what the X rays tell you, then you'd damn well better get the catheter study. When things don't fit together, you have to use another tool."

Friedlich wonders whether the country can afford what it takes to do a careful, time-consuming job of medical detection, and if it cannot, what effect that would have. MGH and other prestigious hospitals are often places of last resort, where patients go because no one else could help. "That takes a lot of unscrambling, and a lot of time. But there's a lot of stress on staff at all levels for the rapid through-put, getting patients through the system fast. And one of the problems with that is that the house staff and students don't have the opportunity to follow a disease process. They see a cross section of disease. It comes in at the last moment and goes out at the first moment. That hour and a half I take with a patient? Well, medical-care people don't pay for that, and they'll probably pay less for it. The influence of financial considerations is great. I've often wondered, in a system like Great Britain's, did they lose caring people when they went into a national health service?"

"Let me ask you . . . what's giving you the most trouble these days?"

"Well, to be honest, I really haven't felt as well as I should since I got this damned congestive heart failure some years ago. But I do feel a helluva lot better than I did, say, at that time. I had a bunch of junk. You know, I used to be in charge of a carrier flight and hangar deck in the navy, and I got little damned sleep then, I'll tell you that. But this . . ."

"Feel nauseated?"

"No."

"Is it just lack of pep?"

"Yes, that's it."

"It's probably due to your cardiac trouble that you feel that way. I've always wondered, you know, whether someone like you, a real athlete, has a harder time dealing with such things because you can't . . ."

"Do everything I want? Well, I sure as hell can't. You know, Doc, I've always wondered how much exercise I can do. Can I have sex?"

"Your body will tell you about the exercise. You walk till you tell yourself to stop, that you've hit your limit. If you can walk up a flight of stairs, you can have sex . . . but not with a thirty-year-old woman."

"Hah. No problem there."

"Watcha been doing lately?"

"Shooting grouse. I'm a name-dropper. Went to the earl's place in Northumberland, seven to eight guns, a terrible slaughter some would say, six hundred birds a day, red grouse. Over here, in Canada, if you get one ruffed grouse in a day, it's a good day."

"Okay, well, I suppose we can close it up?"

"Thanks, Doc. You've looked after me. Hell, if it weren't for you, I don't know what. You did it, pal."

Friedlich has a yes and a no about whether the time he's spent—the kind of time that the master clinicians of yesteryear seemed to have plenty of—has been worth it. "The rewards of medicine are very personal kinds of satisfaction. I have often wakened thinking, God, why do I take all this? And then I think of a few examples of cases that were extraordinarily gratifying, and I decide, That's why I take it. On the other hand, I spent my whole career working ninety hours a week. My family suffered because of it; my wife had a grossly unfair burden of the child rearing. It hurts when . . . I had a good cardiac fellow under my wing one time, and one of my kids said, 'I wish you knew me as well as you know him.' Gradually, as they've matured, I have been forgiven those things, but it comes out of somewhere. But you know, you feel it's the right thing to do, that somehow you're responsible for the kind of place MGH is and you can't undermine that. If you get your kicks out of life by doing a tight job, well done, just right, it is time-consuming. But it results in solving some problems that were not solvable to some other people, and doing something sometimes that is helpful to the patient. So, what does it get you? Well, at least I can sleep at night, feeling that I've done a good job. Those hours can be tiring, but there's nothing so tiring as running your tail off to get things done and still being left with the feeling that you've left loose ends. That would drive me bananas."

11 | Hands-On Training

The student is to collect and evaluate facts.
The facts are locked up in the patient.
To the patient, therefore, he must go.

—Abraham Flexner (1866–1959)

MARCIE IS A HALF DOC, AN *M* IN HARVARD MED PARLANCE, which means she is a second-year student. She is from the Midwest, is blue-eyed, and has Ben Franklin–style glasses and a blond ponytail. A graduate of the University of Chicago with a major in physiology, she wants to be a surgeon, the specialty as yet undecided. She is, like most of her classmates, part of what Harvard Med calls its New Pathway Program for General Medical Education.

Initiated in 1985 by Dean Tosteson, this program is a dynamic approach to becoming a physician: contact with patients in the first year—not in the third and fourth, as had been the case—and problem-oriented, case-based experience in which small groups of students are given responsibility for their own learning under the guidance of faculty tutors. Lectures are deemphasized, and the course work stresses an interweaving of clinical and laboratory medicine; attention to the human organism as a molecular system, as revealed by the "new biology" of molecular genetics; the ethical and economic issues bearing on medicine; health promotion and disease prevention; and the importance of the doctor-patient relationship.

New Pathway students are expected to analyze problems, locate relevant material in library- and computer-based resources, and develop habits of lifelong learning and independent study. There are signs that the program has merit. Compared with other Harvard Med students (students who entered in 1989 and 1990 could indicate their preferences for either New Pathway or a more traditional curriculum), New Pathway types seemed to memorize less and conceptualize more, were better able to relate to patients, generally acted in a more empathetic, less directive manner, and were better at collecting information from patients.

Marcie is going to put it all to the test. She is with a fourth-year student now in a two-bed room at MGH, where she will do a physical examination on a real patient for the first time. It is perhaps the second-most-stressful moment in a medical student's life after gross anatomy, not only because he or she becomes intimate with an actual stranger's body but also because it is well known that most of the mistakes physicians make are due to careless examining techniques. In her Introduction to Clinical Medicine class, Marcie and her classmates practiced on one another, the women examining women, the men examining men. They drew blood, took blood pressures and temperatures, dilated pupils, and used all the tools and techniques of the venerable practice of auscultation, percussion, and palpation. Armed with stethoscopes, they learned not just where to listen and what to listen for but also how and how not to position a patient; with their fingertips, they'd gently tapped chests, looking for lung congestion, and felt necks for swollen nodes and glands. Occasionally, they'd banded into a foursome, two of each sex, with the men usually the examinees and the women the examiners, an arrangement easier for any dads who were paying the bills to understand. When they had to do more intimate investigations, like vaginal, rectal, breast, and prostate examinations, or check for a hernia, they practiced on models, paid volunteers who'd been through it many times and who could tell them if they were probing in the right place and even what to look for. Once, when Marcie was doing a hernia exam, she wondered aloud why they couldn't use a volunteer with a hernia so she could know just how one felt. The volunteer was aghast. "It wouldn't exactly be pleasant," he said coolly, "to get your hernia palpated by twenty-eight fingers for an entire afternoon."

The classroom physicals, Marcie is thinking now as she looks across the room at the patient slumped in a chair beside his bed, had been like playing doctor when she was a kid, or assessing and treating mock injuries as she did during a disaster simulation one time at a teenage summer camp. She is ready for reality, but even though she'd been through all the core courses in metabolism and function of human organ systems, genetics and embryology, pharmacology, immunology, pathology, and biostats, she is still a bit scared now, wishing that what she saw in a recent sci-fi film were possible. In the film, there was a doctor who simply passed a sensor over a patient's entire body and watched a computer screen scroll out his vital signs, along with the diagnosis, cause of disease, and treatment. But then again, fact had already outraced fiction in many ways in this hospital, and Marcie, like all of her classmates, is well aware of it. The finest medical technology available anywhere in the world is here, as much a part of their lives as their intern jackets, stethoscopes, and reflex hammers. For while physicians, students, and nurses are still listening and observing at the bedside and in the consulting room the old-fashioned way, they are also relying on a dazzling array of electronics and other machinery, medicine's new handmaidens, to do the work: ultrasonic waves generated by piezoelectricity to hear what the patient's viscera say; X rays and CT and MRI scans to see inside bodies; air-inflated bubble mattresses to substitute for human touch; recorded voice messages to soothe subliminally, functioning below the threshold of conscious awareness. The ill, no matter in which hospital they lie, have become little more than biochemical sacks of protoplasm, nerve impulses,

and heart rhythms that can be tapped as easily as eavesdropping electronically on a telephone conversation.

Better get a taste of the old hands-on while it lasts, Marcie
thinks, just to be able to tell your kids you did it, for it's going
to be an obsolescent art, like using a manual typewriter, when
she's out there practicing, and she'll probably not be interested
in organizing a local chapter of what one old doc called the
Society for the Preservation of the Use of the Five Senses.

The patient, a very stout man named Riley with a gray
crew cut and a deeply lined, round red face, is staring at a tiny
TV set on an extension arm. He's sweating, and he looks like
he's tired and needs a shave. His eyes go to the ceiling as the
pair walks in, and he says, loudly enough for them to hear,
"Oh, Jayzus, they're double-teamin' me again." Riley knows
this drill well. Marcie is the fourth student and the second
doctor to show up in the last three hours, for the same reasons,
and Riley's already pulling up the right sleeve of his johnny.
"It was one forty over ninety last time they checked," he says
sharply, extending his arm in a Pavlovian response. "Not bad?"

Marcie doesn't know what to say, so she just smiles, hoping he won't see through it. As befits a second-year medical
student who hasn't been near patients but once a week, she's
awkward and apologetic. "I'm sorry for bothering you, Mr.
Riley," she begins softly, her nervousness causing the fingers
of her hands to shake, so that she has to hide them tightly
under her armpits. She's in street clothes, but she's wearing a
stethoscope ostentatiously around her neck in the hope it will
detract from her student status; the fourth-year student has his
tucked away more discreetly—in the side pocket of his jacket,
with just the earpieces showing. "I appreciate the time you're
taking to see me."

She is honestly grateful and understands the privilege she
has been granted, but she's also feeling a little guilty. "Here's
this man," she would tell me later, "who was going to lay

himself bare for me, physically and maybe emotionally, sharing all kinds of personal stuff, and I'd be getting all this information for no purpose other than to present it to my preceptor so he could evaluate me and not the patient."

Riley is more cordial than some. Most MGH patients who've had everyone but the strolling violinists around their beds say things like, "How old are you?" when the students troop in. Or, when they've had enough, they say, "I don't have to talk to you. Get me a real doctor. I'm only talking to the boss." Riley seems to accept Marcie's apology for intruding, even though the prospect of being examined yet again by a bush leaguer was perhaps more irritating than what he was watching on TV, the Red Sox stumbling toward another loss to New York at Fenway Park.

"Well, shall we get on with it, chum?" he says, nodding toward his arm, one eye on the TV screen. He's scowling.

Marcie clears her throat. "Well, first, Mr. Riley," she says, a pen perfectly poised over her clipboard, "what is it that brings you to the hospital?" It was the same bromide that Chris, the first-year student, had used when he met Eddie Conroy. But it was either that or the other favorite variation, "Maybe you can start by telling me why you're here?" She doesn't know what Riley's problem is because they haven't let her see his chart. In her first year, Marcie took a few histories from patients and they'd been perfunctory affairs, as Chris's had been; all she was trying to do then was learn how to establish a doctor-patient relationship and get used to the rote and the rhythm of asking a grocery list of questions. This time, the primary goal is to identify the disorder or disease, focus on it, come up with a plan, and report back. And she has to do it as quickly as possible because this hospital, like all the others, is guided by the rapid through-put, as Dr. Friedlich put it. That's a problem for the medical student. The shortened stays make room for more paying customers, but at the expense of interaction between caregivers and patients; doctors and nurses hardly have time to know much more about their charges than their names, ages, and the nature of their illnesses, no matter what the Harvard catalog proclaims in its ambitious "Plan of Instruction."

What the system really requires that Marcie do is look at a piece of what ails Riley, the part that brought him here and not, as she was taught in Patient/Doctor I, at how his illness has stirred up his life and that of those around him, or, for that matter, how his life has stirred up his illness and perhaps that of his caregivers. "Diagnosis, fixis, exitus," is what one harried chief resident once told Marcie; it's the only routine the health insurers will buy.

"Well, what brings me here is my gut," says Riley, still half-distracted by the ball game and shaking his head.

"What's the matter with it?" Marcie asks.

"Tight," Riley says, turning up the volume on the TV. "Very tight. Ooh . . . ooh . . . goddamn it!"

"Pain?" Marcie asks, startled.

"Naw," Riley says, a disgusted look on his face. "Polonia. Just whacked his first homer in a hundred years, the unconscious shit."

"What about your gut, Mr. Riley? That tightness . . ."

Riley makes a fist. "Keerect. And pain across the whole thing, left mostly, to the right, down low. Here. Tight, like a steel band that's been bending inside me. Feel tired out. That and the pain are why my doc sent me up here."

Marcie plays it smart, going right for the quick answer by asking the best possible question. "Did they tell you what it is?"

"It's maybe a spastic colon, they're thinking. They'll be doing some tests."

Marcie jots down possible irritable bowel syndrome. She tosses her head, flipping her ponytail smartly, and gives herself a mental pat on the back for knowing the jargon already. She relaxes a little. Good start. At least it's not one of those bramble patches like the polycythemia vera she heard about in class once, unknown cause, all kinds of symptoms from enlarged liver, to eye problems, to bone pains, to no symptoms at all. Takes a lot of blood work, a lot of ruling out of other stuff to establish a diagnosis. Where do you begin a physical exam for that one? And the time. Have to be very thorough there, and the way she's been going at it in class, she'd need a couple of hours, and no one at Harvard or any other medical school would ever give her that. Irritable bowel shouldn't be too challenging, although she doesn't know as much about it as she would have had they told her in advance what she'd be examining. Then she could have crammed. But then, this going in blind is supposed to be the ideal learning situation.

"What kind of pain is it, Mr. Riley?" Marcie asks.

"Like I say, tight. Right across here," Riley says, spreading his hand and moving it over his lower abdomen. "Like a knife sometimes. Comes in like ripples. And I got the constipation, no diarrhea like they asked me if I had. Some bleeding, too. Maybe the piles, they tell me is what it might be. And plenty of gas, which they're sayin' maybe comes from the spastic and maybe when I eat a bit of the cabbage and brussels sprouts and all of that other hay. Comes on after I eat. And I'm feeling wiped out. Headachy. I told them about that, but they don't say anything. They give me the Tylenol. And I've got the nausea. I don't take no medicine on a regular basis, thank you Jayzus. And, in case you'll be askin', I just went through a grand old to-do with my boss, the little prick and a half. They asked me about that, too, whether I had the stress, do I worry, do I get pissed. Like they say, it's maybe the spastic colon. And I'm thinkin' they're correct." He folds his arms and glares at the screen.

Marcie doesn't bite. She's thinking he's trying to sound

convinced so she'll figure, Forget it, and just leave him in peace.

"Did they tell you what kind of tests they're going to do, Mr. Riley?"

"Certainly. It's the tubes they'll be sticking up my . . . the colon scopes, they say it'll be. My man already done that and he didn't come up with nothin'. Said it was the piles, but I maybe need a better look around up there. Tomorrow morning, they're goin' to do it."

"Was that a sigmoidoscope your doctor did, Mr. Riley?"

"Sigma somethin', that's correct."

Marcie makes a note. "He did that in his office?"

"Yes, and a terrible embarrassing thing it was, too. Pumped some air up there, and me with the gas to begin with, for Christ's sake."

"Umm, could you tell me what kind of diet you follow, Mr. Riley?"

"Real food, dearie-o," Riley says defensively. "I take my sugar straight because the man upstairs made it natural, not fake like them chemicals they're puttin' in them pink packages they're bringin' in here. None of that phony butter, either, tastes like shit. Gives you the colon cancer is what I hear. Do they tell you that over there? No, I been packin' in the roasts for years, butter on the bread, corned beef, Irish sausage, and the Ben and Jerry and their relatives, Tom and Jerry."

"Tom and Jerry?"

"What? How old are you, anyway, kiddo? That's rum toddy and good old eggnog. Take a taste one day, Doc. You'll give up the squeezed carrot juice is my bet."

The diet is consistent with what Marcie's read about populations with a high incidence of colon cancer. The sigmoidoscopy would have covered about 60 to 70 percent of where colon and rectal cancer would show. He said it turned up nothing. That leaves . . . Does anyone in his family have colon cancer? she wonders. She doesn't know if she should ask, and she decides not to. Why alarm the poor man, and she's not his doctor, anyway. She's aware that the exact carcinogenic mechanism is still unknown, and she can't remember whether it's colorectal cancer that runs in families or large-bowel cancer, and anyway, large-bowel is on the right side, and he's been focusing mostly on his left side. She'll raise it later with her preceptor.

Marcie struggles to come up with more questions. "Did you say you don't have diarrhea, Mr. Riley?"

"Correct. You'll be asking if the pain goes away if I move my bowels?" He cranes toward the TV as an inning ends and the box scores appear. "Balls. They're goin' down in flames. How come they got a guy named Boston playin' for them Noo Yawk fairies? It does go away when, and I say *when,* I move my bowels, yeah. But I ain't been movin' 'em too often, like I say. And they want to know if it comes and goes through the day. That it does. I get it at nighttimes, sometime. It wakes me up out of a sound sleep, and I got to get up and go to the head. But when I'm sitting on the can, I can't go, okay? They're asking me, too, if I have the backache, and I do have that. And the pain inside my behind, too. But that could be the piles is what they tell me. Or maybe the prostrate. That gets me up, too. I ain't had a decent night's sleep since I can't remember."

Marcie makes frantic notes, silently thanking Riley for helping her out. Sounds like irritable bowel. But the bleeding . . . Diverticulitis maybe? That can cause rectal bleeding. Or is it diverticulosis that causes the bleeding? Both, she concludes. But diverticulitis can cause alternating diarrhea and constipation, and he doesn't have diarrhea. So can IBS cause both, or is it one or the other? Carcinoma of the colon? Maybe that, with the bleeding and maybe occult blood, too, and the pain and the lack of energy. Regional enteritis? There's weight loss with that. No, that's usually right side, and there's always diarrhea with it. Or is it constipation? Not colitis, no bloody diarrhea. Ulcers? No, pain too low. Maybe some kind of bowel obstruction? Constipation goes with that. Carbohydrate intolerance? Yes. Symptoms very close to IBS, maybe that's it. Except that causes diarrhea and cramps. He hasn't got either; he's constipated. Maybe a parasite? Shit. I'm playing Dungeons and Dragons, she thinks. Damn this differential diagnosis stuff. Why do diseases have to mimic one another, anyway? Maybe to confuse medical students. Sherlock Holmes had it right: When you've excluded the impossible, whatever remains, no matter how improbable, must be true. Too many questions to ask, and not enough time to ask them. Where're the boss and the DOS? Between them, they'll sort it out. Marcie starts to feel sorry for Riley because of the likes of her. She was the one in anatomy class who wished so many times during it all that she had majored in arts and letters and stayed there.

"How about the blood pressure?" Riley wants to know. "Want to check it out?"

Marcie hadn't planned on it, given the time allotted her and the need to focus on Riley's bowels. And she's wondering if he's just being nasty, trying to waste her time.

"I think we ought to give that a look," says Riley, both eyes off the screen now and on Marcie. "Got to do it right, that's what the last super who was in here with one of your own told him. Got to get my money's worth over here at Boston's best was the way he put it." The fourth-year student nods, thinking perhaps that the super was some savvy attending physician whose word shouldn't be challenged. He motions to the blood-pressure apparatus in a corner, and Marcie rolls it over. She unhitches the cuff, trying to remember all the numbers she'd attempted to memorize: 103 over 70 for a ten-year-old, 123 over 82 for a thirty-year-old, 135 over 89 for the sixtyish.

"How old are you, Mr. Riley?" she asks.

"Just hit the speed limit, love," he says. "Five-five."

Marcie does some arithmetic and gives him 130 over 85, lower than what Riley had told her his was. She wrestles with the cuff, then puts it on upside down and inside out, the guiding ARTERY arrow invisible and pointing upward, the Velcro fastener scratching against Riley's skin. Riley rips it off, twists it around, and positions it correctly, then goes back to watching the TV, shaking his head again. If he's stressed, it's going to show on the gauge, and Marcie doesn't need a high reading to murk things up even more. She slips the disk of her stethoscope under the cuff, sticks the earpieces in her ears, and starts pumping the bulb. The cuff fails to inflate. The fourth-year student doesn't say a word, but Riley looks over, sucks in his breath loudly, points to the knurled knob that controls the airflow, and makes a circular motion.

"Other way. Jayzus, where'd your bosses get their M.D.'s, over to Sears?"

Marcie flushes and makes the change; she inflates the cuff, lets go of the bulb, carefully opens the valve, and listens intently. The air hisses out, and she panics. She didn't pump the needle on the gauge beyond 140 systolic as she should have done, so that's where she starts, and as the needle drops rapidly, she can't recall whether she starts counting for diastolic when she hears the beat slow up or stop; the needle is down to zero, and she mind-fixes at 90, where the beat started to slow. Or maybe because it was where Riley said it should be. My God, she thinks, bring me an L.P.N.

"What was it, then?" Riley asks tartly, but with his eyes glued to the TV, Marcie doesn't know whether his attitude is due to her or the Red Sox, who are now all but dead.

"One forty over ninety," she says, her voice trying to sound doctor-authoritative.

"Is that a fact? Give me something else I didn't know and I'll fall over in surprise."

Marcie starts to fill up. With her lower lip quivering, she asks Riley to loosen his johnny and sit on the edge of the bed. She goes to the opposite side. This is it, she thinks, not a classmate, no professional patient, not a case in a journal. Grumbling, Riley struggles up, pulling the TV around with him so he can see it. She pulls off his johnny. "Deep breaths," Marcie says, holding the jiggling stethoscope against his bare back. She wonders why she's doing this part of the exam, since it's Riley's bowels they're going to ask her about later. She's not even sure if she's hitting the right places, and she feels like telling him what one of her classmates told his first patient: "Look, I don't know what the hell I'm doing, but just be patient with me and I'll have the boss come in when I leave." She doesn't pick up anything on her stethoscope that would cause her to drop the poker face she's trying to adopt even though Riley's not facing her.

"Again." Riley sucks in, his eyes fixed on the TV. A bat cracks on the TV and Riley throws both arms up in the air and yells, "Goddamned faggots!" Marcie jumps and the stethoscope slips from her fingers. The fourth-year student has done a side step away from the bed. Riley takes notice and scowls. "It wasn't you I was referrin' to, pally. It's them. Turn it off, for Jayzus' sake!"

With Boston off the screen, Riley gives full attention to Marcie, who's forgotten about stething his chest. He swings his feet onto the bed and lies flat, panting. "Okay, girl-o, the next thing they do for this trouble is the abominables. Hah. By Jayzus, they ought to give me the M.D. Maybe you can put in a word with your boss? I used to work in a drugstore when I was a kid. It's alls you need to get in these days is what I hear."

Marcie smiles weakly. She starts pressing gently on his expanse of abdomen, looking for signs of tenderness in the colon that would be consistent with IBS. God, she thinks, maybe I ought to reconsider the surgery track. Trying to cut through this omentum would be a trip.

Riley jumps, and Marcie recoils.

"That . . . hurt?"

"No, just ticklish. Maybe a little when you're pressin'."

"Do you have the . . . tight . . . pain now, Mr. Riley?" Marcie thinks she's noted tenderness, maybe some contraction . . . maybe a mass. . . . That could be diverticulitis or IBS. . . . Something, too, on the right side . . . Tumor? Fat pad? Or is it normal for him?

"No. They give me some stuff for that. Domatol or somethin' like that." Donnatal, Marcie notes. They prescribe that to calm an irritable colon. Marcie kneads the lower-left quadrant. Riley winces. She kneads the right, and he winces again.

"That bleeding, Mr. Riley. What kind of blood is it?"

"It's red blood, like with the piles."

"When you have a bowel movement, are the stools black?"

"Maybe. Sometimes greenish black. Blood on 'em. I take a little of the iron tablets every day, and that's what it might be is what they're telling me. I take the stuff because I'm bushed. Good for the tired blood, they say. I been losin' a bit of weight, but not so's you'll notice. I was a bit heavier a few months back. But I'm not too hungry is the fact. You'll be doin' the eyes next?"

Marcie hesitates. "Well . . . yup," she says, accepting an instrument from the fourth-year student. "Please look at the wall." She places her cheekbone close to Riley's forehead, cocks her head, and peers into his eye with the scope. Her hands are shaking, and she jabs the end of the scope into his lower lid.

"Jayzus," Riley says, pulling away. "Care with that

weapon is what you want, lady-o. They's nothin' wrong with the eyes, anyway, they tell me. The pulse and the temperature, that's what you'll be lookin' after now."

Flustered, but not willing to be branded an incompetent by Riley, who was probably keeping a diary so he could go out and bad-mouth Harvard and MGH, and the fourth-year student, who still hasn't said a word, Marcie fishes out a thermometer, sticks it smartly under Riley's tongue, and fingers his wrist while she watches the second hand on the wall clock. "Ninety-eight point six should give you sixty a minute is what I hear," says Riley. He's grinning for the first time.

Marcie can't resist a shot at a curmudgeon. "Well, I make it thirty-seven and sixty," she says, pulling out the thermometer. "Centigrade."

"Well, is that a fact," says Riley, getting the point, his eyes boring at Marcie, the grin stuck on his face. "The rectum is what they like to do, too. That finishes up a grand physical for the spastic colon is the way I hear it."

The fourth-year student intercedes. "Time's up, Marcie," he says, looking at his watch. "Thanks, Mr. Riley. We've probably bothered you enough."

Riley is off the bed and back in the chair. He flicks on the TV. Marcie heads for the door, relieved, and looks back at the patient. "Thanks, Mr. Riley," she says. This time, she isn't so sure. "I hope everything goes okay with you." Riley waves them off.

12 | *To the Bedside*

THE TEACHING OF BASIC CLINICAL MEDICINE AT HARVARD, with its emphasis on physical diagnosis—or bedside medicine—did not, ironically, begin with the founding of the medical school in 1872, but with the establishment more than fifty years later of a summer-only extension facility, the Tremont Medical School in Boston. Tremont was the brainchild of Holmes and Bigelow, both of whom had been strongly influenced by the practice in Paris and London of allowing students to observe signs of illness directly from a hospitalized patient. As obvious as that may seem to us today, most hospitals throughout the world during the nineteenth century, except for those in France and England, paid scant attention to teaching. Boston, for example, even after MGH and the Boston City Hospital came into being in 1811 and 1865, respectively, had no hospital clinics where student doctors could observe obstetrical cases, and young doctors, who often showed up at their first lying-in without ever having assisted at a delivery, obtained practical experience in kitchens, barns, and buggies through the apprentice system.

There were reasons for this seemingly illogical state of affairs. In England, medical schools grew out of the hospitals and were integral parts of them; with no connection to a university, the school usually took its name from the hospital. In the United States, however, as Kenneth Ludmerer writes, "Hospitals tolerated teaching, reluctantly, as long as it was carefully regulated and did not interfere with their other functions. Trustees often professed their desire to participate in medical education, but what they had in mind was instruction of a very restricted sort: amphitheatre lectures, ward walks, outpatient clinics, and section teaching—but not clerkship."[1]

Though Tremont was not a hospital, it managed to incorporate what its founders had learned overseas about dealing with hospitalized patients, both clinically and technically. It was in Paris that the Austrian physician Leopold Auenbrugger introduced percussion of the chest as a method of physical diagnosis; and where René Laënnec first rolled a paper notebook into a tube and listened to the sounds of the heart as a preliminary experiment into his invention of the stethoscope. The techniques were transplanted to Tremont, which soon became an extension of Harvard Med, a place where students who had been deprived of the opportunity to do physical examinations because of the parent school's preference for lectures and demonstrations could learn to diagnose directly by lightly tapping a patient's body and listening with a stethoscope; they also learned how to deal with a woman in labor, a practice that Harvard would not formally institute for many years. Combined with chemical analysis of blood and urine and the use of the microscope, the Tremont School's course of instruction contained the seeds of today's clinical clerkship, with its focus on student participation, ward rounds, and clinical conferences.

In 1858, Harvard Med absorbed Tremont, and instruction in bedside medicine finally crept into the rigid curriculum. Ten years later, when Harvard president Eliot was "turning the whole university over like a flapjack," he made frequent ward-teaching rounds the rule. But, while the patient would always play a central role in medical education, over the years Harvard Med would place more emphasis on didactic teaching, at least on the private services of its teaching hospital, and on the laboratory; demonstrations of intuitive hands-on diagnosis, it sometimes appears, have given way to reliance on esoteric diagnostic equipment and mouse-manipulated computer software with all the possibilities and answers built in.

It is, of course, the fair price of progress, a fee first imposed when Charles William Eliot took the helm at Harvard. For all his good intentions, his appreciation of bedside teaching in the training of doctors, and the much-needed housecleaning he did at Harvard Med, he threw the baby out with the bathwater. The weight he gave to student candidates with solid science backgrounds, the appointment of the first professors to teach and do research full-time, the school's emphasis on the experimental sciences (which were taught before the clinical ones), and the abolition of the apprentice system (which, ironically, would reappear to form the basis of today's residency programs) would play a major role in moving medicine closer to becoming an exclusive branch of science and not, as L. J. Henderson had viewed it, a branch of sociology.

Admittedly, the art of medicine in Eliot's day was, as he said, practiced sometimes by "coarse and uncultivated men devoid of intellectual interests outside of their calling." And it was true, too, that their lack of scientific training contributed to their inability to think critically and solve problems: Most of the early physicians trusted dogma far more than their own minds. More often than not back then, the familiar barbs of medical proverbology applied. Earth did cover up the doctor's mistakes, and God did cure while the physician pocketed the fee for his placebo medicine. Petrarch was not far off the mark when he mourned that life was short enough but that the doctors knew how to make it shorter still, nor was Voltaire, who regarded doctors as men who prescribed drugs of which they knew little to cure diseases of which they knew less.

Yet, for all their faults and failings, many of these "coarse and uncultivated," nonscientific men of the town possessed the other essential ingredients that go into the making of a good doctor, ingredients that science and the men of the gown would soon crowd out, and which today's generation of patients are crying for. The "coarse" practitioners, if not the academics, knew at least how to be kind, if not always clever, how to observe, if not investigate fully, the causes of disease, how to be available, not distant, and, most important, how to listen, not lecture. Their advantage, flawed though it may have been, was their apprenticeship, which allowed those with the good fortune to win exemplary mentors to get close to the sick and dying, to watch and lend a hand. (Those who apprenticed to quacks and humbugs, it was said not facetiously, took their medical instruction by doing chores about the house and taking care of the doctor's horse.) If their diagnoses were often but accurate guesses, these early physicians were no better or worse than their extramural instructors, or, perhaps, than some of today's best diagnosticians, who also still rely heavily on the art of the hunch.

Sixty years ago, the late Joseph Garland, a distinguished Boston physician and editor of the *New England Journal of Medicine*, expressed his reservations about the diluting of the old, patient-oriented art of medicine:

> More and more space began to develop in our medical schools for scientific investigation, and more and more our hospitals began making over their storerooms, their garrets and their cellars into abodes for the muse that sings of bacteriolysins and colorimetric calibrations. The young man with his footsteps hesitating on the threshold of professional life was often lured into these abodes of the intellect and saw in them a shelter, for a time, and perhaps permanently, from the cold realities of practice, of dollar competition and individual aggressiveness. . . .
>
> The result of this has been, in our day, the engendering of a false and warped attitude toward the practice of medicine. The laboratories have wooed and won, not only those pure searchers after truth whose workshops they should be, but many young men . . .

who should be doing yeoman service in the front
lines rather than sacrificing innocent and costly laboratory animals on the ash-choked altars of scientific Mammonry.[2]

Henry Jacob Bigelow would have cheered. "Science
alone," he once said, "is inadequate to the duties of common
medical practice. When the body is diseased, the mind falters
and the invalid looks for sympathy; for heart as well as for
head; for the philanthropist and not the philosopher; and this
difference will often condemn the man of science to yield the
race to his inferiors in intellect and attainments."[3]

Ever since Bigelow locked horns with Eliot, Harvard Med
has struggled (admittedly sometimes as credibly as a professional wrestler) with how best to train its students to be more
directly caring, and how to put the patient back into the curriculum, while at the same time making students proficient in
the new science. The New Pathway—which tries to interweave
laboratory science and clinical medicine in such a way that
the patient-doctor relationship, disease prevention, and health
promotion are better served—has been a step forward;
"patient-doctor" courses, which begin in the first year, cover
virtually every aspect of bedside and office behavior from how
to extract information from patients to how to appreciate the
way they feel about illness. The aim, of course, is to produce
good physicians, men and women who have earned that acco-
lade because of how they view their patients, not just because
of their technical skill alone. In the words of Dean Tosteson,
"Every doctor should have in his conceptual armament three
sets of portraits of human beings. One of man as an organism,
one of man in society, and one of man as an individual person.
These are indissociable dimensions, all relevant to the medical encounter."

Seven of us are sitting around a conference table at MGH: Lloyd Axelrod, who is an associate professor of medicine at Harvard Med and an endocrinologist; some fourth-year medical students; a couple of residents; and a very savvy specialist named Samuel Thier. Axelrod runs a firm at the hospital, not in the usual sense of a business enterprise, but in the British medical definition of a subdivision of an academic department. The one he heads is the James Howard Means Firm, named, as two others are, after chiefs of service. Thier is a nephrologist, a specialist in kidney diseases, but he is with us for more than professional reasons. He has also served as president of the Institute of Medicine of the National Academy of Sciences and chairman of the Department of Internal Medicine at Yale University School of Medicine. At this time, he is the sixth president of Brandeis University in nearby Waltham. He goes on rounds every week at Tufts–New England Medical Center in Boston and every other week at MGH, because, as he says, he does not want to let go of patients. In a few months, he will relinquish his Brandeis post and become president of MGH. Thier is a good role model, a physician who believes strongly in the doctor-patient relationship and also—unlike those who complain about the need to move patients through the system quickly to make it pay and about how too many patients get in the way of empathy—that there is simply no excuse for not finding the time for patients.

The firms, Axelrod is explaining for the benefit of newcomers, function like traditional teaching rounds, but they are more intimate, intense groupings of students and clinicians, with goals that include the proper integration of bedside medicine and technology. The emphasis is on seeing patients—two a day—but more than that, on following them to determine what's transpired in their lives and conditions since the previous visit; this often means taking a fresh and thorough history.

Before and after the patient visits, members of a firm meet

to sift through what they and the house staff know and have learned about their cases, analyzing them much as detectives attempt to solve a mystery. It is what the New Pathway has been preparing the students for: learning how to reason and doctor. To that end, they will, it is hoped, be exposed to the proper role models, the most important formative force they will ever encounter as they move toward becoming good doctors. "Role models shape them even more during residency," Bob Ebert told me before the meeting with Axelrod's firm, "but certainly during the clinical years, as well. If they have people who are understanding, who are interested in them, the students tend to be interested in other people. If people are down on you, hostile, you respond to that, and that spills over. In my view, the environment is enormously important. That's why the new Pathway is a very important venture. It puts small groups with small groups of faculty, where there is an interchange, a kind of respect for one another. I used to tell Michael Crichton to take a close look at the hospital when he began his clerkship because it would be the only time he'd ever see it without becoming an actual part of it. I said the only time you could be objective is when you're a stranger to it. Ultimately, it is in the clinic that you learn how important it is to listen. Too often, people don't want to listen; they want to talk. What will influence students is what they see on the wards when they're taking care of patients."

Axelrod signals that it is time to see a patient, and in a few minutes we are standing around the bed of an eighty-one-year-old man who doesn't look his age and doesn't look sick, either. He sits up as we group about him. Earlier, one of the students, Lauren Solanko, had worked him up, taking his history and gathering all the information she could about his situation. He had told her that six weeks ago he experienced some chest tightness while watching TV, something he had never had before or since. He also said he had been shoveling snow for three days and yet experienced no pain. He said he walks two and a half miles a day in the cold, and still nothing. Two weeks after the tightness, he told Solanko, he felt light-headed, almost passed out, and that's what brought him into the hospital. But Solanko was to discover that when he was interviewed by other staff, he told different stories. He said both that there were recurrences of the tightness and that there were no recurrences; that he had had pain, yes, and that he had had none, no time, nowhere. Later, someone on the staff found out that he had a myocardial infarction in 1965, although nothing else until the most recent complaints.

Axelrod speaks first. "How do you feel?"

"Very good," the patient says loudly.

"What did they tell you about your condition?"

"They didn't tell me nothin'."

"Well, we're going to be able to tell you a little more than that."

"I don't remember that I've ever been sick, and I'm not takin' any medicine."

Thier asks the man if he'd ever been in the military.

"Yeah, 1942 to 1946."

Thier turns to a student and says that he asked about the service because the military is good at diagnosing three things: heart murmurs, high blood pressure, and albuminuria. "Also, induction and discharge." He smiles.

The patient is sizing up the group, and he starts talking before anyone says any more. "Now, the reason I'm here," he says, sounding like the guy next door, who's going to tell you about his operation even though you haven't asked, "is I had a pressure here, on my chest. So I says to my wife, 'I don't know what's goin' on here.' It went away, and two weeks later I was in the bathroom and I got a little light. So I sat down on the floor. It passed. I went into the kitchen and had to hold on to the table. I had two weeks of pressure—

every day, all day long. I had two, three weeks of pressure in 1965, but nothin' special. After I held on to the table, I ate and went to bed, and I slept good, very good."

Axelrod asks, "Any neck pains?"

"Nope, nothin'."

Axelrod leans over and examines the man carefully. He taps his back, gets him to breathe deeply, in and out. He puts a pair of fingers under the man's chin, then on the wrist, then on the inside of his elbow. He prowls over his back and chest with a stethoscope. A resident, Brent Forester, double-checks with fingers and steth. "The murmur is widely disseminated," he says. "Did you feel a thrill?" Axelrod asks. "Felt it all over the thorax," Forester replies. "Okay," says Axelrod, looking around. "What's it called when a murmur changes quality?" Ummm, ummm, ummm. "Hmmm, hmmm, begins with a *G*," someone says. "Gallavardin phenomenon," someone yelps proudly.

The patient beams up at them. He is impressed. Axelrod asks him, "Mind if we let them all take a listen?"

"Naw, I'm glad they're goin' to be good doctors one of these days."

One by one, the students apply their stethoscopes, straining to hear what Axelrod and the resident heard. They nod, but some look puzzled.

"Well, thank you, sir," says Axelrod after they finish and we head out the door for the conference room.

"Thank you. I'll just wait for the good news."

"We've got our fingers crossed with you," says Axelrod.

Around the table again, the firm kicks the case around. Solanko says it sounds like cardiac to her. Axelrod isn't so sure. Someone else suggests a cardiac catheterization. Someone says, "Look, why not just give him a stress test? Guy like that, so active, would sail through like a piece of cake." Question: "Why no pain if it's cardio?" One answer: "Maybe he's had ongoing pain but has a high threshold." Observation: "He's given too many histories to too many people, and I don't like that." "Well," insists Solanko, "what he told me seems like cardio." Someone shakes his head and says, "If it ain't broke, don't fix it." Axelrod offers a verdict of sorts. He says he thinks the man's symptoms, the two straight days of tightness, all day, are noncardiac-related, not consistent with angina, that with all the shoveling he said he did, it was logical he would have had some. Thier says nothing until we are getting up to visit our next patient. "It's worth checking out," he muses. "I wouldn't discount it because of inconsistencies in the man's story."

Later, the heart specialists called in would find that the man did indeed have severe cardiovascular disease. Solanko wasn't exactly crowing, just fourth-year-satisfied, when she would repeat what she'd been saying all along: "When he talked to me, it sounded like cardiac."

The next patient, a twenty-four-year-old obese woman, has pseudotumor cerebra, a rare disorder that causes cranial hypertension, headaches, and visual difficulties. She had also developed bladder problems that required surgeons to put in a patch to enlarge her bladder, which, in turn, upset her acid-base balance. She would eventually undergo a spinal tap to decrease the pressure on her central nervous system.

Prior to the visit, the student who had worked her up summed up for us, performing perfectly what Axelrod called "the ultimately comprehensive and ultimately concise presentation." Now the student goes over the details again, smartly ticking off symptoms, what they do and do not know about intracranial pressure, whether her eyesight is in danger, the medications she is taking, plans for treatment, when she'll go home, who'll be best to follow up.

Now at the woman's bedside, Axelrod and Thier, standing to one side, absorb it all quietly as her mother, seated by the bed, smiles and nods as though she understands it all. The patient lies motionless, encircled by caring people but still alone. Because her illness is so rare, it commands center stage, separate from her persona, the kind of thing that causes the pupils in the eyes of Harvard Med research types to dilate. As the rundown drones on, professionally, painstakingly, I am reminded of those Harvard doctors of yesteryear who communicated with one another in Latin at the bedside.

The recitation is all to form, by the numbers, or, as Thier would say later, on target, well organized, and easy to understand. Still, as the details are presented, he is thinking that while the knowledge of the basic principles has been okay, it's not wonderful. He knows that information about what works before for this kind of pressure is weak, a drawback that will be reinforced during follow-up meetings. Thier knows, too, that about all one can do in a case like this is watch the patient carefully and hope she does okay. But then, he thinks, it's not fair to expect students to understand all the details completely; that's why they're students. There is something else, though. Thier frowns, and Axelrod fades from the bed, aware that a specialist like Thier sits at the right hand of God.

Thier approaches the bed and does something that nobody else in the room has done. But it is not a specialty thing and has little to do with the uniqueness of the woman's disorder. He takes her hand. "You know," he says quietly, a father approaching an ailing child, "there are things you can do to help yourself." The woman looks up guiltily, anticipating a lecture on weight and diet. "Yes," she says, bowing her head shyly. Her mother nods.

"Losing the weight, yes," says Thier, reading the look. "It might keep the pressure down. But, let me ask you, do you get up at night when you feel you have to go to the bathroom?"

"Sometimes."

"Well, I'd like you to think about this. The longer you keep urine in your bladder, you know, the more likely it is you'll have problems. If you could train yourself to empty your bladder frequently, to keep your urine flow rate high, make yourself get up at night to pass it, the chances you will get into serious difficulty with this acidosis will be dramatically reduced. It's not all that complicated, really, and if you can understand what you can do, you'll give yourself that added margin of safety." It was simple advice that should have been offered earlier.

The patient nods. "I will," she says.

"Good," says Thier with a broad smile. "Very good."

As we go, he pats her head and adds, "And the weight, too."

Later, one of the students comes over to me and asks, "Say, who was that masked man, anyway?" Thier hadn't been formally introduced, and most of our group had no idea of his background and current position. Before I can answer, a resident replies, "The good doctor, that's who."

13 | *Talk Medicine*

SHORTLY AFTER ORIENTATION DAY CEREMONIES WERE OVER, TESSA Hadlock got a call.

"Hi. I'm going to be your big brother at HMS, your class adviser," the young man on the phone told her. She replied, somewhat tentatively, "Okay, I was New Pathway, but I'm now HST." There was a noticeable silence. "You're what?" the caller asked incredulously. "Can't you switch back? I can't be your adviser if you're going for HST."

Hadlock, at this time a third-year student at Harvard Med who is doing her clinical work at MGH, recalls how the conversation made her wonder if she was doing the right thing by entering the school's tech-trek program for those with an intense interest and background in quantitative or molecular science who plan interdisciplinary research careers in academic medicine. While HST students, the Pump Room Society, join students of the standard Harvard Med curriculum in clinical clerkships during their third and fourth years, they are encouraged to become involved in research activities early on, and they must continue in that direction through their entire stay at Harvard. Indeed, on an office wall at HST Central, a sign sets the beat: PREPARING A SUPERB PROPOSAL IS NOT A MATTER OF LIFE OR DEATH. IT'S MORE IMPORTANT THAN THAT! HST does, in fact, offer a course in proposal writing, and as a requirement for graduation, students are expected to present evidence of scholarly work in the form of a thesis. Forty percent of the HST M.D. candidates will take it further, doing more in-depth research and picking up a Ph.D. in the process. While still students, they will do things like clone genes responsible for inherited disorders, investigate immunosuppressive drugs, and try to control the AIDS virus and crack the signal codes between cells that govern cellular differentiation. Each year, they will present their findings at Soma Weiss Day, a forum that celebrates the central role of research in training M.D.'s at Harvard Med and is named after the Harvard clinician who is the other half of the team who discovered hemorrhagic Mallory-Weiss syndrome.

Hadlock grimaces. She's not only an HST but she sits on the student admission committee for the society. "You know, the reputation of HST is that they're real nerds, like, they can't totally relate to the human world? So, I'm wondering back then if I was in the right program. I have to agree that if you're going to identify the nerds of the HMS class, you'll probably find more of them in HST. But then, there are also . . . normal people." More accurately, most are relatively normal. "If a person comes into HST with a touch of arrogance, they're nixed," she says. "They focus on the person. Oh, HST will accept a person who's a little maladjusted. They don't like to, but they'll be more apt to take a maladjusted person who's going to win a Nobel Prize. Because they want those people to come from here. They're not going to take a jerk who's maladjusted and going to win the Nobel Prize. So, this means they'll take a nice person who's a little strange."

Hadlock, it turns out, is one of the truly normal people in HST—perhaps supernormal, given that the views she isn't supposed to hold on patient care in the first place go beyond those of even many of the regulars, the New Pathway types. It is not that she was lusting to become physician, someone helping out Mother Teresa in an Indian leper colony, when she was a kid. It is something hard to define, just a feeling she has about people. "I've never even been around people who were dying," she muses. "But in the patient interactions I've had so far, I feel like a kindred spirit with a lot of them. I feel I can really connect with them in ways that can be helpful. But, no, it's not like some big life experience has made me this way and that I'm so great. I just feel that for me, it's easy to be good at it." Strange words coming from an HST.

Hadlock comes from a heady background. Mother, father, and brother all have Ph.D. degrees. She married a medical student after her first year, and both are now in their third year here. "With my family, I had to go to grad school, but the thought of writing a Ph.D. thesis was so horrible for me that I went into medicine sort of by default, but mostly because it has a lot of the things I think about."

Those things had their origin, strange as it seems when it is put simply, in carpentry and masonry. "My big thing that I really loved was problem solving. In my high school days, there were things I liked to build. Like, I'd ask, 'How do I make this doorway and this window? Where does that light have to come out, that wall go?' I got really impassioned about problem solving, and it didn't have much to do with what I was going to be when I grew up. But then I got very into math, because that was more problem solving. When I got to calculus, there were, like, max-min problems and related rates, and I could see again that problem solving was actually doing puzzles and fun stuff.

"So it's turned out for me that this profession I've chosen is a great way to do more of that. I want an M.D. because I want to be a doctor. I want to solve people's physical health problems and deal with patients every day, people who need help and compassion, who need someone to think critically about their state. I chose HST because of that desire to understand medical processes on a really fundamental level. I kind of want to get at the nuts and bolts of things. You know, I have a lot of respect for science. To be totally honest, I think that the most brilliant people go into basic science research because most medicine, though it's really nifty, doesn't require brilliance.

"So I think that to be a good doctor, you have to have

two things, which are equally important. One is a very good understanding of medical processes, a good development of critical thinking. You can't be just a knee-jerk doctor who responds to situation A in this way and B in that. That can only take you so far. You've got to dig deeper. You have to be smart. You need a lot of training in searching things out, and that's how you figure out the really tricky diagnoses. The other thing is to be a really good person, being able to focus on the other person's needs rather than on, say, your own career and where you can get to personally. But that's really hard to teach anyone. It really has to come from who you are. So if they really want to develop a physician population that's caring, the key is to attract and admit people who have a natural knack for it, who are going to be good at it. You can't take a jerk and make him sensitive. You know, in those contrived situations we had with the role-playing and being observed, the people who are slimeballs will probably fake a good interaction. But it's the real situations that count.

"What I really think is that it's a gift to be empathic, and you don't have to spend aeons with your patient. You can go into someone's room and hold her hand and talk, even if you have only two minutes. You can go in for those two minutes and be in a frenzy and totally ignore the patient because you're doing so many other things, but if you can take the two minutes and if you're good at it, you can get the important things done and still make the patient feel like she's really loved and really being paid attention to. I don't know how you develop that skill. I've seen some people who are so overwhelmed by their work that they run around and out and are just terrible with the patient, and others with the same amount of rush and who have to complete the same amount of tasks in the same time period and who are still able to focus on the patient and are warm and really good. That, to me, is the difference between being bad and good in a house officer. What struck me once was, I had this little old lady who'd come in for blood transfusions, and she was a timid, really quiet person. She had been sedated, and the junior resident came in while it was wearing off. She was somewhat arousable, and she and I had been talking a bit, and he came up and said, 'Ma'am, are you awake?' And she hushed him: 'Shh, shh.' So what did he do? He leaned closer and yelled louder: 'Ma'am, can you hear me?' This little old lady who had barely said anything since she came in belted out, 'Be quiet!' It was so funny how she put this guy down. She was just trying to tell him to stop it. She was sedated and he was yelling in her face, and I was like, Wow, tell him, lady!

"I've noticed on rounds that the physicians who are less confident get much more defensive. They tend to be a little antsy around patients and not quite as genuine. I also think that those with no tact came into medicine because they're attracted to the power, the control over human beings' lives, the perceived elevation of themselves. And you know, to me it is totally unacceptable to have people with no compassion. It takes some searching to find people with both that and science, but the two are critical. It should be unacceptable to be loved because you're good at what you do and be a jerk at the same time. You see it all the time. You'd be surprised at the number of totally unacceptable human beings, people who are not good with patients, who throw things across the room, act out of control, and what you hear from the scrub techs and the nurses is, 'Oh, but he's a very good surgeon.' And I say, 'No, I don't care if he stitches good; he's a very shitty doctor.'

"But there's also a problem with the way medicine is done in the hospital. I mean, thoroughness is not really emphasized. People just don't have the time to be thorough, and it's usually the house staff who're taking the histories and doing the physicals, and people just have too much to do. Any hope of being excellent starts with thoroughness."

And, once the details have been gathered, it ends with finishing unfinished business, the soul-satisfying goal of the compulsive problem solver. One time, in the hospital, Hadlock found that end thwarted, and she bristles when she recalls the incident, as few full-fledged doctors would, because most would consider it much ado about not much. "This guy came in complaining of stomach pains, and I ended up spending a lot of time with him, more than with any of my other patients, following his case every day. He'd never been seen at MGH before, but someone doing a routine history found out that he had had a history of syphilis and was also bisexual. They did a syphilis test, and it was high. They did a lumbar puncture and found he had neurosyphilis, and so it had been an improperly treated syphilis infection. So, you're thinking syphilis and bisexuality, and you have to think of HIV. They tested for it, and it came back HIV-positive. Well, the junior resident came to me after that and informed me that he was going to tell the patient about his HIV status. I was bothered by this because I had a good rapport with this patient. I was the person who had spent a lot of time admitting and following the patient, and I felt that he sort of identified me as his primary doctor, even though I was just the lowly medical student. I asked the junior resident if I could at least be there when he told the guy, and he shrugged and said, 'Well, if you want to.' I kinda wanted to sit down with that patient, so I went to see Dr. Potts, the chief of medicine, and I asked him if he thought it was appropriate that the junior resident was going to inform the patient. He thought it over for a while, then talked it over with the resident, who said he thought that since this was a major event, the most senior person on the team should tell the patient. Potts agreed, and the resident told the patient, and I wasn't there. And later, I was embarrassed when I went to see the patient, because we both knew now he was HIV-positive, and I hadn't been there to break the news. The rationale about who should tell him was valid, but I still feel that a sick person doesn't really care who's the most senior person on the team. What I felt like telling Potts later was that this guy doesn't know the senior from the medical student. All he knows is who's watching him every day, and as far as he was concerned, I was his doctor, and I still feel it should have been me." Later, Potts told her he was glad she felt the way she had, because it was representative of a good doctor, that she was really being a physician.

Dr. John Potts, who interned at MGH after getting his M.D. degree from the University of Pennsylvania in 1957, is the Jackson Professor of Clinical Medicine at Harvard Medical School, chief of MGH's general medical services, and an international authority on calcium metabolism. He has a thirty-four-page curriculum vitae, which does not include something about him that greatly impressed Tessa Hadlock. "This patient came in for unstable angina," she recalls. "He had been attending a business seminar, and he had had bypass surgery, and here he was two thousand miles from home and he really had to be dealt with. He had no doctor in town, and no records with him. Before we went in to see this patient, Potts tried to home in on what could be done for this guy—not that we were going to solve all of his medical problems—what was it that we could do to make his situation better. All these questions came up: Is he going to lose his job by missing the seminar? Will worrying about that place him under stress? If he goes to the course, will he have a heart attack? When we went in to see him, Potts so eloquently, I felt, sorted it out for this patient. He told him we wanted to do what would work for him. He asked him if he should write a letter to his boss and to his doctor. He asked him if he wanted us to buck up his medication. He asked him if he wanted us to get him back to the course. 'Exactly what can we do for you?' Potts was asking. What I thought was incredible was that he wasn't getting caught up in what kind of tests we could run. He tailored the man's care to exactly what this patient really wanted and needed. And when I was looking at Potts during this, I felt, I want to be like him. I want to focus on what each individual patient's needs are at that time rather than getting caught up in a frenzy of what this patient's medical issues are."

In his office, Potts talks about connecting with the patient, how he tells his students that they have to have, and keep, peripheral vision. "I believe that we are in great danger of losing, and not paying attention to, the original impulse of compassion. We absolutely have to refocus on it. It is easily the victim of high-tech medicine and it needs to be constantly in focus. As chief of medicine, you represent all the highly technical power that you value very much, and it has enormous impact. The other part of me is aware of having to be natural, and that, too, has enormous impact on the students. A few years ago, we were walking around with the interns who had admitted patients in the morning. Sometimes the patient on the floor is boarded from another floor and is not the responsibility of the attending physician. Well, we walked into a room and there was a woman looking up at us and smiling, and this young intern stepped between us and said, 'That's not ours,' and walked off, adding, 'We go this way.' I didn't do anything right away. It was true: She wasn't 'ours.' But when we got out, I looked at the intern for a minute and I said, 'Sam, why were you so insensitive to that nice lady?' He just hadn't noticed. You have to see everything that's around you and understand all the power that's invested in that physician on rounds. People are looking at you. They're anxious, they're worried, and the slightest radiation of not caring gets magnified by the patient. I tell the students to realize their role, to look around the edges to where the humanity of the person is.

"It's very important, though, not to be patronizing and shallow, or supercilious and feigning concern. Some people are actually weak in skills, and they try to use an awareness of the sensitivity factor as a clumsy defense of their inadequacies. And that must never be tolerated."

But can compassion become baggage as well as a briefcase of personal essentials? Potts thinks about that a moment, then nods his head. "I've known fundamental scientists who have gone into the basic sciences, away from medicine, *because* they were so compassionate. You have to practice displacement. You have to be compassionate, but then you have to turn it off. If you went home every night and carried all the worries of your patients with you, you'd be finished, burned out."

In a caged, dimly-lit warren of rare medical books at the Countway Library, Cliff Barger sits surrounded by antique labware and the dusty papers and letters that will go into volume two of his life and times of Walter Cannon. "In the small Massachusetts town I grew up in," he says, "there was old Doc Ellis, a most compassionate man. Whenever he went into a home, even though he didn't have much in his medical bag, people were relieved, no matter how sick they were, because they knew the doc was somehow going to take care of things. I saw how my parents reacted to him, and I'm sure that played a very important role in my deciding to become a doctor. I thought then that I was going to go back to Greenfield and be like Doc Ellis. So I went to Harvard College and Harvard Medical School and got into physiology. Afterward, I thought for a while that I'd miss my patients. I enjoyed talking with them and taking care of them. Well, my mentors told me, you can have the same kind of relationship with students as with your patients, and that will be multiplied manyfold. I'm so glad I was persuaded. I know now that the good doctor can be doing more than clinical work. A good scientist can also be a good doctor. But there are a lot of physicians who have the notion that if a doctor is interested in science, he can't be a good physician. That is just not true. Some of the best physicians I know are people who are deeply involved in science. In the last analysis, I have to say that the important part is the person's skill and ability, more than wanting to relate and empathize constantly. When I decide who I'm going to use as a physician, I ask who's the best man in that field."

Barger is right, of course, in an either/or situation. So was Petrarch. "Shun the physician who is eminent not for his knowledge, but solely for his powers of speech," he said, "as you would a lurking assassin or a poisoner." Some doctors possess both skill and empathy, and these men and women are arguably the best.

In *The Scarlet Letter*, Nathaniel Hawthorne painted the ideal:

> If the [physician] possess native sagacity, and a nameless something more—let us call it intuition; if he show no intrusive egotism, nor disagreeably prominent characteristics of his own; if he have the power, which must be born with him, to bring his mind into such affinity with his patient's, that this last shall unawares have spoken what he imagines himself only to have thought; if such revelations be received without tumult, and acknowledged not so often by an uttered sympathy as by silence, an inarticulate breath, and here and there a word, to indicate that all is understood; if to these qualifications of a confidant be joined the advantages afforded by his recognized character as a physician; then, at some inevitable moment, will the soul of the sufferer be dissolved, and flow forth in a

dark, but transparent stream, bringing all its mysteries into the daylight.

Such sentiments are, unfortunately, easier expressed than accomplished. Physicians know, as Tessa Hadlock knows, that it is fairly easy to become a competent specialist of some kind. They have, after all, met all the scientific criteria imposed by the medical schools' admissions committees in the first place, and the knowledge they must amass and the techniques they must master to become successful at the specialty they have chosen can most certainly be taught and learned. But becoming a good doctor is something else. The skills necessary to achieve that are not only difficult to teach but take longer to acquire, especially if they are not embedded in one's moral core to begin with. "When students come to us, they are in their twenties," Lloyd Axelrod told me. "They have been in school for twenty years. They are a highly selected group. The people who have instilled their values are their parents and teachers. It may be possible to teach caring, but that's at the preschool and school level. By the time they get to us, if they don't have ethics and morals, we are not going to make ethical and moral people out of unethical, immoral people. We may remind them of what they've learned, and chiefs of service can make an impact. We get into the room. We make sure the door is closed, the lights are on properly, the curtains are drawn, and that we respect the patient's rights and sensitivities and wishes at all times. You can always teach that sort of thing, and I'm pleased that I don't have to address this hardly at all. As we walk in on a patient, people assume these very responsibilities. But it's a bit of hubris to think we teach twenty-five-year-olds values and how to be ethical."

Even what is learned by example on the wards will not always last. Many students will be knocked off course by the socioeconomic tides and storms that swirl about medical practice and will drift from the ideal. They will come to rely on the impersonal telephone consult and the carefully measured office-appointment schedules instead of sympathy, understanding, and communicative skills. They will not have heard Thomas Mann's counsel—if they ever found the time to read it—that they must behave as though the world was created for human beings. They will, moreover, never see the parallel in the words of the proverbial plumber who told a doctor who had called him in the middle of the night about a leaky toilet to drop an aspirin in the bowl and call him in the morning.

For these practitioners, the patient is often the "them" against the "us." And, to be fair, there are times when a physician is justified in relegating a patient to enemy-alien status, for there are bad patients, people who demand, complain, and cling, or who, through the workings of "factitious" disorders like Munchausen syndrome, willingly choose the sick role, deliberately mimicking the symptoms of a disease so convincingly that they often deceive the most competent physicians. "There are many very good people who are not what I call good patients," Oliver Wendell Holmes carped in one of his essays. "I was once requested to call on a lady suffering from nervous and other symptoms. It came out in the preliminary conversational skirmish, half medical, half social, that I was the twenty-sixth member of the faculty into whose arms, professionally speaking, she had successfully thrown herself. Not being a believer in such a rapid rotation of scientific crops, I gently deposited the burden, commending it to the care of number twenty-seven, and, him, whoever he might be, to the care of Heaven."[1]

Some years ago, Dr. James Groves, an MGH psychiatrist, told me the story of a forty-five-year-old alcoholic, known as "Old George" to members of the emergency room staff. They saw him a hundred times over six years for visits ranging from acute gastrointestinal bleeding to a blood clot in the brain, which he barely survived. It became a standing joke that the more carefully Old George was tended, the more furiously he drank. One night, George came in bleeding again. The staff worked him over frantically, pumping in whole blood as fast as he could take it. At 4:00 A.M., the intern pronounced Old George dead. The junior resident shot a withering look at him and muttered, "Thank God." The senior resident nodded and added, "Amen." Old George, Groves explained at length in a piece he did for the *New England Journal of Medicine,* was what doctors know as a self-destructive denier, a member of that gang of "hateful patients" who stimulate negative feelings in most doctors. Groves grouped such people into three other stereotypes.

There is the dependent clinger, the patient who perceives the doctor as an inexhaustible parent and whose dependency eventually leads to a sense of weary aversion toward him. Exhausted by such a patient, the doctor's referral for psychiatric examination may be blurted out in frustrated tones that the patient correctly interprets as rejection. There is the entitled demander, who resembles the clinger except that instead of calling the doctor frequently and flattering him with an overkill of attention, he or she threatens punishment. Such patients, Groves observed, "often exude a repulsive sense of innate deservedness, as if they were far superior to the physician." The entitled demander may try to control the doctor by withholding payment or threatening the physician with litigation— moves that could easily enrage the doctor and trigger a desire to counterattack. Last, there is the manipulative self-rejecter, who, like the last two, appears to have a "quenchless need for emotional supplies." But unlike clingers, they are not seductive and grateful, and unlike demanders, they are not overtly hostile. Instead, they seem to feel that no regimen will help. Appearing almost smugly satisfied, they return again and again to the office or clinic to report that, once again, the regimen did not work. "Their pessimism and nay-saying appear to increase in direct proportion to the physician's efforts and enthusiasm. When one of the symptoms is relieved, another mysteriously appears in its place. What is sought is not relief of symptoms but an undivorcible marriage with an inexhaustible caregiver."

One of Groves's Harvard Med colleagues across the river, Dr. Don Lipsitt, confirms that a few patients kindle aversion, despair, and even downright malice in their doctors. An authority on Munchausen syndrome and hypochondriasis, Lipsitt told me of one patient who had 829 visits to twenty-six clinics in thirty-six years. She said of herself, "I have a bissel of tsuri"—that is, "A smidgin of trouble."

Such behavior, understandably, elicits anxiety in the physician that a treatable illness has been overlooked, then irritation with the patient, and, finally, depression and self-doubt. Still, even when confronted with "hateful patients," physicians are urged at least to try to rise above it all, to understand that it is not how a doctor feels about such pains in the ass that is most important. "It is how one behaves toward these patients," Groves explained. "The doctor who begins to feel aversion should begin to think of setting limits on dependency. The doctor who begins to feel the impulse to counterattack should begin to think of rechanneling entitlement into expectations of realistically good medical care. The doctor who begins to feel depressed with the patient's smug help-rejecting should begin to think of 'sharing pessimism' so that the patient's losing the symptom is not equated with losing the doctor. And the doctor who begins to wish that the patient would die should begin to grasp the possibility that the patient wishes to die." In a word, communication is what's needed. The average physician, it is said, conducts 100,000 medical interviews during his or her lifetime—but it is doubtful, given the lack of training they have had in how to communicate effectively, that many know how to listen to Murray's "music." Fewer still are willing to take the time to talk when the so-called doorknob syndrome is operating—when the patient, whose time with the doctor is up, chooses the very moment he or she is leaving to blurt out some important piece of information.

Dr. Bernard Lown, who was professor of cardiology and director of the Cardiovascular Research Lab at the Harvard School of Public Health, once said that caring is dispensed largely through words. "Talk can be therapeutic. It is one of the underrated tools in the physician's armamentarium. Therapeutic talk is a great art, which dissipates uncertainty and anxiety, instills confidence, augments a capacity to persevere. It enhances both physical and emotional recovery." Lown also bemoaned the fact that the stethoscope, long a symbol of close and direct contact, is being abandoned. "History taking is delegated or automated," he said. "The physical exam is growing more cursory. A skewed cybernetic ensues, wherein inadequacy in bedside skills increases resort to technical solutions. The accent shifts from involvement to indifference; instead of considering the whole person, we focus on our specialties."

Perhaps what patients want, even the hateful ones, is not a doctor who took a charm-school course and acquired a gooey friendliness, but one who took to heart what the ailing Eddie Conroy meant when he told Chris, the first-year student, that the kid might be a patient in the next room himself one day. Patients want information, explanations, and a bit of attentiveness. Most want truth, but told with charity; all want hope.

Dr. Lesley B. Heafitz, Harvard Med class of 1965, pediatrician, teacher in the Patient/Doctor I course, and a woman afflicted with metastatic adenocarcinoma of the peritoneum, echoed Eddie Conroy's message. "Some day, sooner or later," she told an Alumni Day gathering, "every single one of you will become a patient, and I daresay you will not particularly like being on the other side of the bed. However, I know you will find it enlightening, and I am certain that you will discover what a vital role the doctor/patient relationship plays, not only in determining the nature of your experience as a patient but perhaps also in even shaping the outcome of your illness. Empathy is the key to a good doctor/patient relationship. Empathy, for the physician, means the ability to experience the illness with the patient, from the inside out, so to speak, feeling and seeing it through the patient's eyes. Empathy is a gift. For some it is inborn, for others it is learned from the best teachers, and for still others it is acquired by actually being a patient. This was my case."

Then she told this story:

During a checkup at an institution not far from here, I was told by a young physician, "You know, there is a high recurrence rate in your illness, 20 to 30 percent." I never wanted to see that physician again. How much better would it have been if he had said to me, "You know, there is a high cure rate in your illness, 70 to 80 percent." Each of us has a survival instinct, and for the patient, the answer to fear is hope. Today, we all know how much a patient's attitude can affect the outcome of his or her illness. The physician, even in the most hopeless circumstances, must remain optimistic—not dishonest, but optimistic. He or she must see the cup as half full, rather than half empty.[2]

Oliver Wendell Holmes's ghost, still roaming the corridors of MGH that are lined with fantastical equipment that makes his head spin and will send him floating over to the medical school to take a breather in his worn leather rocking chair that sits there yet, heard Heafitz and was pleased.

He wrote in "The Young Practitioner":

You will remember, of course, always to get the weather-gage of your patient. I mean, to place him so that the light falls on his face and not on yours. It is a kind of ocular duel that is about to take place between you; you are going to look through his features into his pulmonary and hepatic and other internal machinery, and he is going to look into yours quite as sharply to see what you think about his probabilities for time or eternity. No matter how hard he stares at your countenance, he should never be able to read his fate in it. . . . It is a terrible thing to take away hope, even earthly hope, from a fellow creature.[3]

14 | *Truth-Telling*

In all our resolves we must decide which is the line of conduct that presents the fewest drawbacks and then follow it out as being the best one, because one never finds anything perfectly pure and unmixed, or exempt from danger.

—*Machiavelli*

RILEY HAD COLON CANCER. THE COLONOSCOPY HAD JUST CONfirmed a large tumor, left colon, and it was encircling the intestinal wall. There was partial blockage. The biopsy was positive. Wide surgical resection was the treatment of choice. The hospital doctors had decided not to mention it to Riley until later in the day, until his family and the physician who'd been taking care of him could come in as a group and sit down with him.

Marcie had all those details. She had thought that cancer was a strong possibility when she saw Riley on her first physical exam, and she said so in her write-up and case analysis. She had been asked to drop in on him again, just to chat it up and get a take on his demeanor, but she had specific instructions not to discuss the diagnosis with him. "Forbidden to," in fact, was the phrase the chief resident used.

On her way to Riley's room, Marcie tried to figure out how to skirt the issue of the cancer and still justify her presence as a student with no real role in his care. She knew he had cancer, and he didn't know it. How could she keep quiet about that? How could she look at him and try to make small talk? Could she lie to him if he asked her if it was cancer? She'd never been in a situation like this one, although when she was going through her admission interviews, Doris Rubin

Bennett had asked her if she thought she could tell a patient he had cancer, and she had replied quickly that, yes, she could. She didn't know why she had said that, except maybe to earn some brownie points. She remembered that Bennett had just looked at her as if to say, Oh really?

Outside Riley's room, Marcie recalled something that Ned Cassem said at a lecture about how patients who are faced with a potentially lethal illness know it anyway and sometimes bring it up before they're told, with some subtle remark or look, and how some caretakers disregard it because they don't want to open up anything. She remembered him saying that if you're going to err in deciding whether to tell someone he is really sick or dying, you err on the side of information; that when there's no conspiracy of silence, patients usually do better; that your main job as a caretaker is to understand the sick person and try to get rid of some of his anxiety and feelings of isolation. But Marcie wasn't a real caretaker yet, and Riley wasn't dying. He had a cancer that is treatable if gotten early, and there are not as many deaths from that as from lung cancer. She caught herself on that. Once, as a high school kid, she had written a newspaper reporter who wrote that, luckily, only one person was killed in the plane crash, and her argument was that that one person had a grieving family and he wasn't just an only. Neither were the fifty thousand deaths a year from colon cancer an only, and the stat comparison to lung cancer would be no consolation to Riley.

Her musings were irrelevant, she decided. She had her orders: Just see the patient and shut up about his problem until everyone's in place. It'll be up to the pros to do the truth-telling.

Riley's door was open, but she tapped politely on the jamb. "It's open," Riley growled, "unlike yer eyes."

He was in a plaid robe, reading a newspaper in bed, and

he still looked like he needed a shave. "Well, well, it's herself."
He grimaced, somewhat weakly, Marcie thought. "Forgot to
do the prostrate is my guess."

Marcie couldn't resist a smile. He really was infectious.
"No, Mr. Riley, I just thought I'd stop by and ask how
you're doing."

"Who knows?" he said, heaving his shoulders. "Who
cares? They don't tell me nothin'. These guys are playin' CIA
here. Had the Roto-Rooter yesterday, and they're pumpin'
the Jayzus out of me veins it seems. For tests, they say. For
experiments, I say. They don't tell me nothin'."

"Did you ask them?"

"No. No point. They'll still tell me nothin', anyways. Say
they'll be doin' some more tests, for Jayzus' sake."

"Well, they have to cover all the bases. You wouldn't want
them to miss something, now would you?"

Riley nodded. His question came at Marcie like an arrow.
"They tell you anything, lady?" He was looking right at her.

Marcie paused. God, I have to lie, she thought, and she
hated that, because she never was able to pull it off, and he
was sure as hell going to know she was lying.

"Oh, they're always telling us things, Mr. Riley. About
your tests, and how they do them, and what they're looking
for." She stopped short of saying, And what they found. "You
know what it is to be a student." Enough, no more. Going
too far. Don't push it. Lie outright; don't try to do it with
charity. Tell him no.

"Never been one," Riley said. "I'm askin' if they tell you
anything about my condition?"

"No. No, they didn't say anything about your . . . condition. You're in pretty good condition from the looks of you."

"Well now," said Riley with a slight smile, "you're blarney-
soaked, but maybe you have a personal opinion? As a student,

I'm meaning, of course. I won't hold you to it, mind you, lady."

"No, I don't have an opinion, Mr. Riley. All us kids are supposed to do is come up with all the possibilities, and we let the big guys check them out."

"And what'd you come up with? The possibilities, I mean."

Marcie wished Dr. Cassem was there. Riley seemed calm enough, though. He was certainly crusty, and his life obviously hadn't been without some knocks. He was, or had been, she had learned, a longshoreman, and that wasn't a job for dainty hands or minds. "Well, the usual things. Maybe spastic colon, like you say, maybe some other bowel problems. It may be nothing at all, like really bad indigestion, because of all that corned beef and jerry you've been eating."

Riley smirked. "Now that's a good one, lady-o. If I get outta here, I'm goin' to get the old lady to fix me up one of them. If them Eyetalians can fry up the veal Marsala with all that cruddy brown wine, why not the good beef stewed up in a toddy? Maybe I can interest the cook over to Dorgan's. Make a grand brunch for before the big parade . . . if I'm able to eat it."

"You will. Call me when you do, Mr. Riley. I'll forget the carrot juice for one day."

"Ah, the carrot juice. So, what else do you and themselves possibility about?" He was smoking her out, she thought. He suspected something. He was giving her a signal.

"I really don't know, Mr. Riley. There're all kinds of possibilities." Marcie hesitated. Don't say it, she told herself. It's not your place. You'll be dead at evaluation. But she let it out before she could stop herself. "Like, you know, it could be nothing at all, on the one end, and the worst would be, of course, cancer, but that's—"

"The cancer?" Riley bellowed. He struggled up and almost toppled out of bed. He scaled the newspaper across the room, his face contorted as if he was in intense pain. "The cancer you're tellin' me? I ain't got no cancer! I'm too young for the cancer! It couldn't be cancer, no way! Jayzus!"

Marcie was as stunned as he. "No, no, Mr. Riley," she stammered. "I'm sorry. I didn't say you have cancer. It's just one of the . . . possibilities that I just tried to tell you about. It's probably nothing at all, you know? Really, Mr. Riley, we don't—"

"Jayzus!" said Riley, staring at his feet and shaking his head. Speechless, Marcie hung her head and let a full two minutes of silence pass. Riley broke it.

"The cancer. Maybe you're right. This sucks, you know that? So that's why them dickheads don't shave were askin' me what my wife's hours at work are, and that they're maybe wantin' to talk to her here this afternoon. They can drop a dime and give her a jingle, can't they? She's a workin' stiff, and this is Wednesday, and they don't take kindly to her takin' the time off over there. The cancer is what they'll be tellin' her and me about here is the way I see it. No other reason for her to come in on a workin' day." Riley's head was nodding from side to side, and Marcie leaned over and patted his arm.

"No, no, Mr. Riley, don't think that. They probably just want to . . ." Marcie didn't know how to finish it.

"Give us the possibles is what they're goin' to give us? Right! It's the big casino, the way I see it."

Marcie agonized. It's all going down, she thought. She was miserable. Riley was miserable and angry, on the royal road to dementia, she figured, and she'd done it to him. Oh God, they were going to cut her to pieces at the seminar. They'd kick her butt out for sure. What a daffodil. Tapioca. She'd be doing physicals for Weight Watchers and the Y after graduation, if she ever sees it. She heard a buzzer go off in the corridor. She prayed it was a fire drill so she could have an excuse to dash out. But she managed to get a loose grip on herself.

"Look, Mr. Riley, let me tell you something," she said, her voice trembling. "Listen, if it is cancer—and I say *if,* because I haven't actually seen any tests that say it is—they can treat it."

"With what, the bag? I don't need no bag to shit, god-damn it!"

"No, no, Mr. Riley, they only do a colostomy as a temporary thing these days. Like, only ten to fifteen percent—"

"Jayzus," Riley moaned. "Sweet hour. The bag it's goin' to be. I'm a goner."

"Mr. Riley, look. You're not a goner. If they have to do a . . . bag, chances are it'll only be for a little while. Most people with this problem live normal lives. You're not a goner."

"So, then, they did tell you somethin'?"

Marcie couldn't keep running this game. She didn't think twice. "Yes sir, they told me that the colonoscopy showed a tumor, that it was operable. Beyond that, I don't know anything more." She had a tight feeling in her chest, and her stomach was rumbling.

Riley lay back, his eyes closed. "What about the radiation, the chemo shit? They goin' to try that, too?"

"I don't know about that, Mr. Riley. I know that the operation is the best thing, and that's what they'll suggest when they see you. You're going to be okay, I promise you."

Out in the corridor, Marcie started to cry. She was thinking that only God could promise. Who the hell was she, anyway? She was shaking so much that a nurse grabbed her and pulled her into an empty room and sat her on a bed.

"What happened?"

"I just blew it," Marcie said. "Jesus, did I just blow it."

The words of explanation, apology, and self-reproach

poured out. The nurse smiled, gave her a poke on the arm, and told her, "You didn't put that in his head. We think it crossed his mind while they were doing the colonoscopy. Someone said, uh-oh. He was tranqued but not out, and he can put two and two together. They told us this morning that they thought he heard. My feeling is, he wanted to know but he didn't want to? And those two scope pilots weren't about to tell him much, since he didn't ask. You got it started."

"The resident's still going to kill me."

"No way. It was a setup. They decided you'd be the one to soften things up for them when they all come in this afternoon. The boss was betting you'd blurt something out under the circumstances—most of you do—and all he's going to have to say now is, 'Well, Mr. Riley, I'm told you already know something about your condition.' "

"And Riley's going to say . . ."

"I took a wild guess."

15 | *Caring on Call*

Man matures through work
Which inspires him to difficult good.

—Pope John Paul II

THE THIRD YEAR AT HARVARD MED IS A GROANING RITE OF
passage from what, for two years, has essentially been a college
experience with panache. The thrill of anticipation—what led
one fledgling student to write in the handbook for incoming
students, "Me, a doctor, wow!"—the kindly reassurances in
Dean Hundert's Orientation Day address, the freshness of the
New Pathway, the security of pass-fail, all are dim memories.
Gone, too, are lazing over cappuccino in North End patisse-
ries, ambling through the Museum of Fine Arts, and hitting
the double dance floor at Man-Ray.

Gross anatomy had been the students' first jolt toward
maturity and the doctoring world, but it was a mere geography
class compared with what they would experience now. In the
gross lab, they did not see the dying—only the end product—
or the diseases that kill, or ailments that cripple; their cadavers
were anonymous and blessedly silent. In their first and second
years, many students, fired with a genuine desire to do right,
or at least live up to what they said in their application essays,
sided dutifully with the patients. They took to heart the words
of St. Matthew, "I was sick, and ye visited me," along with
some of what they heard from mentors of the old school. They
nodded approvingly when they heard that Harvard psychiatrist
Tom Hackett once described some house officers and senior
practitioners as "pathogens who encourage psychopathology
without even realizing it." On the few occasions that they
witnessed undoctorlike behavior, they were duly appalled, as

281

Tessa Hadlock was, and Sonja Short. Short majored in the biopsychosocial aspects of health care at Montana State, and she will never forget the time she was interviewing a patient with a mass in his throat and was interrupted by a surgical resident who flat out told this patient that the thing in his lungs was cancer, that they would take it out, that there'd be chemo, and that there'd be a form to sign, then asked him if he had any questions, running it out just like that. Some, mostly those who were opting for a career in primary care, criticized their classmates, too, the ones whom they felt shouldn't be doctors because they were not listeners at the bedside and had their sights fixed only on their debt loads of $75,000 to $150,000 and the easy bailout of $253,000 a year they were going to make going into radiology, a fat job, where all you have to have is two good eyes to diagnose and a way with numbers, not unlike craps dealers, when you're nuking someone, so you can calculate the rads and give them to the techs, who, for far less dough, do it all, setting up the patients, pushing the buttons, and monitoring the kicks. Those who weren't planning on a Ph.D./M.D. were bemused by Harvard Med's being selected yet again as the "best research-oriented medical school in the country" by *U.S. News & World Report* (an honor that might be construed to mean it wasn't a "medical" school at all) and irritated with the subtle way faculty deemphasized primary care by assigning specialists and not generalists to teach physical examination, or larded their lectures about this and that problem with asides about which of Harvard Med's fifteen Nobels had been won solving them. More than anything, though, they all had time to burn, no matter what their future plans—time to join the Photo Club, the a capella Countway Basies, Medical Students Reading to Children, Medical Students for a Healthy Environment, and the Medical Students' Urban Health Project.

In the third year, they will learn they can neither find time nor make it. Contemplation will give way to action, which will now be graded High Honors, Honors, Satisfactory, Unsatisfactory. They will experience the same sinking feeling in their stomachs they had when they first entered grade school, or started a new job, or waited in the doctor's office for a vaccination. Now they will speak with patients in deep trouble and with their concerned or antagonistic families, not for a few casual hours a week, as they had done while playing doctor in the first two years, but for many dreary hours, nights, days, and early mornings as they begin the two-year rotation through clerkships in the principal clinical specialties, struggling to meet care and treatment responsibilities, and apply their classroom-learned pathophysiology and basic science training to specific, often mysterious clinical problems. They will try to make some sense of fuzzy radiologic images (and change their opinion of radiologists), do lab tests, take an EKG course, get a whiff of anesthesia gases. That is the clean and easy part. Everything else will be down, and sometimes dirty. Their gross cadavers had been drained of the fluids of life, and the embalming process had cleaned them of any odor; now the students will reel from exposure to a noxious collection of human smells—from excrement, mucus, pus, urine, vomitus, and everything else that drips, oozes, and spurts from a live patient. They will attempt, without wincing or gagging, to dress raw, suppurating burns and putrifying wounds, disimpact manually a feces-stuffed rectum when the enemas and laxatives fail, stitch a bloody cheek slashed to the bare bone, set the finger of a screaming, squirming child, go after fish bones lodged in throats and slipped condoms and panty liners wedged into vaginas. They will hang out in emergency and trauma clinics, where they will deal with the victims of violence, treating them and being assaulted by them. They will hear and see things that will leave them bug-eyed: an elderly man, his neck slashed and bloodied from repeated self-inflicted stab wounds, not to kill himself, he tells them later, but to kill the unbearable pain of a cancer eating at his throat; a patient swelling like a Macy's parade balloon before their eyes as air escapes through a puncture in his lung every time he breathes and seeps under his skin, the whole grotesque, crackling thing suddenly deflated when a house officer pricks it with a lancet; a woman who deliberately dashed boiling water on the inside of her thighs so she wouldn't have to have sex with her husband.

With minds awash, they will spend time in the surrealistic chamber of the ICU, where it always feels like three in the morning, and deliver babies in emergency rooms, plucking some, malformed and in the throes of stroke or seizure, out of teenage moms who took a last puff of crack before they came in during the last stages of delivery.

And they will participate in one of medicine's great ironies, the infliction of pain to make a diagnosis. "It's simple, really," says their instructor, "to tell whether the patient is hyper- or hyposensitive. Just press your finger under the ear, near the mastoid process, into the styloid. For your hyposensitive patient, it's nothing; for your average patient, it's just a bit uncomfortable. But for the hypersensitive one, watch out, guys, he'll jump right up at you."

Armed with passwords admitting them to the computerized literature search program, they will cram for a patient visit, and jog through enough rounds to give them shin splints, reread the pertinent literature, and write formal reports; they will stay overnight in the hospital with the night float when on call to cover a team's patients and will meet for weekly sessions on patient management. But much of what they will do has not made the glossy course catalog, and it involves more than (or rather, less than) shadowing doctors and getting involved in the actual management of patients. It is doing things that prove medicine is not always the blessed, humane art of the ancients, but, as Benjamin Rush observed, an occupation for slaves. He meant third-year students: IV-starting, blood-drawing, chart-checking, bedpan-emptying, history-collecting, sheet-smoothing, bed-making, gurney-pushing, coffee-running slaves.

Trapped in the colorless, antiseptic, workaday world of the hospital, they often wonder why they—stars, after all, at the "Medical School of America"—must perform so many lowly tasks; yet sometimes, when they are called upon to assume more responsibility for a patient, their guts clench and they question their ability to make the right decision, which they never questioned while they were acing the four hundred multiple-choice questions of Part I of the National Board exams and composing neat essays that swelled them into believing they were ready to do brain transplants; and the doubts are reinforced every time they hear about some veteran nurses who can tell if you've got cancer by taking your pulse.

It is good that they are apprehensive, for right now, the third-year students are strictly fumblers and dilettantes, ham-handed imposters even, with as much delicacy as a dropped brick. They may be a step above the second-year students, and packing more shiny new tools and accessories and badges on, around, and in their dazzling white coats than a telephone lineman—Harvard ID's, name tags, fat black Mont Blanc pens, notepads, beepers, stethoscopes, reflex hammers, retractors, pocket computers, thermometers—but they're still junior to the forth-year students, who are junior to the nurses, interns, and residents. The doors to the marble wonderland of love and indulgence on the Quadrangle, wide open to them since the syrupy Orientation Day ceremonies, have clanged shut. There are new kids on the block now, first- and second-year students, and it's their turn to nest safely in the Quad. The third-year students' hearts may still belong to Harvard, but their asses are now the property of the hospitals and clinics that fly their school's flag. For the truth of it is that Harvard Med doesn't direct them as much anymore, and they could be doing all this hard labor at Johns Hopkins or Bellevue or Boston City, and no one on staff would give a damn where they're paying tuition. They begin to sense this, as well as that, good as they were to have gotten in to begin with, there are other students from other schools who are just as bright, even brighter. They have been downsized. I once asked former dean Ebert if a doctor's alma mater was any measure of his or her quality and whether one could actually characterize a Harvard Med graduate. "I'll tell you honestly," he said, "it only makes a difference in an interesting way. That is in the perception of the patient, and of the physician. The patient thinks, Oh, that Harvard diploma on the wall! For him, there's a sort of halo effect, which has nothing to do with the quality of the individual. The physician says to himself, I am an HMS grad, therefore I must be pretty good."

Because the third-year students are junior-juniors in the hospitals, they will be under the constant watch of hospital staff, who are well aware that a motivated chimpanzee can be taught how to lop off a leg and shoot dice, but that knowing when not to takes analysis and reasoning and years of experience. They will be verbally abused on occasion, and humiliated, a rarity for most of them when they are growing up. Now, in the hospitals, such treatment is not uncommon, as in, "For Christ's sake, you mean you have only two hands? You're fired, you crippled bastard!" The roses that come after a patient's discharge are usually not for them, they learn tearfully, but for the nurses.

The nurses. Third-year students can work with them or against them, and they are well advised to choose the former because a little trained nurse, as they used to say before men got into the profession, is a dangerous thing. It comes as a shock to some students that these handmaids and handmen in white were not all carried to term by Florence Nightingale, or born with a divine touch, or bound to watch sweetly over the souls and bodies of the sick. One time, during an emergency delivery at Brigham and Women's, a stunned student looked on as a nurse-midwife reached into her pocket for a rubber glove and, like a challenger to a duel, lashed it across the face of the strutting pimp who had bullied his way into the delivery room with his pregnant friend and was interfering with procedures and berating the staff. "They glared at each other for a minute," the student said. "I thought he was going to kill her. But he backed off, not her, and he sat down meekly in a corner and shut up the whole rest of the time." Nurses everywhere often make the point of informing students that they work with and not for the doctors, and if there is any doubt about the equality, perceived or actual, of the doctor-nurse relationship, the story one third-year student told me dispels it. During a routine surgery, a nurse had committed the mortal sin of calling a chief resident by his first name. It was Charles, but she added insult to injury by calling him Charlie. Miffed, he stepped away from the patient, motioned her over to him, and, riveting her with a Harvardian glare, told her never ever to address him that way in front of students. Her response was loud enough to be heard outside the operating suite, and elementary: "I got two words for you, Charlie, and if you have to ask what they are, you're stupider than you look." Concluding from his open mouth that he was, she enlightened him. "Fuck you!" she said, then paused, savoring the moment, and added the punctuation: "Charlie."

Charlie was destined to be a Harvard Presence, the top gun of the hierarchy at whose feet the students must now sometimes squirm, as befits the worms they come to feel they are. Presences are superego superspecialists with academic, hospital, and specialty society titles, and they have usually made national and local magazine and newspaper lists of the top ten doctors. A few also make commendable role models, and all are clearly exceptionally skilled, which is why I, as a local medical reporter with privileged access, for years shamelessly and gratefully accepted, for myself and my wife, their "professional courtesy" treatment of everything that ailed us, even zits, a problem that Presences won't bother about if you just come in off the street. (If they are forced into such garden-variety doctoring, they'll launder it. Once, when I remarked to a Presence that I had heard he was the world's foremost authority on kidney stones, he replied, "Calcium metabolism, actually.") Most are too busy administering, teaching, researching, preparing grants, writing definitive textbooks, and attending meetings to live up to the minimal patient-care component of their media ranking, unless, as is the case in Boston, the patient is what the hospitals refer to privately as entitled demanders, that is, with a Kennedy surname, a throne (exiled included), a medical column with a circulation of better than 100,000, and enough medical insurance to guarantee lifetime job security for the National Association of Underwriters.

It is impossible for Harvard third-year students to escape Presences. The course catalog informs students that "they will be exposed to the ways senior clinical faculty surgeons think through surgical problems," which is not only an exposure to technique but sometimes to showboating. One student recalled his first surgery experience, and fantasizing about doing something grandiose, like helping to hook up a replacement kidney. He had scrubbed carefully and then struggled clumsily into rubber gloves, only to find he merely had to hold the retractors during a routine appendectomy, listen to a Presence, who had deigned to undertake so pedestrian a cutting job— it was his humble offering to Harvard Med—and hope that this man would not ruin a budding surgical career with his slice and badinage style, which was coming dangerously close to lopping off the student's fingers. "I still . . . like to split the . . . muscle with the classic McBurney," the surgeon mused, stabbing his scalpel coolly into the anesthetized, heaving abdomen, his eyes not on the belly but on some distant point of inspirational light, "not . . . the approach . . . that the new kids on . . . the block choose . . . because they want the better"—slice— "exposure of the organ that . . . their transverse Davis-Rockey affords. I"—slice—"prefer . . . the . . . challenge"—he made his point by holding up the scalpel delicately between thumb and forefinger with the other three fingers extended as though it was a teacup—"that comes . . . with finding ways to extend the incision." He resumed the slicing. "And say there, old chum, don't be pulling on that instrument. You'll tear the peritoneum and Lord knows what else in there, and I hope you won't take this personally, but I wouldn't want to have to discuss that with your society master, the man who puts it all in your dean's letter, the one that, as you know, the dean doesn't have time to write and which you ain't going to graduate without."

Painfully aware that they are outsiders, the third-year students cannot even vent much with their peers. Their class, and any buddies they have made, are no longer together at the Quadrangle as they were during the preclinical phase of training; instead, they scattered all over the city, among different hospitals and on different services. They pine for the days of the Second Year Class Show, an annual music and dance review they'd written and directed to satirize the school and faculty, an event that marked the end of their togetherness as a class, and of their innocence. The limerick they roared at during the show has lost its kick after but one night in a "skin" clinic eyeballing syph, chancres, herpes, and gonorrhea in hookers.

There was a young man from Back Bay,
Who thought syphilis just went away.
He's developed paresis,
Has long talks with Jesus,
And thinks he's Queen of the May.

They are on their own, trying to follow the Harvard Med dictum, with its advice and shred of hope: "Eat when you can, sleep when you can, and remember that like renal calculi, this, too, shall pass."

As they slowly learn more and more about disease and malfunction, the students typically become obsessed with medical jargon. "They find themselves compelled to tell everyone they meet about the cremaster reflex and the Maple Syrup Urine Disease," Harvard Med student Benjamin Scheindlin said at a recent Class Day. Ordinary topics, too, are translated into medicalese. "A medical student with automobile trouble might say, 'It's not an emergent problem, so I'll just have the carburetor replaced electively.' Students particularly enjoy borrowing medical terms to describe their emotional lives. The human body has a miraculous capacity to compensate for various diseases—that is, to function reasonably well in spite of them. Yet, when the body cannot keep up with the disease, we say that the person has decompensated. Thus, a medical student will report an unexpected encounter with a former paramour like this: 'So, after not speaking for six months, I ran into her buying a falafel at Sami's and totally decompensated.' "[1]

But at the student stage, a bit of medical knowledge can be disastrous. When a friend or relative asks them for advice, honest third-year students will admit they don't know, or they'll only say things like, "Well, just don't do that" when someone says it hurts when they move an arm and wonders what they should do about it. Or they'll try to help cautiously, but still with sometimes startling results. Scheindlin recalled a friend who phoned to ask the name of the condition marked by pain shooting down the back of a leg. His mother had it and it began with an "a," he thought.

"Do you mean sciatica?" Scheindlin asked.

"Yeah. What can you do for that?"

"Well, what did her doctor say?"

"Oh, she hasn't seen the doctor yet."

"Then how do you know she has sciatica?"

"You just said so yourself."[2]

Few students dare to take on more diagnostics than they should, since the admonition in the course catalog is specific: "The amount of responsibility assigned will be commensurate with the ability of each particular student." This doesn't stop them from diagnosing themselves, however, and in the third year they must, for they have caught the medical student's most notorious disease: hypochondriasis. "Every month I had the illness of the rotation I was on," Shawn Nasseri recalled. "On oncology, I was sure I had cancer; doing neurology, I imagined I was having seizures or a stroke. You get stuck with needles and you say, 'God, I'm going to get AIDS.' You're with kids with AIDS who're bleeding, and there's blood on their hands and on their sheets, and that's why they always tell us, 'If there's blood on their fingers, there'll be blood on their toes, so wear gloves, wash your hands, be careful, careful, careful.' In pediatrics, we'd get all the childhood diseases we never had. In adults, chicken pox is a bad one, so those of us who'd had it would make it worse for those who hadn't. We'd cluck at them, 'Chick, chick, chick.' "

Whether it is from worrying about catching something, actually catching something (colds wipe them out regularly), or from their interminable hospital chores, third-year students are always exhausted. They leave messages on their answering machines that say, "I can't come to the phone right now. I'm either asleep or dead." Or, "You've reached the late Blanche LaVeau, the gangrene queen. Leave your message after the Mozart Requiem. I'm sorry I'll never be able to return your call."

A moon shot has gone off in their heads now, and they start questioning total devotion to the sick as they struggle to balance the patient's needs and demands against their own. They're now doing all this great stuff for patients, things they would never be able to do for themselves or for their families because the patients have dibs on their time. They stay late on the wards, sometimes not always because they want to. "It's a macho thing in medicine," said one, "to tell yourself that you can stay in the hospital forever and take care of patients because you care about them. But what it is, really, is that it becomes gauche to leave early, and you're not a good doctor if you do. And Harvard forbid if something doesn't get done on your shift or gets done poorly, because everyone will be saying that you didn't do the right thing because you wanted to go home. We've had situations here when someone's father died and a mother was having surgery and the student wanted a leave of absence to be with his family. Others had to cover and take extra calls when the student left, and they were saying things like, 'What a selfish person, couldn't he postpone that?' "

The awesome responsibility of caring on call soon becomes a burden that is made heavier by the guilt that comes from not always having one's heart in it, from dreading the possibility of getting stuck with a patient's family because that might take up twenty minutes of allotted time, or from not listening to a patient's "irrelevant noncontributory" problems. They feel guilty, too, for occasionally cursing the range of human variability that has wrecked the preciseness of the science they have learned. The guilt is sometimes good because it gets things done, but it breeds simmering anger, and the students direct it at the patients and families who tell them they're not doing enough or doing the wrong thing, who won't accept a diagnosis after a CT scan, MRI, spinal tap, and enough blood drawn to sustain a vampire coven, who are crybabies with low tolerance for pain, or nasties who hate doctors, or who become ill or pregnant or injured because they screw up and will screw up again and again and are thus wasting everyone's precious time coming in at ungodly hours. The anger makes them judgmental, frustrated. They begin to see that a lot of illnesses stem from self-abuse and are often really just a consequence of social problems. Look, they say, stop smoking, because it's bad for you, and the idiots don't, or they stop and start eating uncontrollably, or start smoking crack and using heroin, or stop using that and start drinking booze. Look, the students say, we'll give you a safe bed in the OB ward so you can hang on to your pregnancy and where your man won't beat you. She'll be grateful for two days, and then she'll go back to the Neanderthal she's living with and he'll whack her again. "You're doing all this great good," one frustrated third-year student told me, "and you tell these bozos and crocks that they can do so much for themselves but that you can do so little if they don't lend a hand. But it doesn't mean a thing, 'cause they don't give a shit about what they're doing or about what you're doing." So you play, you pay, the students think, and sometimes say.

This is when the students often do things for patients not because the patient cannot do them or expects it but because that is what a student is supposed to do. They know now how the weary waitress felt when she brought yet another lighted birthday cake to the enchanted celebrant. They don't ask probing personal questions because they don't want to know the answers. ("So, how do you feel today, sir?" "Well, Doc, I . . ." "Fine, fine, see you tomorrow.") And they start to gravitate toward patients who make them feel useful, while avoiding those who are very draining, incorrigible. Give us this day a leukemia case, they say, because that poor bastard didn't get it from drinking a fifth of vodka every night because he was depressed. Send us your colds and coughs, because we can do the doctor thing, reassure them, say that's a virus, and send them packing, because they're going to get better no matter what we do.

They begin to see clearly how the system conspires to deflect them from practicing compassion at the same time it is being taught. For those who want to, there is no time to get to know a patient, because they see too many on a different service each month, and most of them are propelled through in order to make room for more paying customers. Fresh off an ICU rotation, the students understand and begin to appreciate that most of the saves made there do not come from empathy, which has been beaten out of them anyway, but from the technology armory of a Harvard Med teaching hospital. Increasingly, unless they are tracking toward psych, they begin to protest whenever they hear soma getting overwhelmed by psyche. Unscientific psychobabble, they sniff now, pap that too often substitutes soft theorizing for the real gut questions and the unerring accuracy of those awesome biomagnetic brain-monitoring systems with thirty-seven—just count 'em, thirty-seven—sensors, which are nothing to sneeze at, by God, when you consider that only a few years ago these impressive suckers had only a dozen or so. They shuffle their career choices and start thinking that maybe all those specialties they hadn't thought much of aren't so bad after all, even though there'll be a surplus of 150,000 doctors practicing them by the time they're out of here. Tired of telling people to flee abusive relationships and to stop the booze and dope, they want to make a real, solid difference, and they want to deal with just your kidney, hear? Just your kidney, any problem in the world with your kidney, I'll fix it, but don't talk to me about your liver and how it got that way, or about your mother.

The third-year students will go, too, from never giving even a glance at death over their young shoulders, to a belief

that death is a sentence to be cursed and fought off, to appreciation that it can be a blessed gift not only for the patient but
for the family and, God forgive them, for the caretakers. They
begin to see that their remaining time is finite, too, and the
only difference between them and Patient X is that statistically
he has less time. And after they have passed through the stages
of growth that mark this year, they will, every one, accept that
they cannot be everything to everybody, that all the moral
observations and good advice cannot always be applied. They
begin to suspect that the hurt of their severely ill patients will
always hurt more than the cheer that the students try to bring
will cheer, that when someone is sick and in great pain, they
are truly alone, because no matter how hard the caretaker tries,
he or she will never really be able to climb into the patient's
skin, no more than any human being can truly grasp nature.
Anyway, after recovery, nobody really remembers the severity
of pain, so why bother to assuage it?

Some students seek counseling during this time to reassure
themselves that they have talent and worth and to recapture
empathy; others take time off to "rearrange" their lives with
some whitewater rafting; a few start shadowing Dr. Herb Benson at the Mind-Body Institute, and they choose mantras and
take to reciting Hail Marys, The Lord Is My Shepherd, and
"Ommmm" in an effort to bring on the relaxation response.

But no matter what they do to reshape their psyches, by
the time this third year is over—and most certainly at the end
of their last—they will be very different people: tuned, not
finely, but tuned, goal-oriented, and emotionally older. Many
will firmly justify professional behavior by interns, residents,
and chiefs that they once criticized. They will know that the
pedestrian doesn't always have the right of way. The young
men will chuckle now at jokes like "No ovary is good enough
to save; no testicle bad enough to remove"; the women will
laugh at urologists who are pissed because the penis will never

replace the heart on a valentine. They will guffaw, too, in disbelief when they read in the local papers how one of their highly visible patients, an injured firefighter or cop, say, is putting up a "valiant," or "gallant," "battle for life," because they know he's totally unresponsive and that any "will to live" is in the minds of the writers. All will have learned, too, that if they take on only what they can handle, varnish their insecurities, form a few calluses and crusts, become a little more disattached, and just lie back and punch up the formidable technical backup, they will get through it all and become purveyors of better care, or at least the kind of care the insurers demand. They will have learned how to survive. They are becoming American doctors at last. And they will also want to kill the two students who, in the Orientation Day handbook, were still honeymooning when they wrote, "At Harvard, you are encouraged, even expected to cultivate a life outside medical school"; or "Having completed a full year at Harvard, I can sincerely say that medical school is so much more fun than I ever thought it could be. There really is time to enjoy your twenties and still learn medicine."

Shawn wrote something like that when he was a second-year student and was asked to contribute to the handbook. "Well, let me start by saying, Wow!!!!" he exulted. "What an amazing year. It was much better than *Cats*. I laughed, I cried, I skipped all the way home. . . . Stressed? Roadtrip. Bored? Go dancing. Still bored? OK, so you're probably a lousy dancer, so try concerts, museums, and barhopping instead. Just remember, 'Hello, my name is ———. I'm a Harvard Medical Student, so this year I'm entitled to learn, to grow, and to PARTYYYYYYYYYYYY because next year I will be an academic slave, third year I'll be a hospital slave, and fourth year I'll be stressing about residency.' "

Now, well into his third year, he (and his classmates, he

was relieved, or depressed, depending on one's point of view, to discover) is having nightmares and is, as he describes it, "feeling toxic." He has delivered thirty-three babies, not all of them just slip and slide. If the school would let him and he could get rid of the bad dreams, Rip van Winkle's record would be history. He has fulfilled his prophecy of peonage and is regularly bemoaning his student status as "the lowest form of life in the hospital" in terms of taking care of patients. He has quit playing racquetball, which he had been doing three to four times a week in his salad days. He's not doing any escape reading. He couldn't care less about World Cup soccer, which is under way now and is being followed closely, he says with some amazement, by a few of his classmates. Humor, the black kind that chases the chill from the anatomy lab and lightens the load in the hospital, is his number-one valve. And medicine and his poetry are the dual forces in his life. But the poetry is darker now, full of allusions to splashed blood, ripped faces, horribly disfigured, blue heads emerging from crack mothers' wombs; a woman lying dead in a room with get-well messages scrawled in crayon over the walls by her children; and bucking, strangling patients. His golden banner has dipped, and he is struggling to keep his focus. He still wants to be "the good physician, as well as the good heart and the kind soul," but there are obstacles. "You see these same sick patients, babbling and choking and drooling, and you can't do anything for them. You see the things that could have been avoided if they hadn't used coke or alcohol during pregnancy. And you go home, and you even smell like these people. And you don't want to wake up and go back into the hospital, because you don't want to deal with all the pain."

Shawn's roommate, Steve Frankel, went through it, and his mother noticed a change in him when he went home for spring break. "She was complaining about me because I seemed more stoic, harder. It was probably exhaustion, and two weeks of sleep took care of it, but I wouldn't want to stay that way. At the end of eighteen years of schools and classes, you're a professional student, and taking tests doesn't really make you lose sleep. But now, in the third year, you've essentially got a real job, real patients with real problems, and it goes from the pressure of, Oh, did I get a ninety-seven or a ninety-four? to is Mr. So and So still going to be alive when I get there in the morning? Did I do the right thing, and is he going to bleed? Maybe I ought to have come down on those settings. What if I've destroyed his lungs? You're only a student and, yes, you're supervised, but you get the sense it's your job and your responsibility. There are safety nets, but that doesn't mean you're not taking the hits. You grow up very, very quickly."

For Shawn, that meant growing pains triggered by a couple of his nightmare scenarios that played out in a hospital emergency room. One patient was a thirty-year-old alcoholic male who had had a heart attack at an AA meeting just as he stood up to attest to his addiction. He was unconscious and not breathing when he was rushed in by EMTs who couldn't get a pulse and couldn't resuscitate him. Shawn figured he was probably dead when he hit the floor, because an EMT who was trying to do chest compressions after they brought him in was not giving it his all; he was standing three feet away from the man, and instead of exerting the heavy force required to jump-start the heart, he was just pressing the victim's chest lightly, almost casually. Still, the man was a classic code call, meaning the victim was not showing any signs of life. But maybe there's a chance, so everyone move! Shawn recalled the chaotic scene as though it had happened that morning.

"We all ran to our assigned positions, the guy running the code at his feet, someone at his head, and the anesthetist, who's trying to get an airway down without intubating the guy because he didn't have time. He just put a mask over the guy's mouth, and they started bagging him. That's using this big bag with a release valve. And when you push in and squeeze it, it inflates and fills the lungs, and when it relaxes, there's another valve so that the air doesn't come back to the bag. That valve was pointed right at my face, and I was standing over him doing the chest compressions, and they were trying to run lines into his jugular and subclavian, right where my hands were, and there's this big needle going past me while I'm pounding and someone is bagging. And this man's breath is coming right into my face, a horrid, rancid smell, and I could taste it, and while I'm pounding—it must have been thirty minutes—I'm terrified and thinking, I'm breathing his death.

"It got worse. There was this other patient with cancer in his voice box, too old, too sick to have surgery, so the doctors had radiated his neck, which had so damaged the tissue that it caused what is known as a 'woody larynx,' a tough sheathing that would actually break in two if anyone struck or squeezed it. The patient had had a recurrence of his cancer, and the vocal cords had gone into spasm and closed inside the larynx; breathing on his own was impossible, so a hole had to be made for air.

"They had to sedate him and put a tube down his throat, but because he had such a difficult larynx, it was going to be rough. So we all got around him to do this fiberoptic intubation, where they pass a scope and a tube in while they're watching on a monitor, and while they're cramming this tube down into his lung, he was lunging around, and he couldn't scream because of what he had down his larynx. But just the expression in his eyes . . . He was suffocating, his eyeballs were extruding, and his face was ashen, and all they could do was try to intubate him faster. It was barbaric. But what was bizarre was that here were these four people trying to intubate him and hold him down, but nobody was trying to comfort him. So I took his hand. I had to wrestle with it because he was fighting us, but I managed to squeeze it just to let him know there was some human being nearby. They finally got it down, and he quieted, and the room quieted, and while we were absorbing it all, out of the blue this anesthetist says, 'Don't worry, we've got an amnestic on board, magic stuff, and he won't remember a thing.' And I said to myself, You bastard! *We'll* never *forget* it."

He hasn't forgotten, but he's no longer naïve. "I was with a friend recently," he continued, "who was saying she'd read this disturbing study that showed that at the beginning of medical school students say they want to help patients who are really sick and they want to do great things for humanity, and at the end of their training they're avoiding the ones who are really ill. And she couldn't believe it and was saying, 'How callous.' I told her that when you're dealing with dying every day, and families and emotions and sickness and sadness, at some point you draw a line and say, Stop; yes, I want the easy ones. And because that's almost impossible for most people to understand, she must have thought I was this bad person."

She would have thought he was dancing with the devil had she been with him while he watched with glee one 3:30 A.M. as an intern carried on a lengthy conversation, a mono-logue, with a patient who was unconscious, unable to speak, gorked out.

"Hey, how's it going?" asked the intern. "Great. So, how was your day? Really? Nice. Glad to hear it. Do anything special? No kidding? Whoa, you're somethin' else, you know that?"

Shawn admits the intern wasn't respectful. "But it was the only way he could tolerate putting needles into this guy, changing him, taking care of his bedsores. It was the funniest thing I'd ever seen. You begin to appreciate the gallows humor and you catch yourself saying things in a cold way, like asking patients just to wait a minute, saying that you'll get to them, doing the things you used to criticize as unfeeling, because you're now infinitely more realistic and you're seeing all this horrible stuff. You have a choice. You can take an active role or not, because you are still a student. You don't want to do something, don't. You don't like the patient who's annoying you? Take care of someone else. You can go home."

But those feelings dissipate, like the nightmares before he wakes. He remembers other things, still troubling, but, like the difficult intubation he cannot forget, they are strengthening his resolve to be the best. He recalls the kids born with a devastating combination of oxygen deficiency, neurological difficulties, and severe mental retardation. "You walk into a room and see them, kinda twisted to the side, their mouths open, all whining and crying and breathing in the same voice, and all the faces are shaped the same way because they haven't built up any musculature. They can't pee right, and they all have G-tubes in for feeding because they can't swallow, and when they do, they choke on their own secretions. And some kind soul comes in and cuts their hair and cleans them, and you begin to feel the tragedy of their lives, because the only thing they can hope for is maybe to eat on their own someday and sit up. The names change, but the faces are always the same. And you get guilty for ever feeling negative, and you lose sleep over it, and you end up spending more time in the hospital, because you see your friends, doctors and nurses who couldn't go home, taking care of the kids, cutting open someone else's body, restraining them, drawing their blood, and that's what makes it all worthwhile."

Rafael Allende is also making it through the initial shock and grind of the third year, and he is finding, after weighing it all very carefully when, exhausted and sometimes full of doubt in his apartment a mile from the school with his wife, Rosalina, and two small children, that the experience has done something for him as well as to him. "I realize now," he says, chuckling with satisfaction and on a roll now into his fourth year, where he knows what to expect, "exactly why I came to medical school. I know just when it happened and what I'm going to do with my life."

Allende wasn't so sure when he started out in a small community college in New Jersey, then attended St. John's University in New York City, where he majored in toxicology. He eventually did six years in the navy, working at the Naval Hospital in San Diego as a hospital corpsman and lab tech, and got a degree in biology at San Diego State before entering Harvard Med in Shawn's class. His daughter was born, propitiously, during the Genetics, Embryology and Reproduction block. What he missed in lectures and tutorials, he figured, he could make up in credits caring for a newborn.

He had plunged into the curriculum almost from the moment he entered Harvard Med, dropping by research laboratories in his very first year, then putting in more serious time in his second, and moving to weekends full-time when he started his hospital cores in his third. He worked with Judah Folkman, analyzing growth factor and looking at its levels in patients with prostate cancer. Folkman's commitment to research and to his patients provided Allende with the kind of role model he had been searching for and helped solidify his career goals. "It was basic scientific research applied directly to the bedside, and I knew I wanted research as a corollary to what I wanted to do as a physician."

After flirting with a career in primary care for a time, as many students say they did, Allende has fixed on academic neurosurgery. He's mindful that medical students make specialty choices for a number of reasons: personality, educational background, role models, length of residency, prestige, debts and other financial considerations. "For me, it was definitely gut. I had an open mind, and when I did my first cores in medicine, pediatrics, and neurology, I truly liked them. But it wasn't sitting right somehow; the amount of interaction in terms of direct contact was limited, and it was frustrating. It was management, and this managed-care thing I hear a lot about nowadays is one of my biggest concerns, making me wonder whether quality will be compromised. I wanted to be able to do more than call a consultant or the radiotherapist. I wanted more hands-on, more working with patients. And so when I got into my surgery rotation, I found I loved it in the OR. All the other things I had been doing were fine, but, while you can learn to do a good diagnosis and a great neurological exam, the treatment modalities were, for me anyway, limited. You have a stroke patient, and all you can do is watch and see if he comes out of it. I wanted to be able to do something for the patient, and combining surgery with research lets me do that."

Allende has had more opportunity than most. He's done labwork in the navy and at Harvard. He's drilled burr holes in skulls, opened and closed spinal-disk cases, done some microdissecting. "It's great," he says. "When I was a kid, I used to spend hours making car and motorcycle models, and I've always liked meticulous stuff, small details that took time. And those twelve and thirteen hours in the operating room? When I'm in there, the time flies for me."

A crass question: Did debt load play a role in his choice of specialty?

Allende laughs. "Good question. I've got six figures to pay back. But, in all honesty, that's not why I went into medicine. Look, I knew I was going to make good money as a physician no matter what specialty I chose. So, whatever you make, you can work hard if you have to make it up, and you learn how to invest. But you follow your heart."

One third-year student's ski trip, they say, is another's blizzard. Steve Frankel had started out wanting to cure through surgery, but he has now opted for medicine. "Surgery seemed like a good idea at first, never having done any, and I did my core course at General and my month of peedee at Children's. After three months, it was not what I imagined. The work was great, but the hours were a little difficult to manage. I think I could have handled it, but it was taking more and more to keep me interested. You start out, like, an appendectomy is cool, but then after the fourth and fifth one, they just weren't that exciting. I'd hold the retractors and watch, but I'm thinking lung transplants and colon resections, which I did get to watch, and I realized that if I wanted to get a top spot in that, it was a long shot for me. So I may do critical care, because everything I get is different, interesting, sort of adrenaline-squeezing."

16 | *Primary Care*

There is no creature . . . that works harder and is more
poorly requited than the country doctor, unless perhaps it may be his horse.

—Sir Walter Scott

"AL FRIEDLICH GREW UP IN A WONDERFUL TIME OF MEDICINE,"
says Larry Ronan in his office in the Wang Ambulatory Care
Building at MGH, one of several places where he hangs his
stethoscope. Another is the Chelsea Community Health Center—an MGH facility on the edge of Boston proper—with a
one-half non-English-speaking patient load. He also carries his
stethoscope with him when he makes house calls in Boston's
North End. "But there are two things in great conflict here
and now. You want two things. You want me to be extremely
sensitive, take time with you, and give you a lot of emotional
support. At the same time, they're telling me to see more
patients in a shorter period of time more efficiently. It's all on
volume. It's 'How many patients did you see this afternoon?'
For good or bad, there are two levels of care—care for those
who can afford to find those doctors who can spare the time
to support them and care for those who cannot. Preventive
medicine takes a lot of time, especially when a patient doesn't
speak your language. Health promotion is a lengthy effort. To
work with a patient behaviorally takes time. And I'm given
fifteen minutes to see you, on top of which I have to fill out
a form for you—there are times when I have to give a third
of my time to those forms, some of which are virtually impene-
trable—which you usually need that same day.

"There's that side of you that likes the patient contact—
the thing that sends those of us who choose it into primary

305

care—but at the same time the system is denying that side of the caregiver. If I'm going to spend only fifteen minutes with a patient, what do I focus on—especially if at the end of the exam and the conversation, the patient suddenly tells me that her husband beats her, or if someone else tells me that he's impotent? None of that fits into the fifteen minutes. Unless we change some of the how we practice, we're going to have a hard time attracting high-caliber people into primary care. The kids see this fifteen minutes with a patient and the chaos of insurance forms and they say, 'That's not why I went to medical school.'

"And that's sad, because when these kids write essays for admission, they all use the word *service*. And they say, 'I'm going to care for you.' They're thinking, Tell me what I can do for you. In some sense, the generalist spirit runs in everyone who comes into medicine, and yet we turn out very few generalists. What happened? What happened to that word *service* that appeared in all the essays? How many articles have you read or written on primary care? They're still writing about specialty medicine. It's something to think about."

What happened is not only the chaos of insurance forms that Ronan speaks of; there is also the lack of glamour, of visibility, of prestige that is part of what used to be known as "saddlebag medicine." Opie Read, the American humorist and founder of the magazine *The Arkansas Traveler,* described the workmanlike GP as the man who "bled the ancient Egyptians, blistered the knights of the Middle Ages and poisoned the arrows of the Iroquois. He has been preserved in fiction, pickled in the drama, and peppered in satire." To today's medical reporters, covering meetings of the American Academy of Family Practice is as challenging and productive as covering an awning fire. The relatively low pay of the primary-care doctor—only a third of physicians practicing in the United States are in primary care—is another factor. As someone once said, a fashionable surgeon, like a pelican, can be easily recognized by the size of his bill. Compared with what a cardiovascular surgeon takes in during a year, the GP, thus, would have to be mad to do it if money was the object.

And often, money is. A recent survey conducted by researchers at Ohio State University and five other institutions (Harvard Med not among them) found that 45 percent were either planning to enter primary care or would switch to it with appropriate adjustments in income or loan repayment; none with debts of less than fifty thousand dollars, indicated they'd make a change. When non-primary-care students were given a choice of salaries that would make them change to primary care, the average level mentioned was $180,000 a year.

"In order to reach the goal of having half of all physicians in primary care, a national health care priority," said A. Patrick Jones, an assistant professor of clinical medicine at Ohio State, "somebody has to go out on a limb and start debunking some myths, like the idea that certain types of doctors deserve to make more money than others, or that all family doctors are workaholics."

Ronan, who grew up in Chicago, was a guy who "just wanted to take care of the child's cold and the parent's heart condition"—not an unusual goal for someone from the Midwest who wanted to be a doctor because general practice has been more than norm there than in the East. He also admired his own family doctor, but what settled it for him was that general practice would get him involved with what attracted him the most about clinical medicine, the opportunity to integrate the behavioral sciences into medicine, health promotion and disease prevention, geriatric medicine—all of the things that seem to be gripping the country today but that Harvard Med, for all of its forward motion, lags behind in. Harvard's disinterest—not fair, it's really more a grudging sort of interest—was probably why, when Ronan decided in medical school to specialize in what some call the nonspecialty, he ran into a buzz saw of opposition. "There weren't many of us. Those were the dark days of primary care, and there was a tremendous disincentive to go into it that was often stated by the faculty and my colleagues. They were absolutely shocked at me. Many people in leadership positions in the medical school told me I was making the wrong decision, that generalism was not doable. Specialization was in, and it has been rewarded financially and academically."

Ronan's community-based residency program might goad a few more medical students into primary care and perhaps, if the federal government smiled on it, serve as a model for resident education and how to improve patient access nationally; more students going into preventive and primary care might save the cost of unnecessary hospitalizations, and also might quiet the critics of specialization, who charge that the oversupply of specialists—more than 90 percent of the surplus of 165,000 doctors predicted by the year 2000 will be specialists, according to a recent Johns Hopkins School of Public Health study—boosts medical costs by relying on expensive and often needless procedures. If change ever does come, Ronan's subspecialty colleagues would, as he puts it, "be less likely to crap on family doctors."

Given the deep-rooted specialty-and-research biases of the prestigious medical schools and the dispensers of federal money, however, it will not be easy to rid primary care of its outhouse image. While the changes blowing through the nation's health-care system may eventually improve the image of the family practitioner, no one is expecting that the deans of the old-line schools, their teaching-hospital administrators, and the other bottom-liners who have for some time been exchanging clinical excellence for research leadership—at one time they had both—will suddenly become St. Pauls struck by lightning on the road to Damascus and start cutting back on the number of specialty residencies they offer. Another Ohio State University professor, Dr. Patrick Fahey, suggested recently that he's not optimistic about such a shift occurring, since deans and university hospitals are reluctant to cut prime residencies—especially the popular radiology, orthopedics, and dermatology ones—because their teaching and special-care programs depend so heavily on the specialty residents.

Still, as Ronan sees things, a culture is evolving now that is talking about general practice—even at Harvard Med. A few students, mostly first-year ones who are undecided about their futures, volunteer at community health centers and homeless shelters and attend regular lectures by veteran primary-care doctors who tout the rewards of developing long-term relationships with patients and extol the benefits of diversity in cases. Eric Knight, a first-year student who wants to do solo practice in Idaho, is typical of the group. "I'd be very bored," he says, "focusing on one organ." Except for the solo practice, Jeff Peppercorn, who would like to combine his interest in primary care with academic medicine and health policy, says the same thing. "I kinda like the idea of being able to get into personal issues. I like a lot of variety in life." Andrew Chan is another. He says, "It's one thing to understand the basic sciences, to read the books. It's another thing to know how clinical issues can have significant effect on social problems." And Nancy Rigotti, a general internist in the Women's Health Associates Group at MGH who deals with Harvard Med students interested in primary care, says, "Suddenly, we've become fashionable, instead of knowing we were doing the right thing. It's a good time to go into this."

All true, but unfortunately, despite the Rigottis, the Knights, the Chans, the Peppercorns, et al., Harvard Med is still not exactly where one goes to train to work with Indians in Fargo or set up a dermatology practice in Biloxi. It is, and is likely to remain, mostly a haven for "3-M's"—male medical magistri, gowned gurus who are far more scholar, researcher, and specialist than empathic, readily available healers—and for students who want to emulate them. One first-year student who favors a career in primary care told me, "To look at all the stuff hanging on the bulletin boards around here, you'd think HMS was a hotbed of family practice. That's a laugh. I have friends who've been told they'd be wasting their time going into it, and Harvard's, too. When you're surrounded by very bright, scientifically literate students, most of whom have mothers and fathers who are physicians, your ego takes a bit of a battering, and you wonder sometimes why you're choosing this career that so many faculty and peers think is for underachievers."

Ronan agrees. "You know, you can say we're going to encourage it, but, look, even if you ask all the hospitals to turn out fifty percent more primary-care doctors to correct the deficit, it ignores the real question, which is why people don't go into primary care now. There's not enough emphasis. . . . We just don't take the behavioral sciences as seriously as we do the biosciences. Some of these young kids coming in might be able to figure out the gene for an illness, but if you can tell me how to get my population out of Chelsea, I'll give you the Nobel Prize. If you could turn this country around behaviorally, exercise, no drugs, no smoking, it's the Nobel. But no, no Nobels for behavioral science.

"It may be that everyone should get involved in some part of the community. Maybe the students should be *made* to work with the homeless, or in a shelter. With experiences, people can have enormous revelations about themselves. They can change. Why couldn't Harvard Med insist that its first-year students serve two hours a week in a soup kitchen, attach it to a course like this? Why not get them into the high schools on a weekly basis to get involved in HIV education? If you don't do it, that also sends a very powerful sign. I can get you money almost instantly for the first year of summer research, but I have to scrape and scrape to get the dough to get you to work in a woman's shelter. None of what I'm saying is going to guarantee the empathetic doctor, but I guarantee that the experience won't leave anyone untouched. Imagine, the first day of class they go to a nursing home. Or they see the elderly in the community, not just when they're brought in here. What a message that would send! Disease has to be seen as just one component of a person's life. There is a larger component that is not in the hospital, and not entirely controlled by us.

"Who cares for the patients? We doctors are not the only ones. We try to participate in it with our professionalism. But the family does it. The community does it. The patient does it. I go over to the North End and I visit one of my patients at home. He's chronically ill and he's grossly overweight, but he takes care of himself, his sister takes care of him, and the visiting nurse and I plug in. Most medical students don't see that side. What they see, when he comes in here to the hospital, is a four-hundred-and-fifty-pound old man who smokes and has heart attacks, is sick as a dog, and is not of much value. But out there, it's a rich thing for him. Politicians come to see him. Kids do. He's a tremendously liked person. They can fix his heart in here and send him out, but there's more to it than that. Care is something much larger."

Ronan quits. "I gotta go," he says, looking out the door at a corridor full of patients. He wears a sardonic smile, and he shakes his head. "And you know something? I'll reward that person who runs the MRI scan much more than my visiting nurse."

Eric Knight, a Harvard Med first-year student, has a degree in exercise physiology from USC, a new wife, no doctors in his family, and $150,000 to pay back after he graduates. He has decided to go into primary-care doctoring. He says, "I'm not concerned about whether I make a lot of money, because the way I see it, if I make any money as a physician, it'll still be a lot more than my family ever had. If I make seventy thousand dollars, that's a lot."

Knight figures he'll solo in Idaho, where he grew up, a career choice that seemed to set as well with his Harvard counselors as it did with Larry Ronan's. He recalls, with amusement, his encounter with a tutor on his very first block, a guy who expressed the opinion that people who come into the school are too bright for general practice and that one doesn't really need to know too much to practice general medicine. He went on to say that Eric would get bored, that he knew people who, after being in it a few years, were beating down the doors to get back to where the action is.

"I said, 'Excuse me?' In a lot of places where I grew up, solo practice is the only alternative. The state has one of the worst doctor-patient ratios. He just blew me out. But then, I look at most of my classmates, easily ninety percent of whom are the children of doctors, lawyers, and college professors, and it's easy for me to understand where they'd get bored doing what I want. Sometimes, Harvard students will go down to places, and they have this condescending attitude, and people, intelligent, hardworking people, will say, 'Here's this smart college kid, and he can't even change the oil in his car.'

"You hear people who haven't seen a patient in twenty-five years say that you don't need to know much to do primary care, that you're dealing with sore throats and runny noses, that general practice is not realistic because nobody can have that much knowledge. But you know that people are doing it."

He has concerns, he admits. "I did a family practice mentorship, and some parents called up to say that their daughter was having problems in school. The doctor asked them to have her come in so he could talk to her. He had a good enough relationship with the parents and the daughter to do that. In a managed-care situation, I think we'd have a hard time doing something like that, and I have a lot of problems with business people saying what should and shouldn't be done."

I join Eric, Jeff Peppercorn, and the rest of a small group of first-year students—some planning a career in primary care, others "decidedly undecided," as one puts it—on a visit to the Barbara M. McInnis House, a distinctly unglitzy inner-city facility where homeless people too ill to withstand the rigors of the streets or shelters receive medical and nursing care. The students are part of the Urban Health Project, a student-created, student-run organization that works with community health groups to place first-year students in underserved areas. The student handbook informs those interested that the project "enables students to experience the rewards of primary-care work, the excitement of meeting a pressing need, and the satisfaction of contributing significantly to the quality of the lives of others." It is, along with the other student organizations, billed as "a nice break from the academic grind."

The transition from the immaculate Great White Quadrangle to McInnis, a short drive past seedy bars, storefront check-cashing places, and streets where weeds struggle gamely up through the hot July concrete, is like stepping out of the Taj Mahal and into an Agra clinic for the impoverished and the maimed. "Is this it?" says one of the neatly groomed students as we enter the old yellow-brick building after slipping past a pair of drunks swigging from a bottle of wine wrapped in a filthy towel. "Well," says another, scratching his head. "It ain't the Brigham." The two are wearing project T-shirts with a quotation from Margaret Mead on the back: "Never doubt that a small group of thoughtful, committed citizens can change the world; indeed, it is the only thing that ever has."

McInnis is part of Boston's Health Care for the Homeless Program, which was started in 1985 by the Robert Wood

Johnson Foundation and is now supported by state and federal money and private donations. In a year, physicians, nurses, and caseworkers handle 37,000 visits involving 5,000 people at 42 locations. If it's out there, it's in here, and in the other BHCHP facilities: AIDS, frostbite, accidents, drug overdoses, the DTs, TB, pneumonia, diabetes, mental illness, cancer.

In the lobby, we pass a hand-lettered notice on a wall— "Remember, before you leave the building, talk to a nurse. No permission means a warning"—and sign in. We are greeted by Dr. Jim O'Connell, executive director of the program, an enthusiastic practitioner who has to love what he does, because money (the physicians make less than eighty thousand dollars a year, not bad, but far less than their specialist colleagues draw) is not what brought him and the rest of the staff to this place. He will impress each of these students today, whether they plan to follow his career path or not, for he is a rarity among role models at Harvard Med, where, as Jeff Peppercorn would observe, "They're all in basic science."

"I guess I was grappling with a vestigial, late sixties social conscience while contemplating a fellowship in clinical oncology," says O'Connell, laughing, as he gathers us together in a spartan conference room for what a few HSTs call "the PC Pitch" before we tour McInnis. A graduate of Harvard Med, class of 1982, O'Connell had bummed around—Honolulu, Newport, and Cambridge, England—doing everything from tending bar to studying philosophy. His personal knowledge of the homeless, he has said, was limited to a group of delightful clinic patients who lived on the banks of the Charles River and were self-proclaimed connoisseurs of Beacon Hill leftovers. "Mostly, though, I was drawn to their stories, some real, some woven from fragments of elaborate paranoias, and to their sincere appreciation for a doctor's care."

He tells the students, who are listening intently as we sip coffee around a table, that their school furnishes a lot of moral support (no money) and that his decision to come here was received with enthusiasm by his advisers. "Maybe it's their way of getting rid of me," he jokes. It has been an exhilarating and humbling experience, he says, and the medicine utterly fascinating, but, he warns the students, the medical problems of the homeless, woven into a complex web of poverty and politics, are unique but rarely exotic, which is not especially good news for any Harvard Med types more interested in familial dysautonomia than scabies, weeping ulcers, and winter itch, or for those who were decidedly undecided.

O'Connell flicks on a slide projector, and the images that begin hitting the blank wall, and the patients the students will meet afterward, will have some influence on their career decisions. They see a mournful black kid refusing to leave his street-drugged mother, who lies listlessly on a gurney and who would soon die; a wino who burned his feet on Sterno and later fell asleep on a wintry street and suffered severe frostbite to both feet but still managed to stumble into the shelter every night for a foot soak and conversation. "We had to take him to the OR to cut his shoes off when we first saw him," O'Connell tells the students, who are gaping at how the tops of the shoes had actually dug and fused into the man's bones. Slide. "Okay, these are mites burrowed under the skin. Here's a facial nerve coming right through the skin. You know what this one is? No? This is a classic multiple myeloma. See the breastbone sticking out? Now, this one is clubbing. Know what you're looking for? No? Classic lung cancer association. Squamous CA of the lung." The students do not utter a word. They are still trying to get through the classroom principles of drug-receptor interactions and cohort study design and all of the other methods of epidemiology. A few grimace, but most are trying to be as cool as professional New Yorkers who sit unimpressed, or so they say, across from a celebrity in a restaurant. A slide of a collection of ugly knives taken from some of the patients is to remind the students of the tough world of the shelters. "It's staggering the amount of violence out there." The students nod. "Okay, what's this? Nobody know? Okay, it's gingivitis, a bad case. Oh yes, here's an infiltrated eye that was eventually lost." One student looks quickly toward the door, another out the window. "See this red leg here? No, it's cellulitis, hot, red, edematous."

O'Connell tells them about that one. Guy was an alcoholic, with a 102° fever. He was admitted to Boston City Hospital, where one morning he yanked out his IVs and headed for the package store. Every time they tried to admit and treat him, he did the same thing. So they stored doses of antibiotic at key mileposts along the path they knew he took every day and night—one at a clinic, another at a soup kitchen, and another at a day-care center where he napped. The last dose, they left in the fridge at a local tavern, and the bartender (who also kept insulin in there for another of O'Connell's patients) would take care of things. "Sort of gives new meaning to outpatient care," someone suggests. We laugh. O'Connell gives a few tips on how to deal with homeless people. "One is, be sensitive. They don't especially like waiting in lines, you know. The other is, slow down; they don't give you their history in the first five minutes. Don't push 'em; don't ask if they hear voices. Just learn to wait. It takes an hour to do an evaluation of an IV drug user with a fever. Any questions?" A young woman raises her hand and wants to know, besides how he can take the time, why he's doing this, considering Harvard and all. O'Connell answers quickly. He's been asked the question many times by colleagues who do not do what he does. "I enjoy taking care of people who are ill. Others like wellness care. I hope you can convince your colleagues of that." He does not add a trepidation that he confessed to once in the alumni bulletin. "At times the yearning for the precision of ICU medicine, the intensity of the emergency room, or the constant daily exchange of new knowledge can be a powerful reminder of how far my career has strayed from a world where competency and familiarity came with such ease and excitement. At times, I fear that I will eventually exist, like many of my patients, on the fringe of my professional society."

For the moment, O'Connell has put aside such melancholia. The homeless, he tells the students, have stirred the simple ideals that brought him to Harvard Med in the first place. "I have the gratitude of those with few others to trust and little else to give."

He motions us to our feet and we follow him into the hall. He introduces the group to a man sitting on a sofa. "These are Harvard Medical School students," O'Connell says proudly. "Harvard, huh?" says the patient. "Harvard. Must be goin' to make a lot of money, right?" A student behind me lets out a huge laugh. "Whoa, I hope so. I'm going to be looking at well into six big ones." "Yeah, well, six big ones, huh? You'll make it up fast, pal," the patient says, adding as we walk off, "Want to trade places?"

We walk into rooms where O'Connell is comfortable and we are not. We encounter a patient with blackened feet, frozen this past winter, whose toes, O'Connell tells us in a whisper outside, will eventually end up dropping off one by one to the floor. "God, frostbite in July," a student mutters to himself, dodging a patient exceeding the wheelchair speed limit and sidestepping another with a bandaged head. One man has the shakes; a woman stares out the window at a lone tree; someone else scratches an infestation. We pass a smiling nurse. Perhaps to quiet some apprehension she senses in our group, perhaps to convert any science nerds among us, or maybe simply because she is just one of those good hearts and kind souls that Shawn Nasseri speaks of, she announces spontaneously, "You know something, guys? I love this place. I really do."

17 | *When Skill Fails*

They also serve who only
stand and wait.

—*Milton*

MARCIE HAD JUST BEGUN HER THIRD YEAR AND WAS DOING HER
core clerkship in medicine at MGH when she heard that the
patient Riley had died in the hospital. He had come back a
month after colon surgery because they apparently hadn't gotten it all, at least not the cells that had slipped into his bloodstream and metastasized to his liver. His doctors knew there
was nothing they could do for him, and they were just holding
him at MGH until he could get a bed at Youville, where he
and his family felt he should die.

Marcie had gone to see him once more after her disastrous
meeting with him and had found him depressed.

"You were right, Doc," he had said, not looking at her.
"You called the cancer keerect." He would say nothing more,
and Marcie found herself conducting a monologue with a silent man, as Shawn's colleague had done with his comatose
patient, but for different reasons.

"I'm really sorry about all this trouble you're having, Mr.
Riley," she had said, trying to get his eyes to meet hers. "I
really am. Is there something I can do for you? No? Well, if
there is, please let me know, okay? Okay."

Maybe he'll pull out of it, she had thought as she left the
room. These things take time, and work, and when he's gone
through it, he'll accept it. At least that's what Elisabeth
Kübler-Ross had said when she laid it all out so neatly, those
stages that everyone passes through whether they're dying or
suffering some other loss.

Marcie had gotten the word that Riley was dead from a surgical resident she met when she was first assigned to Riley. She had run into him on one of her stints that required her to be on call every fourth night and admitting patients every other day, and he gave her the news casually. "Oh, by the way, you might want to know that your guy, Riley, the major curmudge, bought it."

The resident's manner didn't surprise her. They called him Catscan Jack, after a mythical—some students say he actually lived—ubiquitous student who seemed to show up at every one of Harvard's teaching hospitals at the same time. The original Catscan Jack got his name when, as a second-year HST, he had allegedly rushed over to the Brigham the day they brought in a two-thousand-year-old Egyptian mummy from the Museum of Fine Arts for a CT scan. The procedure would give the museum, and the research radiologists, new information about their ancient "patient"—medical history, age, cause of death, even the materials and substances used in the embalming process—that was not on the cartonnage inscription, and they'd learn all this without having to open the case or disturb the fragile body. As the technicians slid the mummy, case and all, into the scanner, they say that Catscan Jack, at that moment, decided he would be a radiologist. For here was the ideal patient. He didn't speak, didn't move, couldn't sue, and could be kept in the tunnel for a six-hour whole-body scan, compared with the relatively quick in and out and limited X-ray exposure for a live patient. They say, too, that Catscan Jack had a serious orgasm when the vivid images flashing eerily on the monitor showed evidence of a herniated disk and arthritis, kidney stones, a full set of mint-condition teeth, a neatly wrapped package of bodily organs that had been removed and put between the mummy's legs like the bagged gizzard and heart of a turkey you find where the stuffing goes, and even a gold bracelet. After that, Catscan was hooked on heavy medical metal. He started hanging around the urology department at MGH when they were using an overhead crane to lower patients with kidney stones into a stainless-steel tub so they could blast the rocks with high-energy shock waves and ultrasound; at the Robert Breck Brigham, where they were sucking out synovial tissue from arthritic knees through an arthroscopic straw; at Brigham and Women's when they were unplugging fallopian tubes with Catscan's all-time favorite tool, the hot-light laser, "the light fantastic," he called it.

"Were you there?" Marcie had asked.

"I was having a coffee outside," Catscan Jack said. "He wasn't mine. His wife and kid were there." This Catscan wasn't as bad as his namesake, but he was close.

"Did they say much?"

Catscan shrugged. "The usual."

"What's that?"

"You know, a lot of crying and moaning. It was hard to deal with. The wife was hysterical, saying things like he didn't want to be here in the first place, should have taken him to the Lahey, where they'd have known how to treat him. Right! Daughter said he'd be alive today if they'd never opened him up. Nobody sued, thank God. Yet, anyway. But they're capable of it, believe me."

Marcie asked what Riley's mental state was when he actually died.

"Nothing, I hear," said Catscan. "Depressed as hell."

"Do you know if he ever got angry, like maybe bargaining for—"

Catscan had laughed at her. "You mean like that Kübler-Ross stuff? The program? The paint-by-numbers shit? Come on, sweets. He was depressed when he found out he had CA; he was depressed when they told him they had to operate; he was depressed before he died."

Someday, Marcie was thinking, you'll call me Dr. Sweets, you nerdy prick. "So, nobody could talk to him?"

"Nobody. He was staring at the ceiling. A couple shrinks came by. But there was nothing to do."

Catscan stared at Marcie. "Look," he had said gently. "Some unsolicited advice. You've got a lot ahead of you here on this core. You've got emergency, you've got the EKG course, complication rounds, all-nighters, special bedsides with the firm, clinical lab. You might learn that people are hydro-electric, biochemical systems and that when it all goes down, you can't talk it back. You fix it if you can, but that's really all you can do."

Marcie was suddenly angry—not so much at Catscan Jack, because he was probably right, and he represented what medicine was all about today. She did have to grow up sometime if she was to survive in this. She was angry at herself for her gullibility, accepting stages too readily, as she had when she read Gail Sheehy's pop-psych *Passages*. "Screw you, Elisabeth," she had muttered. "Get a life."

But she had also remembered Ned Cassem again, something he'd said about when skill fails, it's the relationships that count. But what if they don't hear you, like Riley hadn't? Well, then, she reasoned, you do it for yourself. But maybe Riley had appreciated what she'd said that day he didn't respond, and perhaps she had done some good after all. Yes, there was another story that Cassem had told. There was this patient with an infection, and the odor from it was terrible. The student who came in couldn't stand it, and he became so nauseated and repelled by it that he couldn't talk, so he just put his head down on his arm to try to calm himself. He stayed that way for a half hour. Then he got up and patted the patient on the head and went out as fast as he could. Later, he felt awful because he'd failed. So he talked to a chaplain, who told him that everyone is weak and to go back in and try again.

So the student did. He sat down, put his arm on the patient's shoulder, and said, "Hi." And the patient said, "I just want to tell you how much that did for me yesterday when you came in and prayed for me. I really needed someone to do that." The only problem was, Riley hadn't been around long enough to thank her.

18 | *The Patient Redux*

First, the patient, second the
patient, third the patient, fourth
the patient, fifth the patient,
and then maybe comes science.

—*Bela Schick* (1877–1967),
*discoverer of the Schick test
for determining
susceptibility to diphtheria*

JEROME, A PRODUCT OF SMALL COLLEGES IN SAN DIEGO, SAN Francisco, and Seattle, was intimidated when he showed up at Harvard Med for his personal interview, intimidated when he heard Dean Hundert say that it was normal to be intimidated here, and intimidated even more when he started listening to some of his classmates.

"I was a very good undergrad," he said when I first met him a week after Orientation Day, a hint of defensiveness in his voice, "even though I always confused Medicare with Medicaid." He was doing gross lab, struggling through the dissection and to keep his breakfast down, and hoping he wouldn't prove what he heard an instructor say: that if anybody drops out of Harvard Med, it comes during gross because they can't hack it—pun intended.

"Sometimes I do wonder what I'm doing here with students who seem to know much more science than I," he said, "and what kind of a doctor I could possibly be. It's years away, the debts I'm going to have to pay and the kind of medicine I'll practice—all totally, absolutely unknown to me at this moment. I just don't know. I'm thrilled to be here, of course. Who wouldn't be? But I just don't know what it's going to be like or what's going to happen."

Jerome—"short, dark, and round," as he described himself when I telephoned to set up a meeting and asked how I'd recognize him on the steps of building A—majored in medical anthropology and the history of medicine, an admission he had made somewhat apologetically. He chose it, he said, because he wanted something "medical-sounding" if he was going to apply to medical school, and also because he figured it would be less cutthroat than the biology all the regular premeds were taking, and he didn't want to deal with that kind of competition. "An end run into medicine is what I was looking for, I suppose." He also had a minor in Early American literature. "Yeah, I had the basic science requirements. You know, I knew the difference between an amoeba and a paramecium."

All medical students have ready replies about why they want M.D. degrees. They say it is so they can heal, combine a love of science with people interaction, have job security, and get an easier shot at clinical research grants than they would if they just had a Ph.D. But while they may know exactly why they want to be doctors, and have aced their MCATs, they rarely have a clear understanding of what doctoring really entails, or, equally important, of the extreme diversity among doctors.

To most premeds and first-year students, doctors assist Mother Nature and get paid pretty well for that awesome job description; at Harvard Med, students think doctors step in when God runs out of miracles, and that they get reimbursed with Nobels. The exceptionally bright ones figure they're destined for specialty and research greatness, and the average bright believe them and settle for what the brightest feel is less. All of them, unless they have physician fathers or mothers or have had the time and inclination to pay attention to such matters, have but a TV generation's knowledge of the litany of nonscientific aspects of medicine, the socioeconomic bedsores that plague the profession. Few can offer much that is memorable and worth quoting about mounting insurance premiums, profligate and litigious consumers, greedy pharmaceutical companies, misdirected and costly research that has not significantly extended life spans or wiped out disease, lack of universal coverage, the unequal distribution of health services; at this stage in their education, the vast majority are, despite the popular lay perception of medical students as intellectually blessed, fairly limited, or outright one-dimensional. Most here at Harvard Med, unlike Jerome and a handful of others, are science-smart, noninterdisciplinary majors who have crammed and rammed their way through the appropriate premed courses that will buy them the hot ticket. They are liable to have their minds bent upon practical matters, as an eighteenth-century physician once put it, long before they are able to comprehend their rationale. They also know zip about patients.

If Jerome had perceived this about his classmates, as he knew it of himself, it would have improved his self-esteem markedly. He was honest about his limitations. He wasn't really sure what it took to be a doctor—the ones he had had limited contact with did not impress him one way or the other, and he did not know any kindly country doctors he wanted to copy. In fact, his father, a Portuguese immigrant who eked out a living in commercial fishing, mistrusted doctors and hospitals, making the point over and over that they had bankrupted him and that's why they were driving Jaguars, when he couldn't afford a new radio for his dragger. He was also fond of repeating a Portuguese proverb: "If you have a friend who is a physician, send him to the house of your enemy." (Despite such barbs, when Jerome announced he had been accepted at Harvard Med, his dad was proud and congratulated him. But he had to add, "You going to charge me when I need something?")

Given his father's low opinion of the medical profession,

Jerome was also not one of those students who had wanted to be a physician from birth. He started thinking about it only after his junior year in college, while working a summer job as an orderly in a well-equipped community hospital. Never having been hospitalized, one aspect of the place quickly intrigued him. "It was the constant changing, the different faces of patients coming and going, the kinds of emergencies. One day, we had shooting victims from a bank holdup; another day, it was a big fire, and they brought a lot of them in to us. I couldn't get bored, because every day varied. There'd be different people—doctors, nurses, and patients—and different chores." Mostly, he was a transport guy, lifting people onto gurneys and pushing them into the X-ray department, the hyperbaric chamber, ICU, and the OR. But he made friends with technicians and hung around the labs and treatment rooms on his breaks. Sometimes he'd sneak into rooms when patients were dozing and memorize their charts, then speak knowledgeably about their illnesses whenever he got a doctor's or nurse's ear, even though he didn't know what he was talking about. He scanned journals in the hospital library, more to prepare for the medical school interview he was starting to think about than out of any real interest in the subjects he didn't understand. Every so often, after he had wheeled patients into a room after an X ray or some other nonsurgical procedure, he'd lag behind when the nurses left and, if the patients seemed willing, he'd ask questions about their illnesses, their families, their plans. Given that his ideas about medical school were still forming, he admitted that he wasn't exactly sure why he was doing all this. "I thought for a time that a medical degree would help if I decided to make a living studying skull trepanning among the Mesopotamians," he said. "Or maybe I was playing Fantasy Doc, the Pseudo Doc." (This was a role he did play later in his second-year class show at Harvard Med.)

What was becoming clear, however, was not only that he enjoyed the live-patient contact but that he saw the patients—all the patients—were invisible to the visitors who came in to see only one. He had the opportunity to see and talk with many, and he had started looking at them not as isolated citizens but as members of a community, in the sense of a group of people with a common interest living in a special area. The common interest was the desire to get well. He also began to realize that being hospitalized meant giving up something—dignity and privacy. The standard argument he used to hear around the wards was that patients weren't medical authorities and that they usually brought up trivial matters, like rudeness, condescension, overly long waits. Patients complained too much, one nurse had told him—they demand to know exactly when their meals will come, why they can't have pain meds, why the nurses don't have enough time for them. Some of what she said, Jerome reasoned, was valid. But most, he concluded, was not. Patients were right. They are often treated like children, and any sense of self-confidence, self-reliance, and self-respect disappears the moment their clothes are removed from them and hung in a shared closet by the bed or when they have to use a bedpan. He saw them paraded around the corridors, embarrassed, in open johnnies, and wheeled like cripples into the CT suite, where they were run through an assembly line of paperwork and snapped instructions; and he heard many a testy admissions bureaucrat giving them a hard time about their insurance. He saw doctors show up late for appointments or not at all, and those times he remembered something Ollie Holmes said about a colleague of his who always carried two watches, to make sure of keeping appointments. All of it started Jerome thinking about what it was, exactly, that patients wanted, as well as what they should have.

When his time was up in the hospital, he knew something else: The best doctors and nurses not only had a strong scientific foundation and an appreciation of technology but a "mild case of the touchy-feelies." The best doctor he saw used to warm up his stethoscope on a cold day before he placed it on a patient's bare chest. He had also become enamored, from his anthro reading, of traditional forms of health care—acupuncture, moxibustion, leeching, herbal medicine, and the use of the mind to heal the body. The only doctor his father trusted was a chiropractor, and the one time Jerome went to him for a strained back, he had been impressed by the deft and comforting way the man used his hands. He had listened, too, to the chiropractor's careful advice on how to stay healthy, how to bend and lift, how to follow a proper diet, and how to learn to relax. It had all worked for him. They were right, he thought, those ancient Chinese patients who rewarded their doctors as long as they were well and withheld payment when they got sick. So, back in his last year at college, he wrote a senior essay on the ideal physician, with Oliver Wendell Holmes's ability to combine medicine, science, and communication with the patient as the focus, incorporating his own view that the good doctor also does not rule out alternatives or what organized medicine has deemed unacceptable, but combines them with the standard. He wrote of the power of touch:

> It may well be that the non-conventional therapists are more in tune with the total needs of the patient, don't act as superior as doctors, or as hurried, and that they're more apt to use language that patients can understand, more willing to offer them sympathy and patience. Perhaps, too, there's something in their hands, some kind of power that doctors can learn to appreciate and tap into. Not a divine power that heals directly with a hand pressed to a fevered brow. Too many doctors have convinced themselves and their

submissive patients that they had that kind. Rather, the kind that comforts and demonstrates caring through a simple touch, the kind that befriends and inspires confidence and trust with a firm handshake. The ideal doctor must be a person who has learned that he can use his hands as an extension of his compassion.

He also put in this quotation from Holmes: "A man may be much valued by the profession and yet have defects which prevent him from becoming a favorite practitioner. If you cannot acquire and keep the confidence of your patient, it is time to give place to some other practitioner who can. Take down your sign or never put it up. Your estimation of your own ability is not the question, it is what the patient thinks of it."

Jerome applied to eight medical schools. To his great surprise, he was accepted at two, Harvard among them. "That I lucked out," he said, "was amazing. My college and MCAT grades were right up there—I crammed like hell for the physics section with all the published sample questions I could find in the libraries—but I thought to get into this place you needed a golden shoehorn, as well." Unbeknownst to him, he already had one of those shoehorns, and he would pick up another one minutes before his interview on the Quadrangle.

The first showed up one night while he was working in the hospital, in the form of an article in the *Annals of Internal Medicine* on enriching the doctor-patient relationship. Written by a physician-professor at Harvard, Thomas Delbanco, it made the point that doctors and patients were drifting apart and that patients were increasingly questioning physicians' motives and quality of care. The piece had greatly impressed Jerome, and it tied in nicely with his own thoughts about the nature of the ideal physician and what it was that patients wanted. The other golden shoehorn fell into his lap while he was sitting in the lobby of a campus building, waiting to see his interviewer. "I had picked up a newspaper and was browsing through this interminably long article on HMOs and why they're not all what they're cracked up to be. When I went in, the doctor asked me a broad question about my volunteer work, what I enjoyed most about it, and how medicine might change for the better, all the stuff I was ready for. I gave him my impressions of hospital life, how I felt about patients, what they wanted, what the medical profession doesn't give them, what it could give them. I slipped Delbanco's *Annals* report in, figuring that one of their own couldn't hurt. I gave him some Holmes, and Jonathan Edwards and how maybe his being a combination of mystic and logician would be a good role model for doctors, which was a mistake, because I didn't have to be Edwards to see my interviewer's eyes were getting misty. I told him I felt there had to be more emphasis on prevention and diet control, and that alternative medicine, things like meditation and massage and even placebos, had their place not only because patients wanted them but because they'd been shown to work. He seemed to like it, and he told me he agreed with some of the things. Insofar as Delbanco was concerned, he told me that some people around here didn't agree with him on everything, that he was known around campus as 'Terrible Tom, the angry man.' I figured I was going to die, especially since my second interview was bound to be with someone who was one of those 'around campus' guys. Then he asked me what I thought were the most fundamental ethical and existential questions in medical practice, and I thought I was definitely dead. I gave him something loose about euthanasia and AIDS, and tossed in a little Camus, and after I did, I thought I was buried. Then he dropped the big one: 'What do you think about HMOs?' Man, was I psyched or what? I ran with it like Hillary Clinton, and I must have impressed the ass off him, because he said, 'Well, you've certainly done your homework. Delbanco, HMOs, and Camus, too. Not bad.' I wasn't sure whether he was being sarcastic or not. My next interview was with a nervous fourth-year student who told me it was his first time and asked me to please bear with his inexperience. I'm definitely out, I told myself. But he only asked me to talk about my senior thesis and what I thought was the doctor's role. I told him it was to consider the whole patient and his environment and that disease was only a piece of the puzzle they should be trying to put together. He beamed and said, 'Oh, you want to be one of these new biopsychosocial practitioners who figures the patient is someone who has a life that itself may be as life-threatening as a narrowly defined illness?' I said, 'Something like that.' And he smiled again and told me he was sure I was in, because Harvard could use a few oddballs, no offense."

The nickname "Terrible Tom," which has been given to Dr. Thomas Delbanco, an associate professor at Harvard Med and chief of general medicine at Harvard-affiliated Beth Israel Hospital, has nothing to do with how he treats patients, which is admirable. It has something to do with how he views medicine's slowness to make patients partners, and even with how he has treated some of his own colleagues, notably, in his words, in an "infamous study" on iatrogenic deaths at the hospital where he works. *Iatrogenic* is a medical euphemism for anything unfortunate that happens to a patient because of an attitude or action of a physician.

Delbanco's study, the results of which had been suppressed since 1981 and have only recently been published in the *Journal of the American Medical Association,* had found that of 203 deaths from cardiac arrest, 28 were due to treatment errors, 18 of which were labeled as avoidable. The most frequent errors were prescribing the wrong medication, administering incorrect dosages, and failing to recognize harmful side effects. Next in line was failure to act on unusual test results and on additional signs of distress, such as shortness of breath.

"I got into a lot of trouble with that," Delbanco said with a quick-vanish glare. "And no, I'm not an angry man," he added, anticipating the question.

Owning up to errors is difficult enough for ordinary humans, but it is devastating for physicians, to whom death and illness represent defeats comparable to a peasant army destroying a battery of cruise missiles. On the surface of it at least, Beth Israel handled the situation well. As soon as it became aware of the study's findings, procedures were instituted to get test results to doctors more quickly, along with a crash course for staff on preventable errors.

Sensitivity to such issues, which translates into concern for patients, has been a quality of Beth Israel Hospital since its founding by Boston's West End Jewish community during World War I. In those days, Boston's hospitals were generally a Protestant-run lot that dispensed care that didn't always serve the needs of Jewish immigrant patients and that had few Jewish doctors on staff. Jews would check in, often to find a crucifix over their beds, a Waspy doctor who didn't speak even pidgin Yiddish, and bacon for breakfast. A facility was needed that could provide the kind of care that would meet the language, dietary, and psychological needs of Jewish patients, whose numbers were growing steadily with a new wave of immigration from Eastern Europe. The first fund-raising drive was low-key, to say the least. Every home in the West End—where MGH was then putting the finishing touches on its pricey Phillips House, which would feature upper-class care and hotel-class cuisine arrayed on fine china—kept a *pushke,* a small box into which spare change was squirreled. The pennies and nickels, along with miniature bricks sold for fifty cents apiece by a group of mothers who met in the Three and Nine Cent Store in another Jewish neighborhood, spurred a more dynamic drive, which finally built the hospital. There were forty-five beds, twenty-three physicians, kosher food, and a charter, soon to be a model for others in the area, that specifically pronounced a nonsectarian policy that welcomed patients of all racial, ethnic, and religious backgrounds.

The next step was affiliation with a medical school. In the 1920s, Beth Israel hired a New York consultant to assess possible teaching links, expressing the desire to affiliate with Harvard. "Don't even think about it," the consultant told the trustees. Harvard had still not shaken loose from President Lowell's reservations about Jewish students, medical and otherwise, even though its discriminatory quota system was crumbling and more Jews were being admitted. However, largely through the efforts of Harvard Med dean David Edsall, who knew the capabilities of the handful of Jewish physicians in the area, affiliation came in 1928, along with a converted boiler room for BI's first laboratory.

Beth Israel today has five hundred beds, four hundred doctors, five thousand employees and is one of the country's largest recipients of federal research grants. It is also the sort of place where a thornbush like Delbanco belongs, a hospital where criticism is accepted. This is evident in the often-told story of the patient who asks to be transferred to BI from MGH's Phillips House. The admitting doctor asks him, "So, why do you want to come here? Is it the nursing that was lacking over there at Fancy Schmantzy?"

"No, I couldn't complain," says the patient.

"Well, was it the medical care?"

"No, no, I couldn't complain."

"Maybe the food? They stopped the five o'clock martinis?"

"No, I couldn't complain."

"Then why?"

"Here, I can complain."

If Delbanco, a BI physician, could complain about his own

colleagues' behavior, point a finger at their wrong moves, help to straighten things out, and get away with it, then why shouldn't nurses, orderlies, technicians, laundry and kitchen staff, and janitors? They do: As members of participative-management work teams, they offer opinions and solutions to problems ranging from how to stop patients from stealing diapers and rubber gloves, to how to cut the seven-hundred-dollar-an-hour cost of running a CAT scan, to whether there's been an overkill of broccoli on the cafeteria menu.

It is the complaints of patients, however, the people who have been characterized as every hospital's most underused in-house consultants, who have contributed mightily to improving care and staff attitudes, not only at BI, which fosters such a once-unheard-of input and which indeed was founded to make things better for those who had been accustomed to accepting care passively, but at scores of other hospitals here and abroad. An eighty-seven-year-old woman writes to BI's chief executive officer, Dr. Mitchell Rabkin, wondering why a physician introduced himself as Dr. Smith and called her Gertrude. Another complains that she overheard two young doctors talking about a patient's personal problems on an elevator; they didn't identify him, but she knew whom they were talking about, and she knew he would have been mortified at what they were saying publicly. Rabkin prints both complaints in his weekly "Dear Doctor" letter.

Rabkin is another "Preparation H"—Harvard College, magna cum laude in biochem, and Harvard Med, cum laude—who started out in clinical medicine and endocrinological research. A professor of medicine as well as an administrator, he likes students who argue, task forces, lifetime staff commitments, skilled nurses (he pioneered primary-care nursing, and his department of nursing, with a clinical nurse in chief who has the same status as chief physicians, is arguably the best in the world), doctors who care for patients in the humanitarian as well as the technical sense, janitors, and bedpan jockeys.

His first day on the job as president of BI, Rabkin, who sees his hospital as an urban village, walked into the cafeteria and yanked down the curtain that separated the doctors' dining room, with its white tableclothes and other trappings of exclusivity, from that of the plebians. As befits a BI doc, a number of them complained. Rabkin's response, based on his firm belief that everyone in the hospital is involved in interactive patient care, twenty-four hours a day, was, "You feel like eating together, that's okay. Just sit at the same table, that's all." Rabkin has done other things like that. He refused to put in a Phillips House–like luxury suite for the high rollers of health-care consumerism. Instead, he upgraded all the beds to deluxe.

Delbanco has listened to patients, too, and he has surveyed them, collecting and assessing their complaints and their perspectives on medical care. There is a fascinating medical paradox here, and Delbanco spoke of it. "Medicine has been very arrogant," he said, "very self-centered, very conservative in the sense that it's a one-service business. It's probably the last one to go to the customer and say, What do you need? If you think about every service business around, bankers, car makers, and the like, they kind of say, What does the customer want? And then, We'll take care of it. Medicine doesn't do that. It says, We know what the needs are and we'll do it for them."

That seems to be changing, he says. Increasingly, the focus is on bringing the patient into the system—for a calling that, it would seem, was supposed to be devoted to just that, the new awareness is somewhat like suddenly appreciating that a director needs an actor if the show is to get on the road—and this, Delbanco believes, is going to be the salvation of medicine. "If doctors can't get closer to patients and hear the things they want," he said, "we're going to be in bigger trouble than we're in already."

Delbanco begins his own relationship with new patients by asking them if they want to call him by his first name or last. "I strike a bargain that I'll do the same with them; that's the deal I cut. Then I ask them what they want me to be like, and I always get different responses. Some of the best doctors are a little chameleonlike. One patient wants to be told what to do, bang bang, and goes to a businesslike, last-name, white-jacketed doctor who says, Do this, John, and call me if it doesn't work. The next patient wants to be very much in charge of the decision making and gets two or three opinions."

To find out what a broad range of patients wanted from their health-care deliverers, and, not incidentally, to draw closer to them, Delbanco and a team from BI, Harvard Med, and the School of Public Health surveyed some six thousand patients at sixty-two American hospitals. They learned that patients did not focus on prettier waiting rooms, better food, or adequate parking lots. Rather, they were concerned about issues of clinical significance. "They want to be able to trust the competence and efficiency of their caregivers," Delbanco reported. "They want to be able to negotiate the health-care system effectively and to be treated with dignity and respect. Patients want to understand how their sicknesses or treatments will affect their lives, and they often fear that their doctors are not telling them everything they know. Patients worry about and want to learn how to care for themselves away from the clinical setting. They want us to focus on their pain, physical discomfort, and functional disabilities. They want to discuss the effect their illnesses will have on their families, friends, and finances. And they worry about the future."

Funded by the New York–based Picker Foundation and the Commonwealth Fund, which has been based at BI since

1987, the survey turned up a number of specifics that only patients could accurately assess. Among them:

- Nearly half complained that they were not told about the hospital's daily routine.

- Some 20 percent reported that no single doctor was responsible for their care, or that the doctor was unavailable to answer questions.

- A third of those surveyed said they were not informed of important side effects of their medicines.

- A quarter of the respondents felt that no hospital staff went out of their way to meet their needs and said that nurses seemed too busy at times to attend to patient needs.

- A third said they were not told what foods they should eat or what danger signals to watch for when discharged; they complained they did not know when they could resume normal activities, when they could go back to work, and, equally important, what they could do to speed their recovery.

- Nearly a quarter said that their doctors spent less than five minutes with them discussing what to do at home, and more than a third said the nurses also gave short shrift to that aspect of care.

Given the reticence of many physicians to get too close to their patients or give them too much authority—doctors have already objected to Delbanco's study because they feel that asking patients about their hospital experiences might trigger a wave of malpractice suits—it would be a small miracle if the survey touches off the widespread and positive impact that

Delbanco believes it will. When Mitch Rabkin wrote and implemented the nation's first Patients' Bill of Rights in 1972—considered radical then, it covers, among other things, the right to privacy, to receive all necessary information, and to be treated with respect without undue familiarity—a physician came into his office, angrily shaking a copy of it. "This'll bring every nuthatch out of the woodwork," he shouted. It's also common knowledge among doctors that when patients bring formal complaints to state medical boards for what they perceive to be bad treatment, the grievances result in far fewer disciplinary actions than when hospitals or other doctors blow the whistle.

Delbanco has this vision of the future of medicine, one that makes more efficient use of a doctor's time and yet helps narrow the gap between the practitioner and the patient. "You'll come into my office having done a lot of work beforehand. You will have interacted with your TV set at home, discussing the issues you want to discuss with me, and you'll come in with a medical history that you've written. We'll be able to focus on what's bugging you, and you'll go home with a transcript that we've gone over together. Even now, when I see patients, I type notes with them. I write, 'John says he wants to lose weight, but I don't believe it.' Then I hand it to him and ask him what he thinks and whether I ought to leave it that way, change it, or what. Then we write it again together, and I send him home with the note.

"As you leave, there'll be a set of questions—for example, 'Did Delbanco answer your questions properly?' We're going to get instant feedback from you, and we're going to expect you to do a lot more work as a patient with us."

At the end of his second year, Jerome was no longer trembling at his classmates' imperious behavior. He was paraphrasing Harry Truman's remark when he first got to Congress. "When

I first came to Harvard Med, I looked around and wondered how I ever got in here. In my third year, I started to say, How the fuck did they get here, on Amtrack? A few faculty included."

Much of what gave him confidence was the self-directed learning environment offered by the New Pathway. He liked the way it wove the basic science into the clinical, and the faculty seemed to bend over backward to see that a nonscience major got through it all. "I saw very quickly that they wanted us to pass—wouldn't look good to flunk the chosen, right?—and there was a lot of individual structuring. For example, I stayed out of labs as much as I could, but in them we worked in small groups, and there were plenty of instructors who would come back in at night if you needed a review session."

Jerome did best, as he figured he would, in core courses that dealt with psychosomatic mechanisms in physical disorders; culture, illness, and healing; preventive medicine and nutrition; and social factors in health status. Unlike many of his classmates and most faculty, he kept his mind open to alternative therapies and exhausted the literature, quack and professional. There were a few kindred spirits, and one course that interested him. It was a new, month-long elective called Nonconventional, Unorthodox Medical Techniques: Implications for Clinical Practice and Research. The teacher was Dr. David Eisenberg of Beth Israel Hospital. He had published a 1993 study in the *New England Journal of Medicine* estimating that Americans—mostly well-educated, middle-income whites from twenty-five to fifty years old—spend $13.7 billion a year on alternative therapies but rarely inform their doctors.

From fifteen hundred telephone interviews, Eisenberg and his colleagues concluded that in 1990, 61 million Americans used therapies that included diet, massage, relaxation, chiropractic, acupuncture, spiritual healing, herbal medicine, and homeopathy. Moreover, those who visited therapists returned to them an average of nineteen times in a year—which translated into 425 million visits—more than the number of visits patients make to internists, general practitioners, and pediatricians combined. Patients wanted alternative therapy, it seemed, most often for chronic conditions that resist conventional therapy—back pain, insomnia, headaches, anxiety, and depression. Eisenberg also studied Chinese medicine and other alternative therapies at Beijing Institute of Traditional Chinese Medicine and served as an adviser to a newly created NIH office for the study of unconventional medical practices. This office has conducted clinical and basic science studies of the safety, efficacy, and cost-effectiveness of the alternatives; it also directs Harvard Med's exchange program with Peking Union Medical College and the Chinese Academy of Medical Sciences, both of which are not quite ready to drop some three thousand years of emphasis on the influences of the cosmic forces, the negative yin and the positive yang, on health and disease, and whose practitioners still take pulses at the "heavenly spot," the "earthly spot," and the "human spot."

To his credit, Eisenberg feels that more scientific studies are needed not just on whether but also on how the various unconventionals work. "It is conceivable," he says, "that physical manipulation, or acupuncture needles, or active ingredients in particular remedies are in fact physiological. But if for certain patients, in certain instances, faith or belief can cause changes in physiological function in a reproducible way, then we have to bring together the best scientists from a variety of disciplines, including the neurosciences, psychiatry, endocrinology, and physiology, and ask them to figure out why. That's an area for a very provocative search, and I think ultimately that's where this field will be going in the next decade."[1]

Inspired, Jerome became his class's resident authority on everything out of the mainstream, from acupuncture to zoopsia. The science dweebs were now coming to him for guidance when considering anything offbeat (typical question: "Is this bullshit or angel droppings?"), as he had gone to them. Someone started calling him Saint Jerome, after the third-century Doctor of the Church, the patron of librarians. In his third year, he studied Herb Benson's work with the relaxation response, learned how to teach it to patients, and, in a course called Caring for the Caregiver, how to apply it to his own stresses. Benson is the associate professor of medicine who founded the Mind-Body Institute at Harvard-affiliated Deaconess Hospital. A fervent promoter of meditation, repetition of words and repetitive muscular activity to break the chain of everyday thought, his technique aims to induce a physiological state of decreased blood pressure, heart rate, respiration, and metabolism, as well as slower brain waves. In a bygone generation, Benson—who is the first incumbent of the Mind-Body Medical Institute Chair in Behavioral Medicine, the first in the field of behavioral medicine—and Eisenberg would not only have been assaulted with withering looks of donnish faculty scorn but sure as hell sent packing after their Harvard chairs and labs were torched. Jerome was in synch with Benson. He learned about Benson's goose in the bottle. As Benson explains it, "Imagine a goose in a bottle, a big, fat, live goose with a long neck. The trick is to get the goose out without breaking the bottle and without injuring the goose. Tough? Well, it's simple. How did the goose get in the bottle? I told you to imagine it there. So, okay, imagine it out. How many geese are you carrying around with you? This person doesn't like me. That person is going to do me in. I'll never be able to do that exam. The overriding concerns of medical students are that they don't have enough time and that the competition is fierce, and in this school they're thrown in with people as bright as they are, probably for the first time in their lives. All of these concerns are conjured up in their heads. I tell them, if you put them there, you can get them out."

Jerome was at MIT when Benson brought in the Dalai Lama to give the keynote address at a symposium designed to explore the union of Eastern spiritualism and modern medicine, a meeting that caused not a few of Harvard Med's hard-science clinicians to pass the Compazine around at a couple of faculty meetings. Held at MIT, safely across the Charles River in Cambridge, and not, good God forbid, on the sacred green swath of the Great White Quadrangle itself, the meeting would legitimize the views of those who wanted the opportunity to blend the behavioral sciences into medicine, prevention, and health.

So here he was now, the Dalai Lama, recognized as the reincarnation of his predecessor when he was but two years old—a succession not, needless to say, recognized by Harvard Med's geneticists—droning on mystically before a rapt audience of twelve hundred general practitioners, psychiatrists, neurobiologists, nurses, social workers, religious leaders, and a few Jeromes about the link between mind and body and how that ties in with the Buddhist concept of emptiness, which is the ultimate nature of reality and into which the individual must peer if he or she is to become more flexible and open to possibilities. He talked about the importance of meditation in gaining insight into the ultimate reality, how meditation helps one attain the "clear light of mind," that separation of the mind from bodily influences that takes a person beyond anger, envy, and fear. Even so, he went on, as Jerome listened, rapt, Buddhists are aware of the inextricable link between mind and body, between the state of the mind and physiological processes, and it is because of just that that meditation has such a powerful effect. The panelists were not about to be upstaged by such good stuff. They raised heady questions: How can the mind effectively study the mind? In what context do Buddhist teachings deal with addiction to crack cocaine? How is karma related to the mathematical principles that govern the natural world? Definitely not the sort of questions that Jerry Foster and his cohort of interviewers would ever dare raise—if they ever even thought about such things—when grilling already-nervous candidates for admission. Sitting in front of Jerome was an elderly gent in a gray vest and a black-and-green-plaid bow tie. "What the hell," he groaned softly, exasperated at the physician who had organized this, "is that madman Benson up to now? Next thing we'll have around here is the materialization of Mary Baker Eddy."

For Jerome, the symposium was more than a simple connection between mind and body. "It was an appendage," he said, "a third leg." That was another Bensonism. "Medicine is a three-legged stool," he says. "One leg is pharmaceuticals, the other is surgery, and the third is what people can do for themselves. Mind-body work is an essential part of that, along with nutrition, exercise, and how to change your way of thinking. Is the glass half empty or half full?"

Jerome sought extra credit for an independent research project on the benefits of chiropractic, but scrapped it, along with another suggestion into how the physician writers Holmes, Chekhov, Maugham, and William Carlos Williams portrayed their fellow doctors, after an adviser told him, "Ahem, N.E.H.M. Not exactly Harvard Material. Get a little more . . . sciencey?" Jerome settled for kidney disorders in uranium miners.

But it was on the wards in his third year that Jerome was happiest. He even liked something that Mitch Rabkin did to him and a few other students on one rotation. In an effort to teach a new way of interacting, Rabkin ordered that Harvard Med students, whom nobody in the hospital knew, dress in a varied wardrobe of uniforms—housekeeping, laundry, maintenance—and be made to spend two or three days a week with service personnel so they could see the hospital as they did, as well as how others treated them. "What really horrified the students," Rabkin said, "was that they didn't realize how many so-called professional people treat these individuals as nonpersons. They'd never been in an environment where they were treated that way. It's a very compelling experience. They come to realize something a lot of doctors don't, and that is, if your first experience as a medical student is with a white coat and stethoscope, you fail to realize that life goes on in some very important ways when you're not here."[2]

Dressed as a maintenance man, Jerome met up with the best and the worst of physicians and nurses. "One guy, a cardiologist, actually called me in to change a lightbulb in the OR, when there was a box of overheads and a stepladder in the corner, and all he had to do was climb up and screw. I don't know what possessed me, but at the risk of blowing my cover, I asked him if he had arthritis in his arms. He said, 'Pal, you've got your job to do, and I've got mine.' "

In the hospitals, Jerome gravitated toward anything he could handle with diet, exercise, and meditation. "This guy thinks that even rusty ratchet nuts will improve with deep breathing and push-ups," said a classmate. Mindful of Delbanco's finding that a lot of patients complained about doctors who didn't tell them what they should eat or what kind of self-care they should be following at home, he incorporated such advice in as many of his patient contacts as he could. And he was distressed to learn that it didn't always produce the desired results. One night, he sat with an obese woman who had just had her gallbladder removed. She wasn't sure what she should eat when she got home.

"What did your surgeon tell you?" Jerome asked.

"He said I just had to try things. If they bothered me, don't eat them."

"Didn't he tell you to start eating gradually? I mean, you're not going to go and pig out on a pint of ice cream, are you?" Jerome recalled that he was weighing her mentally, and he came up with around 210.

"Pint?" she mocked. "Say quart, which I was doing a day."

"Not good," he said. "Not only for the recovery, which takes about two months, but for everything else that makes you tick. Did he tell you that being overweight might have been a factor in why you developed the stones?"

"No. When I asked him, he said it probably runs in my family, or something to do with the kind of food I eat. And yes, gallstones do run in my family."

"Well," Jerome said, "I don't doubt that. Any other members of your family overweight?"

She giggled. "All of us are big people—my mother, father, and one of two sisters."

"They had gallstones, did they?"

"My mother and one sister and an aunt did."

"Any heart problems?"

"My dad, my mother, and my aunt. Mom and Dad died in their sixties. My aunt had a heart attack, but she's okay."

"Okay," Jerome said, "this is what I'd suggest. You've had one problem that may have something to do with your overweight, one of your parents had a problem that may have had something to do with overweight, and the other had two problems that most likely had something to do with that. Now, the way I see it, we've taken care of one of yours. Now it's up to you to take care you don't get another, especially if it runs in the family, like heart trouble. I suggest you start by holding off on the ice cream for at least two months. It takes that long for your digestion to get back to normal. After that, maybe you should try to cut back on it, try working on the weight. This is serious stuff, not funny. And watch the fatty meats. It'll help your heart. Because we can't take that out as easily as your gallbladder, can we?"

She gave him what Jerome called a look, then thanked him. The next day, he ran into her surgeon. "Hey, swami," he said sharply. "I hear you're into doing social service and diet workshop on a surgical rotation, telling my patients they shouldn't eat ice cream and meat after a cholecystectomy. Didn't they inform you here that there are no dietary restrictions postop and that it doesn't cause any nutritional difficulties?" Jerome said he was aware of that but that he also thought his advice on moderation and fat intake was appropriate, if only because of the family history of heart disease. He was about to add that in his preventive-medicine class he'd been taught and encouraged to counsel patients on behavior change when obvious, but he swallowed it. "Look," the surgeon said, both hands flailing the air, "next time, you check with me first before you talk to somebody I've cut. You probably scared the shit out of her, and as we speak she's home dialing my office for an appointment for a dietary consult and a referral to the Framingham Heart Study and Oprah Winfrey. She comes in for the consult, and my secretary asks her for the cash up front because her insurance doesn't cover a half hour of bullshitting that she can read in the health section of any women's magazine. My insurance company is telling me, Cut the shit, Doc. You know, unless you're a medical student, that gallbladder surgery doesn't result in any dietary or nutritional problems. Tell her to spend a couple bucks and read last month's issue of *Glamour*. You know what I'm saying?"

Jerome felt like telling him, "My dad was right—I'd like to send you to my enemy," but he knew the cutter had a point. "He didn't have the time to diddle around with counseling. And, even if he did, he'd have to send Mother Teresa over to Blue Cross to collect, and they'd tell her not to slam the door on the way out. They'd tell her it takes technical skill to pull out a gallbladder and that's what they're willing to pay for, not commonsense advice. And that sucks."

Immersed in his fourth year, he saw other things that he thought sucked. He learned that doing good sometimes meant having to do bad. He knew of physicians who prescribed treatment for a covered condition that didn't have to be treated, just because the flulike symptoms the patient came in for weren't covered (the doctors called this, "Buy one, get one free"); or doctors who cut flat-fee deals with the elderly if they could pay up front and forget the Medicare with its 15 percent cap over what Uncle Sugar was willing to pay. If market forces weren't mucking up the system, the patients themselves, unfortunately, sometimes were. This came as a shock to Jerome, who still believed that what the patients wanted was usually right-on. One time, at MGH, learning how to evaluate and prevent workplace disability, he met a patient who wanted plenty of the former and already knew enough about the latter apparently to have stuck his hand under a drill press accidentally on purpose. Jerome was unaware of that fact and was asking the man whether his company had employee classes on safety. "Look, kid, like they say in Vegas, all's I need from you is some numbers," the patient told him, dangling bandaged fingers in the student's face. "Like, how many weeks can I collect?"

When I last saw him—on his way to a residency in internal medicine and kidding about opening up "the Psyche-Soma Clinical Nutrition Center, where the opening question for a patient would be, 'So, how's the family?' instead of 'Where's the pain?' "—Jerome was still "Steady Eddie, the Harvard Meddie," a fervent believer that disease prevention was largely a matter of education and behavior change and that what patients wanted, needed, and should have should predominate. "Generally," he added with a smile. "I'm into qualifiers now that I'm finishing fourth year." But, perhaps because of the encounter with the gallbladder surgeon, perhaps only because he was close to becoming a real doctor, he was worrying more about his future and had become more preachy. "I'm starting to fear now that the system isn't going to change drastically—and I don't care how it changes so much as that it changes to make room for comprehensive care that includes the stuff I'm interested in—and that it'll be a long time before someone starts paying a little more for a doctor's time. I'm hoping, but not very optimistic. All I know is that if it doesn't change, the patient's right to participate in his or her care is going to be compromised. And that should be the bottom line—the patient. This HMO and managed-care debate? It used to be confusing to me, but then it hit me what the opposition was all about. The critics, physicians, tell you it detracts from the patient-doctor relationship because it's too impersonal, limits patients' choices of a doctor, and means inferior care. That makes it sound like they're concerned about the patient. But what it really is is money. Managed care means the specialists and surgeons are going to take a financial hit, while the primary-care guys are going to make a pretty decent living for the first time.

"If you press me, I'll say that some HMOs are good and some stink. If you ask me, I'll say that I believe solo practice as we've known it is dead. Medicine has become too complicated. It relies a lot more now than ever before on technology, and that can be good, but the way I see it, it's also very bad. No, I'm not a Luddite. Close, though. I don't think anybody can survive alone out there unless they're the only doctor for a hundred miles around. And even then, he's going to need some backup, he's going to get overworked, stressed out, and he's eventually going to get a bunch of other docs together to share the rent and the equipment, and whoa, here comes managed care, an HMO, a clinic, a health-care center. I'll give you my opinion that a good HMO and these other systems where docs join a group and charge less are as personal as private practice, maybe more, because the patients belong to this little community that has a wide range of generalists and specialists who do know them and can give them what they need and who are willing to make less money. These solo guys make me laugh sometimes when they talk about the demise of personal care. It's as if they're conducting a social hour every time they see a patient, and we know goddamned well that nobody is paying for that kind of soiree. I kinda like the idea of a salary. I may not be able to buy the Jag, but I'll sure as hell have enough left over to buy my dad his new radio. You've got to ask yourself how much money is enough.

"I'll tell you one thing, I ain't graduating High Honors with my background. Last week, one of my would-be role models had the balls to tell me that I was great with people but should be working a lot more on my technical skills. 'All oil and no wheels is career stasis,' he said."

In Henry Jacob Bigelow's inner consulting room there was, along with a showy oriole who cavorted in and out of his sleeve and forty caged Japanese sparrows, an elegant mynah bird he had patiently taught to speak. The mynah could pronounce Bigelow's name with a range of inflections and whistle a variety of airs. One day, a Boston dowager entered Bigelow's outer offices and heard a crackly voice from within ask, "What's your name?" Outraged that she hadn't been greeted at the door by Bigelow, and assuming that the voice was his, she replied icily, "You had better come and see if you want to know!"

Bigelow was fond of his mynah, as he was of the ant colonies that he safeguarded in shallow glass-topped boxes; his pampered pigeons, which took the gold medal at every show in England; his collection of well-groomed monkeys; the domesticated family of terns he fed supper to each night on his piazza; and his horses, which he chloroformed when they reached old age rather than order them sold. A vocal opponent of vivisection, he protested regularly against cruelty to animals. "The instincts of our common humanity," he said, "indignantly remonstrate against the testing of clumsy or unimportant hypotheses by prodigal experimentation, or making the torture of animals an exhibition to enlarge a medical school, or for the entertainment of students, not one in fifty of whom can turn it to profitable account."[3]

Bigelow was also fond of his patients, whom he could read, as one of his colleagues said, as a scholar reads books. He knew quite well what they wanted. And he had both the oil and the wheels. Lordly and obstinate though he may have been with his peers, he was keenly aware—these were not the times of frantic specialists working on volume—that a visit to a doctor's office was often only a social one, the sort of "soiree" that Jerome rightfully suggested cannot happen today. Bigelow knew how to make each encounter agreeable. Suffering painfully long narratives from talky patients, he listened intently. One time, a longtime patient sent for him to discuss a trivial problem. Bigelow sat quietly, allowing her to go on without interruption for nearly an hour. "Well," he said when she had finished, "as near as I can gather, the position of things is this. You have sent for me in order to tell me that you had thought of sending for Dr. A. to ask him whether you had better send for Dr. B., but that upon consideration you have decided to take a remedy which Dr. C. prescribed for Miss D. for a different disease."[4]

If, after hearing the story, a Harvard Med student failed to grasp the message of practicing patience, he would most likely have it driven home in one of Bigelow's celebrated lectures on bedside manners. Learn to listen patiently, he would advise, "to sympathize, and to re-establish a facility in the manifestation of that tenderness which is generally upon the surface in early youth, but which sometimes gets embedded beneath a stratum of indifference and insensitivity."[5]

Bigelow was, perhaps, the epitome of what he called the "practising doctor," not only a skilled surgeon but a physician who would routinely camp out in a patient's home when he thought it necessary. "The first duty of a physician," he once said, "is to his patient, who has a right to expect that his disease shall be thoroughly investigated and skilfully treated, with charitable consideration for his mental peculiarities or infirmities." Once, he sat uncomfortably on the floor through an entire night, his finger compressing a bleeding abdominal artery to avert a fatal hemorrhage.

Bigelow also had a legendary distaste for something that his colleagues and their descendants could never appreciate: making money out of medicine. He rarely received large surgical fees; his bookkeeping was primitive; his bills, when he chose to send them, were mailed late. He became annoyed when a patient sent goods in lieu of fees, more so if they came from merchants seeking an endorsement of some allegedly medicinal product. "Do not send me any more wine!" he wrote to one fawning dealer. "We have a code of medical ethics here, which I wrote myself, prohibiting any medical man from publicly puffing any such thing—whether mineral waters, patents, medical preparations or the like—and so lending their aid in public advertisements to weaken the distinct line between the regular practice of medicine and the practice of quackery. . . . Besides, at the price you affix to some of this wine the obligation incurred by the present of a box of it does not leave one free to do otherwise than speak civilly of it."[6]

Early in his career, Bigelow established a "Charitable Surgical Institution" in a church basement. Here he offered patients advice, consultations, vaccines for referring physicians, and operations—all for free. Some of Bigelow's colleagues were unimpressed. One of them printed up a rather nasty circular, which was distributed to practitioners.

"We are prepared," the flyer proclaimed, "on receiving

from a country physician a carefully written account of any case, to send gratuitously our opinions, with medicines and a coffin; and that our facilities for giving an accurate diagnosis may be appreciated, we are happy to add that we have recently obtained a stethoscope of six thousand ordinary stethoscope power, by which means cerebral auscultation can be practised at a great distance, and many things heard which do not in reality exist." It was signed, "Festinans Bigblow, equal to two Surgeons, and Mr. Externus, recently from abroad."[7] The unorthodox, in medicine as well as in other endeavors, has always prompted criticism and suspicion, even when it does good.

Epilogue

It is all over at last for yet another Harvard Med class. The Great White Quadrangle is June-resplendent. The grass is lush and green, and the breeze-blown Hippocratic plane tree bows reverently as the happy graduates parade by to take their seats under a bright yellow-and-white-striped tent; there are crimson banners and gowned faculty; parents, standing on collapsible chairs, watch, necks straining and cameras cocked. Everybody is smiling: the students uncontrollably, because they've finally finished twentieth grade and because close to 80 percent of them have been accepted for training at their first-choice hospital; faculty smugly, because, as one observes, "Let's admit it up front, these kids are stars"; the chiefs at Children's Hospital grimly, because their former head of cardiology is on the verge of being indicted for stealing a quarter of a million dollars from group practices at the hospital; and the dean, Tosteson, jubilantly, because he's just received the largest gift ever in the school's history, $60 million for the study of neurobiology.

There are speakers. Tosteson, summoning up Variation Number 9, to the students: "I call on you to develop a profound and proud humility which will strengthen your work as physicians and scholars." Tosteson to the parents: "Let me say thank you for shaping the imaginative minds of our students. You have made a major contribution to the health of the people on this planet." Columnist to the lovelorn, Ann Landers, who has some amorphous connection to the school: "Patients want competence, compassion, and above all, time." Marian Wright Edelman, president of the Children's Defense Fund, exhorting, "We must maintain our capacity to give hope and make it a part of the treatment." The year before, it had been Donna Shalala, U.S. Secretary of Health and Human Services, who said with a stroking tone, "You are among the most powerful men and women in the world. You have the power to help people every day." And the year before that, a few months before he died of AIDS, Arthur Ashe, the Wimbledon and U.S. Open tennis champion, putting it a bit more candidly: "You are supposedly the most well-trained new physicians extant. If you're not, and for what you paid for tuition here, you certainly should be."

The oath is administered and taken. In years past, those of Hippocrates, Maimonides, and the Declaration of Geneva bound the grads. They swore by Apollo Physician, by Asclepius, by Hygieia, by Panacea, and by all the gods and goddesses to make house calls, to share their substance, and to supply necessities and teaching without fee or covenant. But today, gods are the embarrassing, irrelevant, and shadowy stuff of mythic lore; they have been replaced by other patrons of the medical arts, NIH and NSF, Medicare, Medicaid, and, perhaps, a new federal MacSomething.

This year, the class oath is a combination of the old standards (with snippets from one written by the class of 1991), written by three class members who felt a need to offer a pledge that reflected their vision of what a doctor should be in today's world. It says, in part:

> Now being admitted to the profession of medicine . . .
> I pledge myself to the service of humanity. I recognize
> my obligation to serve my patients, my community
> and my profession.
>   I will use my skills to serve all in need, with open-
> ness of spirit and without bias. The health and well-
> being of my patients will be my first consideration. . . .

I will not subordinate the dignity of any person to scientific or political ends. I recognize that I have responsibilities to my community: to promote its welfare and to speak out against injustice. The high regard of my profession is born of society's trust in its practitioners; I will strive to merit that trust.

They are serious. And they may actually believe that their experiences in classrooms and clinics and hospitals allow them to boast that they have seen life and have prepared them to take on any challenge. But it is not over till it's over. They are the successors of a long line of Harvard Med physicians and scientists, but the art of medicine is not inherited, and they will have to put their pledges and promises on hold. "In a few short weeks," says graduate Robert Vonderheide, "probably around three or four a.m. because that's when these things happen, we might be handed a jagged, irregular cardiac rhythm strip and be so addressed: 'Doctor, Doctor? What do you want to do?' First, denial: 'What arrhythmia?' Then, anger: 'Why am I the last to know?' Guilt: 'I should have paid attention in medical school.' Bargaining: 'What would you do in this case?' Finally, acceptance: 'I'll call the junior resident.' "[1]

Eventually, when their residencies are over and the thirty thousand dollars a year they were paid is finally increased, most of the ones who have opted for practice instead of attempting to pick apart the short arm of the Y chromosome or steer a gene into a retrovirus will curse that even if they did swear by Apollo, he was out cruising in his chariot when they came up with socioeconomic forces, malpractice insurance, mountains of insurance forms, and meddling ombudsmen who advocate patients' rights. The practitioners will also not work unobtrusively in the silence of instinct and intuition, but amid the costly, overamplified humming, ticking, whirring sounds of hands-off technology; the places where they work will be troves for Rube Goldberg, housing everything from high-performance, special-purpose biomedical recorders to three-stage alarms that compensate for intermittent breathing patterns, not to mention the refractometers, photometers, monochromators, and viscometers.

They will soon be overwhelmed, these former oath-takers, by data from their machinery and tests. Many will confuse technical values with human ones, and in so doing they will miss vital information the computers, the bloods, the creatinines, and the spinal taps cannot supply. Some will telephone-consult, sheepishly charge for it, and that will suffice for patient interaction. Coolly professional and emotionally distanced, these new doctors will try desperately to live up to their oath, but many will struggle to cure without comforting, rationalizing that competence cannot be sacrificed for concern; in so doing, they will fail more often than not, for many have not yet grasped the impact of fear and other stresses on human ills, or the fact that medicine is based on sympathy, or that "headaches in living" have driven an overwhelming number of patients to their offices.

The students continue to speak, and, because it is Commencement Day, without sounding a sour note to mar the festivities. They say:

"Today, all the power and prestige of the Harvard Medical School comes together to issue diplomas that call us doctors."

"Coming from a developing country, I am interested in how to provide the best possible care to the largest number of people at a reasonable cost."

"Most of the patients are waiting for us, not to be heroes, but to be there with them. Being there is the first duty of a doctor."

Mitch Rabkin, however, bravely shares his worries about the future. It probably falls on deaf ears on such a day as this. "Years ago," he says, "when I was in private practice, one of my patients was my great-uncle. At the end of each session, he would reach into his pocket and put two one-dollar bills on my desk. 'Uncle,' I would say, 'please, I don't want your money.' 'Mitchell,' he would reply, 'relatives is relatives, but business is business.' I am concerned whether we are being drawn into a vortex where 'ethics is ethics, but business is business.' If that occurs, where will be the excellence of Harvard Medical School tomorrow?"

As he speaks, a few of the students' eyes glaze over. They know where the excellence will be. These are the uppercase Doctors, who will lapse into the genetic code they will send to their fellow uppercases via their journals, all of it mystifying to the patients they study and to the doctors of the lowercase. In the Doctors' reveries are grants, Nobels, and General Motors Cancer of the Year awards, not wreaths fashioned from the leaves of Hippocratic plane trees; and the best way to publish first, short of, but not necessarily ruled out, pouring Karo into their rivals' lab cultures.

The rest of the graduates have no such dreams, because the entire workaday medical system they are plunging into is under a klieg light and needs a prescription, generic if possible. It is being written by experts even as the graduates file out to their residencies, but nobody can read the handwriting or understand the formulations because the experts are from Byzantium. They are economists and politicians, insurance writers and drug makers, academics and doctorologists. None has ever been hospitalized or has had to pay for their own insurance. They speak to themselves of alternative dispute-resolution tribunals, insurance-purchasing alliances, the consumer price index, plus population growth and 1.5 percent, which is the formula for keeping the premiums down and the quality of care high. They do not doubt the thinking power of humans, but they prefer computers, which know what is best and can come up with the answers without missing a byte. The computers do multiphasic health testing. They gather many megas of data, then rearrange, correlate, and evaluate. They diagnose, prognose, dose, and overdose.

The festivities are winding down. The students doff their caps, put their concerns on hold, and gleefully fling inflated rubber gloves and a condom or two to the wind. They fall into the arms of family and friends as starry-eyed as they were on Orientation Day.

When Michael T. Myers, B.A., General Honors, Johns Hopkins University, African-American, tall, lean, and green, graduated from Harvard Med not so long ago, he was, as he said, filled with egalitarian notions of helping to save the world. "I became the embodiment of my medical school application essay, spewing forth all sorts of wonderful reasons why doctors had to take their services to the streets, so to speak. I was Dr. Quixote."

He had $85,000 in loans to pay back (his wife had another $65,000) and an idea that his Harvard mentors had tried to shoot down: a decision to go into general internal medicine and start up a solo practice in an underserved working-class part of Boston, Dorchester, where not many doctors visit, let alone live, as Myers did. In a "savior mode," he convinced a neighborhood bank to loan him $160,000, which, when added to his other indebtedness, would force him to make hemorrhagic payments of better than $5,000 a month.

He hung his Harvard degree and a collection of impressive prints on an office wall in an old brick building, put in fancy fixtures and soft chairs, and waited for patients. They didn't break down his doors. So he hustled. To make ends meet and to drum up some referral patient trade, he put in three shifts a week, six to midnight or seven at night to seven in the morning, in the Carney Hospital emergency room. He brought his mother in from Kansas City to help with his new baby, be his secretary, and come up with marketing ideas like printing up purple handbills, which they passed out shamelessly to commuters at the nearby T station. He took out ads, mailed out patient guides, wrote newspaper articles, and did free cholesterol screening. Sometimes, his mother pushed the envelope, dispensing homespun medical advice over the phone. His colleagues at Carney nominated him for the American Hospital Association's "Physician Marketer of the Year Award." But between the two of them, they picked up twenty-five or so patients, and in two years the load was jacked to two thousand.

Buoyed, Myers gave himself a nominal salary of $18,000 a year, a pittance compared with what his classmates were making or going to make. But revenues were unpredictable, the forms and codes of the 257 insurers he was dealing with overwhelming. A typical scenario went like this. Chain-smoking, obese patient comes in, LDL cholesterol of 173, a time bomb. Myers spends an hour with him taking blood, doing an EKG, counseling, and setting up stress tests at the hospital. The fee is $115. He bills, and three months later, he gets a check for $18.56. Appalled, he resubmits. Another check shows up, this time for $27.02, with a note explaining that this is the final, full payment.

Broke and with his blood pressure hovering around 134 over 90, Myers looked for some moonlighting less stressful than the Carney ER. He signed up for a four-month hitch at the hospital as a day intern, a doctor who fills uncovered slots as a daytime freelancer. It was a throwback to his days of beeper madness and endless questions from families and staff. He was doing better financially, $27,000 a year, but his bank had folded, the FDIC had a firm grip on his loans, and the IRS was auditing him for back taxes. Moreover, his pride was battered. "Here I was, an attending physician, a Harvard great, reduced to the ashes of inserting Foley catheters and disimpacting elderly nursing home residents once again."

Exhausted and frustrated, Myers gave up. For prospective private practitioners, he had these curt parting words, "You can have it."

I meet Mike Myers in the pleasant atmosphere of the well-appointed MIT Medical Department, where he is now a full-time, salaried internist, and loving every minute of it. Walking leisurely across the street to a cafeteria, we are stopped at least three times by passersby—students, faculty, and staff—who know him either as patients or colleagues. The counterman greets him. Over a deli sandwich, several students stop by to chat.

"You see this?" he says happily. "I feel as though I'm a village doctor."

It was what he wanted while he was a student. "Being on the trail of a 'good' case, exploring a variety of diagnostic possibilities with lab tests and X rays, the real stimulation of morning reports and work rounds, seeing patients' appreciative faces when they are discharged from the hospital, being seen as the patient's doctor—these were the images I had when I first thought about medicine in my early years."

Back in his office, he is critical not only of the current system that has focused too much on insurance and not enough on access and the unfairness in the availability of health care but also of the way Harvard Med students see the practice of medicine.

"They won't say to you that they want to be radiologists because of the dough. They'll say they want to do something where they can learn everything about one subject. That's bull-shit. Just look at the definitive textbook on gastroenterology. It's ten volumes! There is no area of medicine today where you can understand every scientific aspect of a specialty. Being a doctor is not that. It's making decisions; it's being a counselor, an advocate. It's not being an encyclopedia or some walking computer that spits it all out. But that's how students are taught on rounds, how we breed them at Harvard. It's no wonder that they come out choosing a specialty, wanting to become a superdoc. That's bullshit, too.

"On the other hand, they'll also say they want to be a general-care doc because they can't learn it all. Well, to them I say, I can't learn it all, either. I don't know it all, either. Every single day, there's something new I have to look up, or call someone about. That's the wonder and beauty of being a physician."

That there are no blood tests to order for his patients is a welcome change for Brent Forester, who has made the switch from internal medicine to psychiatry, something he had wanted to do since his MGH days because of his interest in really taking the time to talk with patients. There are other concerns, though, now that he is a resident at McLean Hospital, where he has found his new experience an unexpectedly difficult transition and, though fascinating, not without its disappointments.

"One of the problems I foresee for the future," he says, "is that because of this emphasis on managed care and the limited time we can spend with a patient, instead of the traditional psychotherapy, where you'd have an hour a week with a patient, we're getting paid to prescribe medicine. That became evident to me very quickly. I came into it thinking I would spend more time with my patients than I did, and you do, but you're sort of like a medical doctor for the medical illness."

To Brent, medicine in general seems to be in complete chaos. Everything has shifted around. There are budget cuts, psychiatrists fired. He wonders, Is there going to be a job for me when my residency is over? What will I be doing if there is? His mentors are being told what to do. It's a very uncertain time.

Still, he tries to keep his focus. "When you're a student, you have a lot of idealism, you want to help, but you lose it in the middle of your training, and you're taking care of too many patients with too little time to know your worth. Now, in my residency, I'm beginning to see that whatever I do, it really does help people, and that it's possible to remember why we went into this in the first place. But the hardest thing is to hold on to that."

Shawn Nasseri has decided to go into ENT—ear, nose, and throat—not primary care. Money is not the reason he chose a specialty. It is, however, a factor, a fleeting thought sometimes, sometimes a gnawing one. Distancing himself from such thoughts, he switches to the second and third person, as he does on occasion when he's giving me his take on a topic of concern.

"As you get older in your training, people talk about money and perks and good things and how people respect you. But that begins to seem so superficial. This is not why you went into medicine. Anyway, with the new health-care reforms that'll probably occur over the next twenty years, there's just not going to be the kind of money that's been around the last decade. Still, they like power, prestige, how you're going to be appreciated by your colleagues. So it is an issue in terms of loans and picking specialties. It's well known that people will go into surgery instead of pediatrics to make this much more money, and if you've got one hundred thousand dollars in loans it becomes a . . . selection . . . especially if your friends are driving Saabs and Mercedes and you can't even afford a car. It's sad. It should not be the case."

In his fourth year now, he's chosen his specialty because it's one that offers him a unique set of organ systems that tend to have similar problems—without the hassle of social considerations. "If someone comes in with an earache," he tells me, "they don't want to talk about the person who's abusing them." He adds hastily, "But you can incorporate that, of course, if you want to." Early on, he enjoyed working with deaf kids, and he even learned sign language in college. "Aggressive people who want to solve problems go into surgery; the ones who love their families and want to spend time with them tend toward internal medicine and pediatrics. ENT? I guess, like in ophthalmology and OB-GYN, there's a mix of internal medicine, a lot of disease management, and surgery. And there will still be situations where you can be the good physician, in heart and soul. And you don't want to miss those opportunities."

Notes

1 | "Thank You for Coming Here"

1. *Focus*, Harvard Medical Area, March 1992, p. 4.

2. Oliver Wendell Holmes, *The Poet at the Breakfast Table*, section V.

3. Henry Jacob Bigelow, *Anesthesia: Addresses and Other Papers* (Boston: Little, Brown, 1900), p. 266.

4. Bicentennial Report, Harvard Medical School, April 1981, p. 3.

5. Mark G. Perlroth, "More on the Halloween Incident," *Harvard Medical Alumni Bulletin* 66 (Fall 1992): 4.

2 | The Fatigue Lab and the Good Doctor

1. Bernard Barber, ed., *L. J. Henderson on the Social System: Selected Writings* (Chicago: University of Chicago Press, 1970), p. 8.

2. L. J. Henderson, "Physician and Patient as a Social System," *New England Journal of Medicine* 212 (1935): 819–823.

3. Steven M. Horvath and Elizabeth C. Horvath, *The Harvard Fatigue Laboratory: Its History and Contributions* (Englewood Cliffs, N.J.: Prentice Hall, 1973), p. 15.

4. Barber, ed., *L. J. Henderson on the Social System*, p. 27.

5. Henry K. Beecher and Mark D. Altschule, *Medicine at Harvard: The First Three Hundred Years* (Hanover, N.H.: University Press of New England, 1977), p. 492.

6. Horvath and Horvath, *The Harvard Fatigue Laboratory*, p. 12.

7. D. B. Dill, "Case History of a Physiologist: F. G. Hall," *The Physiologist*, April 1979, p. 13.

8. Beecher and Altschule, *Medicine at Harvard,* p. 493.

9. Horvath and Horvath, *The Harvard Fatigue Laboratory*, p. 43.

10. Barber, ed., *L. J. Henderson on the Social System*, p. 36.

4 | *Getting In*

1. George Bascom, "Unsung Heroes," *Harvard Medical Alumni Bulletin* 65. (Spring 1992): 17.

2. "Report to the Alumni Council," *Harvard Medical Alumni Bulletin* 55 (Fall 1981): 22.

3. Lisa Belkin, "The Less Traveled Road to Medical School," *New York Times,* June 17, 1992, p. 1.

4. Francis Burns, "Why It's Hard to Enter Harvard Medical School," *Boston Globe,* May 30, 1952, p. 1.

5. Marcia Graham Synnott, *The Half-Opened Door* (Westport, Conn.: Greenwood Press, 1979), p. 50.

6. Saul Benison, "Walter B. Cannon and the Politics of Medical Science," *Bulletin of the History of Medicine* 1991, p. 240.

6 | *Young Veritas*

1. J. C. Furnas, *The Americans: A Social History of the United States 1587–1914* (New York: G. P. Putnam's Sons, 1969), p. 336.

2. Howard W. Haggard, *Mystery, Magic and Medicine* (Garden City, N.Y.: Doubleday Doran, 1933), p. 92.

3. Robert A. Kaplan, "Diversity, Humility and the Quest for Knowledge," *Harvard Medical Alumni Bulletin* 56 (Fall 1982): 18.

4. Thomas F. Harrington, *The Harvard Medical School: A Historical Narrative and Documents* (New York: Lewis Publishing Co., 1900), p. 51.

5. Lloyd E. Hawes, *Benjamin Waterhouse* (Cambridge, Mass.: Countway Library of Medicine, 1974), p. 50.

6. Joseph E. Garland, *Every Man Our Neighbor: A Brief History of the Massachusetts General Hospital 1811–1961* (Boston: Little, Brown, 1961), p. 14.

7. Audrey D. Stevens, *America's Pioneers in Abdominal Surgery* (Melrose, Mass.: American Society of Abdominal Surgeons, 1968), p. 47.

8. Bicentennial Report, Harvard Medical School, June 1982, p. 4.

9. "Attainments," *Boston Surgical and Medical Journal,* October 3, 1849, p. 185.

10. Bicentennial Report, Harvard Medical School, June 1981, p. 2.

11. Oliver Wendell Holmes, *Medical Essays, 1842–1882* (Boston: Houghton Mifflin, 1892), p. 377.

12. Ibid.

13. *Henry Jacob Bigelow, A Memoir* (sketches by his Boston colleagues) (Boston: Little, Brown, 1900), p. 80.

14. Ibid., p. 134.

15. Bicentennial Report, Harvard Medical School, June 1981, p. 3.

16. *Henry Jacob Bigelow, A Memoir,* p. 132.

7 | *"The Beginning of an Evil"*

1. Henry K. Beecher and Mark D. Altschule, *Medicine at Harvard: The First Three Hundred Years* (Hanover, N.H.: University Press of New England, 1977), p. 476.

2. Ibid.

3. Ibid.

4. Ibid., p. 461.

5. Lucy Sewall and Anita Tyng, letter to the faculty and dean of Harvard Medical School, January 22, 1866, in the Francis A. Countway Library of Medicine, Cambridge, Massachusetts.

6. Letter to Dr. George Shattuck, dean of the faculty of Medicine, Har-

vard, January 25, 1868, in the Francis A. Countway Library of Medicine, Cambridge, Massachusetts.

7. Nora N. Nercessian, *In Celebration of Life: A Centennial Account of the Harvard Medical Alumni Association 1891–1991* (Harvard Medical Alumni Association), p. 58.

8. Beecher and Altschule, *Medicine at Harvard,* p. 464.

9. Mary Roth Walsh, *No Women Need Apply* (New Haven: Yale University Press, 1977), p. 8.

10. President's Report, 1916–1917, pp. 144–45.

11. "Women at HMS," *Harvard Medical Alumni Bulletin* 55 (retrospective issue, Spring 1981): 44.

12. Leon Eisenberg, "The Early Years," *Harvard Medical Alumni Bulletin* 64 (Fall 1990): 13.

13. Ibid., p. 15.

14. Robert C. Hayden, *African-Americans in Boston: More Than 350 Years* (Boston: Trustees of the Boston Public Library, 1991), p. 144.

15. Beecher and Altschule, *Medicine at Harvard,* p. 480.

16. Bernard Davis, "Academic Standards in Medical Schools," *New England Journal of Medicine,* May 13, 1976, pp. 1118–1119.

17. Eisenberg, "The Early Years," p. 16.

18. "Celebrating Affirmative Actions," *Harvard Medical Alumni Bulletin* 64 (Fall 1990): 12.

19. Frances K. Conley, "Breaking the Glass Ceiling," *Harvard Medical Alumni Bulletin* 66 (Winter 1992/93): 40–41.

20. Ibid, p. 41. See also *1993–1994 Medical School Admission Requirements,* (Washington, D.C.: Association of American Medical Colleges, 1993).

8 | *"I Heard Your Cry"*

1. Francis Weld Peabody, "The Care of the Patient," *Journal of the American Medical Association,* March 19, 1927, pp. 877–882. See also Peabody,

The Care of the Patient (Cambridge, Mass.: Harvard University Press, 1927; New York: Macmillan, 1939).

12 | *To the Bedside*

1. Kenneth M. Ludmerer, *Learning to Heal: The Development of American Medical Education* (New York: Basic Books, 1985), p. 156.

2. Joseph Garland, *The Doctor's Saddlebag* (Boston: Massachusetts Linotyping Corporation, 1930), pp. 9, 10.

3. Henry Jacob Bigelow, *Anesthesia: Addresses and Other Papers* (Boston: Little, Brown, 1900), p. 213.

13 | *Talk Medicine*

1. Oliver Wendell Holmes, "The Young Practitioner," *Medical Essays, 1842–1882* (Boston: Houghton Mifflin, 1892), p. 390.

2. Lesley B. Heafitz, "The Empathic Way," *Harvard Medical Alumni Bulletin* 56 (Fall 1982): 32.

3. Holmes, *Medical Essays,* p. 387.

15 | *Caring on Call*

1. Benjamin Scheindlin, "The Great Medical School Conspiracy," *Harvard Medical Alumni Bulletin* 64 (Fall 1990): 31.

2. Ibid.

18 | *The Patient Redux*

1. "Study Reveals Wide Use of Alternative Medicine Therapies," *Focus,* January 28, 1993, p. 1.

2. Claudia Christie, "M. Rabkin, New England Business Profile," *New England Business,* March 19, 1984, p. 52.

3. *Henry Jacob Bigelow, A Memoir* (sketches by his Boston colleagues) (Boston: Little, Brown, 1900), p. 151.

4. Ibid., p. 59.

5. Ibid., p. 60.

6. Ibid., p. 66.

7. Ibid., p. 26.

Epilogue

1. *Focus*, Special Commencement Issue, June 10, 1993.

Index